THE
GREATEST
VIKING

THE GREATEST VIKING

The Life of Olav Haraldsson

DESMOND SEWARD

BIRLINN

First published in 2022 by
Birlinn Limited
West Newington House
10 Newington Road
Edinburgh
EH9 1QS

www.birlinn.co.uk

ISBN 978 1 78027 795 0

British Library Cataloguing-in-Publication Data
A catalogue record for this book is available from the British Library

Designed and typeset by Hewer Text UK Ltd, Edinburgh
Printed and bound by Clays Ltd, Elcograf S.p.A.

For Frederick Lesser, a lover of Norway,
who suggested that I write this book

Contents

Prologue

The Sword in the Burial Mound

> This is the sword called Baesing
>
> *Legendary Saga of St Olav*[1]

One summer in about the year 995 (the precise date is unknown), heavily pregnant and confined to bed at the house of her father Gudbrand Kula, Åsta Gudbrandsdatter found herself incapable of giving birth.[2] Worry or rage, or both, may have been the cause, because her husband, Harald Grenski, King of Grenland,[3] had cast her off to go to Sweden and court the widowed Queen Sigrid the Proud, whose wealth he coveted. Nor was Åsta soothed by learning that, irritated by his advances, Sigrid had persuaded Harald and his housecarls to drink until they dozed off into a stupor, then sent men to fire the hall where they slept – and, as the burning rafters were falling on them, to kill all who ran out from the flames.

The news of Harald Grenski's death and her widowhood was brought to Åsta by Hrani Vidforli ('Far Travelled'), who had been his right-hand man. He survived because in the wake of a recent victory over the Jómsborg Vikings, Harald had left him behind in charge of the main body of his *hird* – his armed retinue – when he went to woo Sigrid.

According to the *Legendary Saga of St Olav* (a thirteenth-century life based largely on stories told by the skalds) a majestic figure who wore a red cloak and a massive gold arm ring then appeared to Hrani in a dream. 'I am Olav Digre,' it said. 'I want you to break into my burial mound at Geirstad. There you will find a man in clothes like mine. Go up to him, take his arm ring, belt and sword, and finally cut off his head. There will be other men in there, too, but have no fear of them . . . If you do not do just as I say, all will go wrong, but if you do, then all will be well . . .

'Next, you must go to the Upplands, to King Gudbrand Kula's house, where you will find his daughter Åsta in childbirth but unable to deliver. Gudbrand is broken-hearted, distraught from a humili- ation for which there is no remedy. All this has happened because Harald Grenski sent Åsta and her women back in disgrace to her father who, with his daughter, is prostrate with misery. Wait until they ask for your advice, then tell them to gird my sword belt around her.'

The mound was that of King Olav Geirstad-Alf, 'Olav Digre', who had been killed sixty years before. He and his half-brother Sigrød of Trondheim had refused to pay tribute to another half- brother, King Eirík Bloodaxe. Through a howling gale, Eirík and his army 'sailed night and day, coming faster than the news of him'. Defiantly Olav and Sigrød drew up their men in a shield-wall on a ridge near the farm Haugar close by Tønsberg in Vestfold but, outnumbered, they were soon overwhelmed. Their housecarls built howes for them on the ridge where they fell.

There were many kings' burial mounds of this sort in Norway, such as the famous Gokstad howe. When in 1880 archaeologists discov- ered a ship underneath, they found seated on a chair the skeleton of a huge man covered with terrible wounds received in battle, all in front, and for many years people believed, wrongly, that he was Olav Geirstad-Alf. Norsemen usually gave such places a wide berth. The god Odin, 'Ghost Sovereign and Lord of the Mounds', did not care for trespassers while elves lived in them, not pretty little fairies of the English sort but spirits of the dead who, if angered, might send a storm or cast a spell that would ruin the harvest. Prudent people, especially farmers' wives, offered sacrifices to placate the *álfar* in their area.

Most fearsome of all were the *draugr*, the 'undead' or 'again-walkers' for whom the howes had been built and who, guarding their treasure, attacked anybody trying to enter. The *Saga of Grettir the Strong* tells how Grettir breaks into the howe of Kari the Old, whose ghost is terrorising the local farmers. In the foul-smelling darkness he stumbles against a high chair on which sits undead Kari, surrounded by heaps of gold and silver, with a gleaming sword at his feet. As Grettir is climbing out with the treasure, a bony hand grips his shoulder and he wrestles for his life with the again-walker until it collapses with a rattling crash. Before leaving, Grettir draws his own sword and cuts off the draugr's skull which he lays between its thigh bones.[4]

However, Hrani was an exceptionally brave man. Breaking into Olav Geirstad-Alf's howe, he hacked off his head, taking his arm ring, belt and sword. Then he went to Gudbrand Kula at Hringerike in the Upplands, wild forest country to the far northwest of what is now Oslo, where he told his story. With Gudbrand's approval, he placed the belt and sword on Åsta's belly as a charm and soon after she gave birth to a son. Bitter at Harald Grenski's desertion, Gudbrand ordered it be left to die from hunger and exposure, as was often done in pagan Norway with unwanted children – a custom known as 'out bringing'. Despite Hrani's protests, the child was placed in a ruined hut.

That night Hrani, woken by the baby's cries, saw a strange light shining over the hut, and went to its grandfather, prophesying that it would grow up to be a wonderful man who would do his kindred great honour.[5] When Gudbrand Kula refused to take it in, Hrani brought a friend to the hut who also saw the light. Still the old man remained adamant. ('Kula' means 'lump', which does not suggest high intelligence.) Eventually, Hrani persuaded Gudbrand to come and see for himself. This time, the light was almost blinding. Shaken, Gudbrand gave orders for the baby to be taken into the house and brought up as a member of the family.

Having agreed to be foster-father, Hrani gave the child the belt and the arm ring to play with. He also named him 'Olav' after the king in the howe, an act of great significance for pagan Norsemen, some of whom believed strongly in the transmigration of souls. Bearing the same name could even imply that the boy was Olav Geirstad-Alf born again.

At the same time, Hrani entrusted Åsta with the sword Baesing, to keep for her son.

Introduction

Norway's Once and Future King

'warriors dared not look into the serpent-shining eyes of terrible seeming Olav'

Sigvat Thordarson, *Erfidrápa Óláfs Helga*[1]

This is the life of a Viking hero who became *Norges evige Konge*, 'Eternal King of Norway'. He was Olav Haraldsson, who reigned at the beginning of the first millennium, and we know more about him than about any other Viking. For Norwegians, he haunts their landscape, even more important to them than Arthur is to the British. But unlike Britain's 'once and future king', he really existed, and like Arthur and Excalibur his story begins with a sword, taken from a burial mound instead of a stone. Unlike Arthur, his life was ended by an axe that became his symbol.

Each year his shrine at Nidaros attracts more and more pilgrims. Part of his spell lies in the contrast between his life as a peculiarly ferocious Viking and as the man who made Norway Christian. Demon haunted and god haunted, he emerges from the company of Odin and Thor into the High Middle Ages – the world of illuminated manuscripts, Romanesque sculpture and Gregorian chant.

When a very young man, he was dramatically successful in raids along the Baltic, in France and Spain, and above all in England. Yet he also doomed the Viking way of life to extinction by ensuring that Norway abandoned its ancient gods. What is seldom taken into account is how strong was the hold of the old pagan deities on the Norse people, which makes his achievement in overthrowing them all the more remarkable. Understandably, he made many enemies.

He was long remembered in Britain as well as Norway. In 1009 he joined a wide-ranging Viking raid on England that turned into a bloodbath. He himself pulled down London Bridge, then stormed and burned Canterbury, whose inhabitants were massacred. He also acquired quantities of loot, receiving a huge sum in Danegeld. His surprising popularity stemmed from his gift for healing. At least forty churches were dedicated to him in the British Isles and a fifteenth-century screen at the church of Barton Turf in Norfolk still has a painting of 'St Olofius', carrying the axe that helped to kill him.

Olav's story was best preserved by the Icelander Snorri Sturluson (1179–1241) in his astonishing *Heimskringla* ('Circle of the Earth'), the sagas of sixteen Norwegian kings, which until recently was the most widely read book in Norway. Among the sagas is that of Olav, the masterpiece of a man who anticipated the great psychological novelists.[2] He was not always accurate since he lived two centuries after Olav and his chronology is erratic, but he had the benefit of folk memories handed down from generation to generation and of contemporary skaldic verse. Beyond question, Snorri is our most important source of information.

Nowadays the Vikings are a cult, inspiring television programmes and novels that command a huge audience, yet Olav is largely unknown outside Norway or the academic world. My own interest in him began during a Christmas spent at Oslo when my host told me that the *pilgrimsleden*, the ancient pilgrims' roads to the king's shrine at Nidaros, had been revived.

Chronology

I

The World of a Young Norse Chieftain

'Odin owns the nobles who fall in battle and Thor owns the race of thralls'

Harbard's Song[1]

Olav's foster-father, Hrani the Far Travelled, is often called his uncle, but although he was Harald Grenski's foster-brother and like Harald came from Grenland where he had a farm, there was no blood relationship. Even so, he was Olav's first great ally and because of the dream that brought the boy into the world he sensed something uncanny in him. As soon as his first tooth appeared, Hrani placed the sword Baesing beside his cradle.

Old Gudbrand Kula died when Olav was five, and his mother Åsta had married again. Her new husband was Sigurd Syr, King of Hringerike. Despising Sigurd's preference for farming instead of war or raiding, neighbours nicknamed him *Syr* ('Sow'), inferring that he spent his time snuffling and rooting in muddy fields. Snorri Sturluson was nearer the mark in calling him a 'careful householder'.

When Olav was eight, he saw a mysterious object in one of his mother's chests that gleamed with a cold, blue light. Fascinated, he asked her what it was. 'That is the sword called Baesing', Åsta told him, 'given to you by your foster-father. Once, long ago, it belonged to King Olav Geirstad-Alf.' The boy insisted on taking possession of it at once. No doubt he thought it possessed magic powers.

> The shield-destroyer, with gold it shines.
> In the hilt is fame, in the haft is courage,
> In the point is fear, for its owner's foes[2]

Made of tempered steel, with a plain cross-guard, Baesing would have had a double-edged blade two and a half to three feet long, lightened by a 'blood groove' running from hilt to point. Swords like this were so sharp-edged that the sagas describe a single blow slicing off a man's head, even his buttocks. Despite a rounded point, they could be used for thrusting, but were primarily designed for slashing. The blade and pommel were frequently inlaid with gold or silver, and the hilt wound round with gold or silver wire. Occasionally the blade was inscribed. The *Lay of Sigrdrifa* advises, 'Victory-runes you must cut if you want victory, and cut them on your sword-hilt; some on the blade guards, some on the handle.'[3]

Passed down from father to son as an heirloom, and credited with magic powers, a sword of this sort was indispensable for anybody who hoped to become a famous warrior.[4] Like Baesing, outstanding ones were given names. King Hakon the Good owned a sword named 'Quern-biter' that he claimed could split a millstone and on one occasion he cut through the helmet and skull of a hitherto all-conquering berserker with a single blow.[5] Rulers rewarded favourites with them. Olav would present his skald Sigvat Thordarson with a sword that had a silver pommel and a gold hilt.

Much too big and heavy for Olav, who insisted on wearing it all the time, Baesing's scabbard dragged along the floor, clattering behind him. When with the kindest intentions Sigurd offered to exchange it for a smaller sword until he grew a bit older, the boy snarled back that while he might be little, he would never let anyone else own Baesing. He spoke so fiercely that Sigurd told him to keep it.

As Baesing's owner, Olav saw himself as heir to King Olav Geirstad-Alf in the howe at Haugar, which increased his pride in the weapon. It gave him not only a claim to the land in Vingulmark, but to some distinguished supernatural forebears. 'Geirstad Alf' means 'Elf of Geirstad', the name of a King of Vingulmark long ago whose mother, the mythical Alfhild, was the daughter of Alfarinn, King of Alfheim (Elfland). She had born children with such striking good looks that everybody thought they must be kin to the elves.

We know from the sagas that in later life, besides a sword, Olav owned a long-shafted broad-axe called 'Hel' after the death goddess. Designed for fighting, not for cutting timber, its head, thinner and lighter than that of a woodman's axe, was sometimes inlaid with silver or gold like a prized sword blade and had a broad, razor-sharp edge of specially hardened steel. Using both hands, a man who knew how to fight with an axe like this could smash shields with ease and decapitate a horse.[6] Some were said to be so magical that they gave a ringing sound if you touched them.

Olav was also a fine archer and adept with a spear. Some spears were heavy, close-quarter weapons for lunging, used not unlike the old bayonet and rifle, while lighter spears were for throwing with the aid of a thong, capable if hurled strongly enough, of going straight through a man who did not wear a mail shirt. He may also have learned to use the sling, that too-often overlooked instrument of death.

We may guess that it was Hrani who taught him how to handle weapons, as well as the skills needed for sailing, rowing and navigating a ship. He was an apt pupil, learning quickly. Snorri says that when very young the boy was already 'expert in all bodily exercises', an unusually strong swimmer, and a smith who could work every kind of metal. Determined to excel, he wanted to win in every sport or game.

As he grew up, Olav Haraldsson felt less and less respect for his unwarlike stepfather. Snorri pictures Sigurd overseeing the harvest in clothes that are not what one might expect of a Viking: 'A blue coat and blue hose; shoes laced about the legs; a grey cloak, and a grey wide-brimmed hat; a veil before his face [against midges]; a staff in his hand with a gilt-silver head.' Normally, unless in the banqueting hall, Norsemen of all ranks dressed plainly at home, wearing wadmal – a coarse, undyed, homespun cloth.[7]

When he ordered Olav to saddle his horse, the boy saddled the biggest billy goat on the home farm and brought it to his door. Sigurd said resignedly, 'Your mother thinks it right that I order you to do nothing against your own inclination,' then added, 'I can see that we are of very different dispositions and that you are far prouder than I am.' Olav laughed and strolled away.

Yet the peace-loving Sigurd made young Olav an excellent step-father who was tolerant and, one suspects, affectionate. Not only was he rich but a survivor, the last petty ruler in Norway able to call himself 'king'. Olav grew up happily, in comfortable, aristocratic surroundings.

Living in a land without books, young Olav was illiterate but learned to read and write runes, a clumsy, sixteen-letter script for carving memorial stones, for inscribing protective spells (or curses) on ships, weapons or amulets, or for writing questions on sticks, twigs or wood shavings then thrown up into the air in order to tell the future – told from the position in which they landed on the white shirt or cloth laid out to catch them.

> Hidden Runes shalt thou seek and interpreted signs,
> many symbols of might and power . . .[9]

But throwing them could be dangerous, because it attracted evil spirits.

He learned, too, about the Norse gods and how to worship them since as a chieftain he was a *gothi*, a priest, who when he grew up would sacrifice to them, the only way of ensuring that his people had a good harvest and lived through the winter. The long *julblót*, the midwinter sacrifice at Yule, was a happy interlude during so bleak a season, a pleasant change from feeding farm animals, or mucking out stables and cow byres, even more enjoyable than feasts in better weather, such as the *sumarblót* in mid-April for victory in battle, or the winter ale in mid-October for a good year. The feasts were attended by the *bonder* (farmers) on Sigurd Syr's estate with their families and servants.

The sacrifice might take place at a sacred spot near the chieftain's homestead, in one of the rare temples, or under a holy oak or on a *horg* (altar) in front of a howe, provided the local elves were not being troublesome – as they are sometimes said to be in Iceland even today. However, it is likely that the first sacrifices which Olav saw were in Sigurd's mead hall. Each *bonde* brought a horse, the most valuable animals after men, with other gifts.

The ceremony began by hanging the horses whose throats were then cut by Sigurd as priest. Pouring their blood into a cauldron, he sprinkled it with a bunch of twigs on the walls and ground, and over everybody present like Christian holy water. Sometimes other animals were sacrificed, even, although rarely, men – criminals, captives or slaves – who were killed in the same way. After the horses had been butchered, their flesh, credited with magic properties, was boiled in kettles, then handed out as meat and soup in goblets blessed in a prayer said by Sigurd. Toasts were drunk to the gods, especially Odin and Thor, and to departed kindred. The bonder brought plenty of food with quantities of ale and mead, so that feasting went on for days with singing and dancing.

In the Viking age the houses of Norse aristocrats were glorified cabins of logs and wattle-and-daub, with 'staves' (tree trunks) that carried low-pitched roofs covered with layer upon layer of birch bark held in place by sods of turf upon which enterprising sheep grazed. (Roofs like this can be seen today on Norwegian farm buildings in remoter areas.) A nobleman's homestead was basically a long *innhus* with three dark, windowless rooms filled by smoke from the long, trench-like hearth that ran along the middle of the hall, the main room, escaping through a smoke hole in the roof – the sole source of daylight.

The innhus of a wealthy chieftain such as King Sigurd Syr usually possessed an outside gallery, with a banqueting hall close by, as well as detached guest rooms and sauna-like bathhouses. Next to these was the *uthus* – barns, stalls and sheds – the nearest of which was the stable. A complex like this was the nearest thing to a capital in Sigurd's tiny domain.

Although a time when the temperature was warming, the winters with their howling gales and drifting snow must have seemed interminable. It is hard for us to imagine the cold, damp, smoke and all-pervading stench accepted as normal indoors while there was always the worry that provisions might not last. 'In many places their life would be a constant battle against semi-starvation, cold and disease.'[8] Should stocks run low, infants would be allowed to die and the old and sick discreetly knocked on the head in a desperate struggle to save food.

However deep the snow, Vikings went out into it to hunt for elk (moose) and red deer, game birds and mountain hares, to supplement a basic winter diet of oatmeal or barley porridge in which a piece of half-rotten meat, salted or pickled in whey, or of dried cod came as a treat. They also hunted for the furs they needed to keep warm – bear, wolf and lynx, marten, otter, fox and squirrel. It was vital to know how to travel fast on skis or snowshoes, to cross frozen lakes and rivers on skates made from cow or deer leg bones, to cope with snowstorms. Snorri describes a trapper caught in a blizzard sleeping through it under the snow, a survival skill still taught in today's Norwegian army.

The Viking world was essentially aristocratic. At the top of a highly stratified clan structure were the chieftains and their closer kindred, although chieftains were far from all-powerful. Feuds between clans about murders or theft, or over ownership of land, had to be debated at the local *Thing*, an assembly of freemen. A man found guilty of a serious crime such as murder would have to pay compensation to his relatives, in livestock or crops. If he had done something really atrocious, he might be outlawed, which gave any freeman the right to kill him.

The wealthier freemen (bonder) owned their farms, although there were many landless ones who became housecarls or worked as farmhands. At the bottom, since this was a slave-owning society, were the *thralls* (slaves) captured on slave raids overseas who formed 20 per cent of Norway's population. For the Vikings were people traffickers as well as pirates, carrying off strong men and handsome girls.

As Neil Price sums it up, when captured the thralls underwent 'the disbelieving experience of passing from person to property in seconds'.[10] Most were sold overseas but a fair number were brought home where, inadequately dressed in rags and with shoes of birch bark, southerners found the cold winters a new nightmare. Sleeping in the stables, male slaves did all the rough work – digging, dunging, felling trees, cutting turf, herding sheep or pigs. They were indispensable for running a farm while the master of the house was away with his men on a Viking expedition, but when a thrall grew old he could expect to be put down like any other farm animal that had outlived its usefulness.

The fate of female slaves varied. The ugly became sweated labour who were forced to toil until they dropped or were put down, weaving wadmal or sail-making from sunrise to sunset, or at best as house servants or dung-spattered dairymaids. Pretty ones suffered a fate worse than death until they lost their looks and were put to work with the less attractive. However, DNA evidence shows that more than a few had better luck, especially those from Ireland or Scotland. Viking Scandinavia was polygamous, well-to-do men taking concubines, which caused a shortage of nubile young women from freemen's families, so that often the only way for a poor freeman to find a wife was to marry a slave girl.

Obviously, women were the losers in a society like this, especially female thralls who might be buried dead or alive to serve their owners in a future life. There is a famous account of a Norse chieftain's funeral by a tenth-century Arab chronicler, Ahmad ibn Fadlan, who met Vikings on the Volga. He tells how a young slave, persuaded into going to the next world with her master, was kept drunk for days, then ritually raped by mourners who finally beat and strangled the screaming girl to death. (The rites were presided over by a terrible woman, known as the 'Angel of Death', almost certainly a witch.) Another tenth-century Arab, Ibn Rustah, says that when a Viking chieftain died his men built a howe and 'put his favourite wife in the grave with him while she is still living'. How, asks a historian, did onlookers 'articulate the knowledge that inside that grave a woman they knew was slowly suffocating, dying in the dark beside the rotting body of her partner, and that one day the same fate might be theirs?'[11] Mercifully, such burials seem to have been rare.

Even so, wives and daughters of the free classes enjoyed a certain level of respect and had rights such as inheriting property, even a degree of independence, since common sense dictated that they were the bedrock of the family. A wedding ceremony gave legal status and a wife might divorce a husband and recover her dowry, if she could prove he beat her without cause or was impotent, while there were penalties for rape. Yet she had to put up with concubines or her husband sleeping with any female slave who caught his fancy. She herself was restricted to a single man and might be put to death if found guilty of adultery.

A strong wife could bully a weak husband into letting her do a man's work and a very few even set up as traders. A *ringkvinna* was a spinster who in the absence of adult male kindred took over as head of a family with full legal rights when her father or brother died. The *Poetic Edda* tells of 'shield maidens', female warriors with the hearts of wolves, such as the young Hervor in *The Waking of Argantyr* who, dressed as a man, goes into her father's howe to retrieve his sword.

The greatest shield maiden in Norse legend was Lagertha, known only from the *Gesta Danorum* ('Acts of the Danes') by the Dane Saxo Grammaticus who wrote in the twelfth century. Sent to a brothel when the Swedes invaded Norway, she escaped and, clothed as a man, fought at Ragnar Lodbrok's side when he attacked them. Fighting with her hair loose over her shoulders, she astonished everybody by her heroism, winning a battle by charging the enemy from the rear, alone. Ragnar married Lagertha, then deserted her to marry the King of Sweden's daughter. She found a new husband, a kinglet, whom she speared to death after he proved unsatisfactory, taking over his little realm and ruling it by herself.

Writing in 1991, Judith Jesch dismissed Saxo's Lagertha as a product of male imagination and all reputable historians would then have agreed that female warriors were literary flights of fancy.[12] But in 2014, DNA analysis of a tenth-century burial at Birka in Sweden of a helmeted chieftain who was armed with sword, shield, battleaxe, bow and spears, and accompanied by a stallion and a mare, revealed that the body was a woman's. No less an authority than Neil Price concludes that other female chieftains must have existed, although rare exceptions.[13]

It must be said, too, that the *Poetic Edda* can show a sensitive response to femininity found nowhere else in Western literature at that date. 'You weep, gold-clad girl, cruel tears . . . each falls bleeding on the prince's breast, chill as rain, searing, clotted with grief.'[14] There are many poignant love affairs in the sagas, as in the *Saga of Gunnlaug Serpent-tongue* that tells of the skald Gunnlaug's ill-fated passion for Helga the Fair.

A poem from this time, the *Rigsthula* ('List of Rig') contrasts the lives of the classes. Two ragged thralls have a son with a scabby face, horny hands and a back bowed by carrying firewood, while their daughter-in-law, bandy-legged from farm work and with badly sunburned arms, has mud on her bare feet. Their grandsons, who have brutish names such as Horsefly, Shagger or Smelly, do all the rough work on the homestead. The granddaughters are Stumpy, Tatty-Clothes or Bondwoman. The only food the couple can offer a guest is some thin broth and a coarse loaf full of bran.

A freeman leads a much better life. With his neatly trimmed beard and smart shirt, he sits in his house by a roaring fire, carving wood for a loom-beam while his well-dressed wife, who is spinning with a distaff, wears nice brooches and gives a visitor a really good meal.

One day their sons will tame oxen, build barns, make carts, drive ploughs and till the fields. These were the rich bonder, well-to-do yeomen farmers, tough and independent minded.

The description of how a nobleman of royal descent lives is that of Olav's life as a boy. A chieftain, the *Rigsthula* tells us, owns a great hall, south facing, with rushes on the floor. Wearing a long-skirted dress and a blue linen blouse, his beautiful, white-skinned wife lays a cloth of fine linen over the table on which she puts white bread, before serving a guest with game, pork and roast chicken in silver-mounted bowls, washed down by wine in silver goblets. As their son grows up, he learns to shoot with a bow, use a sword and hurl spears, to ride and hunt with hounds. Fighting his way to still more riches, by the end of his life, he will own many homesteads, rewarding his housecarls with jewels, gold arm rings and thoroughbred horses.[15]

Much admired as a Viking, Erling Skjalgsson from Rogaland was a chieftain of this sort, a magnificent looking man with an attractive personality. His lands were so broad that he was a king without a title, his estates stretching from the mouth of the Sognefjord to the Naze. Every summer he went raiding in a longship crewed by 200 men, while 'winter and summer' he housed and fed ninety housecarls, who were given a lavish allowance of drink. The thirty thralls on his farm were allowed to grow their own corn if they worked in the evenings or at night and then sell it, so that energetic ones gifted with green fingers could buy their freedom within three years – replaced by fresh slaves purchased with the money. He employed the new freedmen in the herring fishery, on his farms or clearing woodland, which enabled them to build their own huts. 'He helped all to prosperity' says Snorri.[16]

However, there was a less likeable side to Erling. From being no more than a member of a clan who had for many years governed west Norway collectively, he became its sole ruler when he married King Olav Tryggvason's sister, and his autocratic ways made him revengeful enemies. They included most of his kinsmen, led by a certain Aslak Fitjaskalli.[17]

*   *   *

Young Olav would have learned all about his distinguished ancestors. An Yngling 'of Yngve's race', he belonged to the country's oldest family, the Ynglinga, who descended from the god Frey. His unfortunate father Harald Grenski had been a great-great-grandson of Harald Fair Hair, first King of all Norway, through a son Bjorn Farman (the Seafarer) whom Fair Hair fathered on the concubine Svanhild.

On his mother's side Olav descended from Ragnar Lodbrok, the legendary hero who had killed a giant serpent to rescue his future bride before setting out on an enviable career of mass slaughter, rape, pillage and general mayhem. With poetic justice, Ragnar ended his life in a pit filled with adders into which he was thrown by his intended victims after a raid on Northumbria went wrong. But the defiant way he died and his death song, with its last line 'Laughing shall I die', sung while waiting for the snakes' venom to kill him, were an inspiration for all true Vikings.

We do not know when Olav decided he was King Harald Fair Hair's successor and that the kingdom of Norway was his by rightful inheritance, yet it may have been during boyhood. In an oral culture, there were many Norsemen who recalled Harald. We know that Sigurd Syr was among them and no doubt he took care to see his stepson knew that all the great king's male line descendants had a right to the throne.

The *Legendary Saga of St Olav* says he grew up 'handsome, magnificent of countenance, stocky, not tall, thick-haired, and bright-eyed with curly, light chestnut hair'. A Norwegian who about 1190 wrote a brief history of his country's kings agrees that he was good-looking, saying his hair was red, his beard even redder.[18] However, Snorri Sturluson states that he was impressive rather than handsome and very strongly built, adding that he was an early developer, highly articulate. Much loved by those who knew him well, he was called Olav 'Digre', which can be translated as fat, but in his case probably meant thickset. He did not object – it had been Olav Geirstad-Alf's nickname.

Echoing the skald Sigvat Thordarson's memorial poem to Olav, Snorri also tells us he had strange eyes with so piercing a gaze that 'one was afraid to look him in the face when he was angry'. Everybody knew this was a sure sign of a man born to rule – 'the glow of his eyes is like gleaming snakes'.[19] Beyond question he possessed the traditional Viking virtues, which (as defined by Tom Shippey) were 'independence verging on insubordination, refusal to show pain and . . . taking certain defeat and death as motivation rather than discouragement'.[20]

2

Harald Fair Hair and His Successors

'There were skalds at Harald's court whose poems the people know by heart even at the present day, together with all the songs about the kings who have ruled in Norway since his time; and we rest the foundations of our story principally upon these songs.'

Snorri Sturluson, *Heimskringla, c.*1230

We tend to forget the sheer vastness of Norway, whose coast stretches for over a thousand miles beside the Atlantic. The eastern border – mountainous, densely forested, with wide tracts of bog – is with Sweden while the southern is across the sea with Denmark. The coastline's northern stretch lies within in the Arctic Circle, including much of the region the old Norsemen called Hålogaland. The north-ern-most inhabited territory was that of the Sami, 'solitary rovers and nomadic', whom Vikings feared for their witchcraft, but who supplied them with exotic furs, rare falcons and walrus ivory.

In AD 1000 the population may have been under 200,000 since only 3 per cent of the terrain was fit for farming with the primitive methods of the time. 'Most infertile of all lands, fit for beasts alone', wrote Adam of Bremen seventy years later. Yet there was enough good soil to grow scanty crops of barley or oats with a little wheat, and plenty of grazing for hardy little short-tailed sheep, which provided small, isolated clans with a bare living. Everybody knew that a spell of bad weather in the summer might result in a winter famine that would kill old people and the very young – either directly or indirectly. Many men emigrated or lived by trading, or by plundering and slaving abroad.

Gradually the clans grew closer, linked by trade and a common language (Old West Norse), although Norway's geography made it a difficult country to unite. Four areas with good soil were reasonably well populated. These were the Trøndelag, which had some of Norway's best arable; the west coast region down to Stavanger, but only small fertile strips along the fjords; the land in the southeast on both sides of the Oslofjord; and that around Lake Mjøsa. Elsewhere, there were tiny, isolated communities. However, all of the clans inhabiting them, great and small, developed separate identities which with the natural barriers formed serious obstacles to union.

Harald Harfagre (Fair Hair) from Sogndal, who in about the year 870 became King of Vestfold to the west of the Oslofjord, was the first man to unite Norway. At first only one among several 'sea kings', he based his power on a hird of well-armed warriors and a large fleet, as well as a string of coastal farmsteads and island depots. To defend his merchant ships against pirates, he allied with Hakon of Lade who ruled the region around the Trondheimsfjord. Joining forces, they sailed their joint fleet along the coast, defeating each rival in turn.

After a decisive victory at Hafrsfjord (a little south of modern Stavanger) in the 880s, Harald was recognised as King of all Norway by the kinglets, who paid him *scatt* (tribute tax). Yet except on his own estates in Rogaland in the southwest where he spent much of the year, Harald was no more than overlord of the west coast, king only in name, as he did not establish any sort of administrative system apart from jarls who if called on would supply him with troops from their area. In the north real power belonged to the great Lade jarls.[1]

Some modern scholars deny that Harald ever existed, but the skalds' evidence for him is compelling. Snorri says he was known as *Harald Luva* (Shock Head) from vowing not to wash or comb his hair until he had conquered all Norway – a vow taken to persuade a girl to become his concubine. When he did so after ten years it looked so fine and silky that it gained him the name 'Fair Hair'. A skald who clearly knew his court well, Tórbjorn Hornklofi, wrote a poem in his praise, *Haraldskvaedi*, a dialogue between a Valkyrie and a corpse-eating raven that tells how generously he rewarded skalds. He gave them, boasts Tórbjorn, red, fur-lined cloaks, silver-mounted swords, chain-mail shirts, gilded helmets and gold arm rings, with beautiful slave girls from Wendland.[2] Less poetically, Snorri says that Harald appointed an 'overseer of guests' named Wolf the Unwashed.

When Harald Fair Hair died about 930, the succession was disputed, his twenty sons by at least nine women fighting each other to the death. Eventually, Eirík Bloodaxe (otherwise 'Brothers' Bane' from killing so many of them) whom Fair Hair had wanted as his successor, was driven out and Hakon, the youngest, took the throne. Nicknamed 'Athelstan's Foster-son', Hakon had been brought up in England as a Christian at the court of the great King Athelstan.

An able administrator, Hakon set up a centralised Thing system that worked well and made him popular, as did reducing the chieftains' scatt. A fine soldier whose hird included berserkers, he fought off two invasions by his brothers. However, he was not so successful at converting Norway. Three English missionary priests, probably monks of Glastonbury whom he had brought home with him, were murdered and their churches burned to the ground, while he himself was forced to attend the Yule sacrifice and pretend to eat horse meat.

Like Fair Hair, he might have achieved the rare feat for a Viking ruler of dying in his bed from old age, but in 961 he was mortally wounded by a barbed arrow in the armpit during a final battle with his brothers. Buried in the old pagan style beneath a huge howe, in his armour and finest robes, he had been 'greatly in favour of all the people', who now named him 'Hakon the Good' and wished him a hearty welcome to Valhalla. His skald Eyvind Skáldaspillir lamented that because Hakon had departed this life, Fenris Wolf, whom even the gods feared, would go unchained and devour numberless human beings.[3]

Some believed the arrow that slew Hakon had been guided by his Danish stepmother, Queen Gunnhild, Bloodaxe's widow, a tiny little woman as cruel and evil as she was beautiful, who always did her sinister best to help her sons. The rumour that she had learned witchcraft from Sami warlocks made her widely feared, while she was credited with changing into a swallow whenever she wanted to spy on her many enemies. (Her stepson Dag owned a sparrow with prophetic powers.) Milton's lines on the 'night hag' in *Paradise Lost* suit Gunnhild very well:

> In secret, riding through the air, she comes
> Lured with the smell of infant blood, to dance
> With Lapland witches, while the labouring moon
> Eclipses at their charms . . .

Despite mother's spells, Eirík Bloodaxe's sons, grim, crafty and warlike as they were, only succeeded in establishing themselves on the west coast and, after their leader Harald Wolf Skin was murdered in 970 by Jarl Hakon Sigurdsson of Lade, they were driven out altogether. The Danish King Harald Blue Tooth then became nominal King of Norway, but for twenty years the country's real ruler was Hakon who a Christian chronicler tells us was called 'the Evil' because of 'his unbridled cruelty of temperament'.[4] Blue Tooth had the jarl forcibly baptised, on a visit to Denmark, sending priests with him when he left for Norway – thrown overboard by Hakon as soon as he set sail.

Hakon was terrified that Gunnhild might cast a spell on him and at his request Blue Tooth lured her to Denmark with a proposal of marriage, saying they were both getting on in years and would make a fine old couple, but when the witch queen arrived he had her drowned in a bog, in ancient Danish fashion.[5] A mummified corpse found in a Jutland fen in 1835, thought to be Gunnhild's, was reburied in a marble sarcophagus with full Lutheran funeral rites at

Roskilde Cathedral among the Danish royal family, as befitted a princess of Denmark. Embarrassingly, her body was later identified as that of a man a thousand years older.

At first Jarl Hakon, handsome and pleasant mannered, made himself popular by lavishing gifts on his supporters and, as a shuddering chronicler put it, because he was 'a slave of demons to whom he was always making sacrifice and calling on for help'.[6] He did so at the famous temple to Frey set up at Trondheim by his family while, proud of his descent from Odin, he encouraged everyone to worship the ancient gods. Many, perhaps most, Norwegians approved of such commitment to the old faith. They knew that on one occasion Hakon had made a most effective blood sacrifice after which two ravens flew over his head, croaking loudly – a sure sign of divine support. This was when he beat off a Danish attempt to take over Norway in 986, routing at Hjörungavágr Bay a fleet of longships sent by King Blue Tooth that included a group of Viking mercenaries, the Jómsvikings.

The sacrifice had been the jarl's own seven-year-old son, a promising child, whom he offered to the goddess Thorgerd Holgabrud – 'Thorgerd Shine Bright'. When he saw that the battle was going badly, he took the boy into some deep woods and asked for her help, ordering his thrall Tormod Karke ('Thick Skin') to kill him. In response a storm blew up and won the battle for Hakon, Thorgerd and her sister Irpa blowing huge hailstones into his enemy's eyes and shooting arrows from their fingers that invariably brought death.[7] Later, on Shine Bright's advice, the jarl made a man from driftwood, inserting a heart cut out of another human sacrifice. After the goddess brought the thing to life, Hakon gave it an axe, with orders to go to Iceland and kill a skald who had insulted him. The wooden man's mission is said to have been a great success.

Hakon was respected for more than worshipping goddesses or winning battles since he enforced good law and order, while successive years of fine weather ensured that his sacrifices coincided with excellent harvests and the biggest shoals of herring in memory. It looked as if the gods were on his side. However, as time went by his rule became tyrannical. Nor could he control his womanising, abducting and raping not only common women but highborn ladies, which turned their menfolk into enemies bent on revenge. When in 995 he tried to kidnap a certain Gudrun known as 'Sunbeam' because of her beauty, her husband Orm Lugg, a rich Trøndelag bonde, sent round the war arrow – burnt at one end, a hank of rope at the other – which set off a serious revolt.

Already threatened by a rival, Olav Tryggvason, of whom he was terrified because of his descent from Harald Fair Hair and whom he had tried to have kidnapped or killed, Hakon lost his nerve while his goddess abandoned him. He fled with his thrall Tormod Karke to Melhus, to the farm of his main mistress Thora of Rimul, who hid them in a hole under the pigsty in her farmyard where nobody would think of looking.

Unexpectedly, Olav came to her farm with the bonder army whom he reviewed in the yard, and the pair heard him offering a reward to anyone who killed Jarl Hakon. The thrall fell asleep and, when he woke, he whispered to the jarl how he had dreamed of Olav putting a gold ring round his neck. Hakon whispered back that it might be a red one. Although by now suspicious of his companion, eventually the exhausted jarl dozed off but began screaming in his sleep. Karke took the opportunity to cut his throat, then hacked off his head.

Climbing out from beneath the pigsty, he took the head to Olav, expecting to be rewarded with a gold ring. Instead, just as Hakon had predicted, Olav gave the thrall a red necklace, ordering him to be hanged on the spot. As for the jarl's head, it was stuck on a stake so that passers-by could throw stones at it.

Born shortly after his father's murder by Harald Wolf Skin, Olav Tryggvason was a great-grandson of Harald Fair Hair. Captured by

Estonian pirates at the age of three, after six years as a child slave he was rescued by a Norwegian merchant who, realising who he was, bought and freed him, then took him to Scandinavian Novgorod where he spent the rest of his childhood. When about twelve, seeing his former owner in the marketplace at Novgorod, Olav, unrecognised, snatched the man's axe and killed him.

Modern historians question this background. 'Olav must be considered a self-made man', writes Sverre Bagge, who believes his descent from Harald was a fabrication.[8] Tom Shippey agrees: 'What the legend of Olav's early life seems to say is that an adventurer from the southern Baltic appeared on the Norse scene with a story of his ancestry that was mostly or entirely self-authenticated.'[9] Yet all early sources accept Olav's account of himself.

What is beyond dispute is that Olav Tryggvason grew up to be a young man who was a magnetic combination of charm and ferocity. Soon after being given command of the *druzina* (bodyguard) of Prince Vladimir of Kiev and Novgorod, he fell out with his employer and became a Viking, raiding along the shores of the Baltic Sea. During this period, he married the King of Wendland's daughter, Geila.

When Geila died, Olav joined the Danish King Sveinn Tjúguskegg (Forkbeard) in 991 in a raid on England, ravaging today's Home Counties with fire and sword, wiping out a little band of Essex men who dared to challenge his army. Their self-sacrifice inspired a famous Anglo-Saxon poem, *The Battle of Maldon*, in which the heroic old thane Byrhtnoth, fighting to the death against Olav's Vikings, shouts to his comrades:

'Thought must be the harder, heart the keener,
Spirit shall be more as our strength lessens.'

But Byrhtnoth's sacrifice was in vain. Shortly after the battle, King Ethelred the Unready (whose name meant 'ill advised') bought off the invaders with 16,000 pounds' worth of silver, setting a disastrous precedent that attracted further swarms of Vikings.

Now in his late twenties, Olav Tryggvason was the classic Viking, who impressed his crew by juggling with three daggers, throwing two spears at once or running along the oars of a longship. 'Merry and frolicsome', he was generous, good company and wonderfully brave in battle, but horribly cruel when angry, apt to have captured enemies burned alive or thrown from mountain tops. He owned a huge dog, probably an Irish wolfhound acquired during a raid in Ireland, with whom he developed a close bond. Highly intelligent, Vige went everywhere with his master, more than once helping him to run down and kill an enemy. When he was badly wounded by a sword cut, Olav had him carried back on board his ship and took pains to see that he was nursed back to health.

Having decided to make himself King of Norway, Olav had the good fortune to arrive in Trøndelag in 995 during the revolt against Jarl Hakon led by Sunbeam's husband. Using his share of Ethelred's silver to buy the bonders' support, he was elected king by a Thing at Trondheim and soon people throughout Norway acknowledged his right to rule the country as Harald Fair Hair's heir. He quickly established his capital at Nidaros (now Trondheim), starting to build a new town where until then, according to *Fagrskinna* (a catalogue of the kings of Norway), there had been only a single house.

Olav had been converted to Christianity during the previous year, by a clairvoyant hermit in the Scilly Isles who told his fortune with startling accuracy, warning him of a mutiny about to break out aboard his ships that he would put down – which was precisely what happened. Soon after becoming king, he set about bringing his subjects to the same faith. He had brought several priests with him.

Bishop Sigurd, an Englishmen, was a 'wise and good man and a great scholar', so holy that Olav was afraid of him. The German Thangbrand was rather different, however, a giant with a glib tongue and a furious temper. Appointed priest of the church on Moster, he robbed several pagans, who in his eyes were beyond the law. As punishment, he was sent to Iceland where he made many converts. However, with aid of a neophyte he then murdered two men for mocking him. The last straw was when he challenged a pagan berserker to a trial by fire and the berserker mysteriously fell on his own sword, after which Thangbrand was outlawed and run off the island.

The first step in Olav's own missionary activities was to hold a Thing at Maere, at the head of the Trondheimsfjord where there was a famous temple, and order everybody in the Trøndelag to convert. Staunch conservatives, the bonder, who all came to the meeting fully armed, told him bluntly to stop preaching this new religion. Their leader, Jern Skiaegge ('Iron Beard'), insisted that Olav must sacrifice to the old gods. Pretending to agree, Olav gave a lavish feast for the bonder at which he made them very drunk with heroic quantities of ale and mead. They did not realise they were drinking 'tainted' liquor that had gone bad in a way undetectable by those who swallowed it. Next morning, when the guests awoke with appalling hangovers, they were summoned to his presence.

'You say no sacrifice is so pleasing to [the gods] as the killing of men, who then feast with them in the other world,' he announced. 'I now intend to offer you as a sacrifice to them, to promote peace for myself and perpetual honour for you.' In his Latin life of Olav, the monk Oddr Snorrason tells us that 'there was great dejection in the hall'. Quickly and eagerly, everybody asked for baptism, whereupon the king announced that he was cancelling the sacrifice.[10]

His next step was to go with his men to the Maere temple where they smashed all the idols into pieces. Jern Skiaegge, who came running to try and prevent the sacrilege, was cut down outside. The king proclaimed that those refusing to convert must expect death or mutilation. He also took hostages, sending men all over the Trøndelag to see that everybody accepted baptism. 'And no man in the Trondheim country opposed Christianity.'

To show that he would obey Norway's laws, as part of the blood price for Jern Skiaegge's killing he married his only child, Gudrun. A fine, high-spirited girl who had not forgiven her father's murder, when in bed with the king on their wedding night she tried to knife him as soon as she thought he had fallen asleep, but Olav was awake and managed to disarm her. Snorri informs us, a little unnecessarily, that 'Gudrun never came into the king's bed again'.

Unfortunately Olav made enemies all too easily, due to a certain lack of tact. When he offered to marry the dowager Queen Sigrid of Sweden, Harald Grenski's one-time flame, and she brusquely declined to join his new religion, he slapped her face with his glove, sneering, 'Why should I want to have you, old wrinkle-face, a faded old woman who is a heathen bitch?'

'This means your death,' retorted Sigrid, already furious that a massive gold ring he had given her had turned out to be gilded brass. She kept her word after she married the King of Denmark, Sveinn Forkbeard.

In September 1000, as Olav was returning in his ship *The Long Serpent* from a raid on the Wendland Slavs, Jómsborg Vikings lured him into an ambush at 'Svoldr' that Adam of Bremen places in the Øresund – the great stretch of water between Sweden and Denmark. Led by Hakon the Evil's son, Jarl Eirík, who brought a band of Norwegian exiles, the enemy included Sveinn Forkbeard and King Olof Skötkonung of Sweden, Sigrid's son by her first marriage. Their joint fleet numbered between sixty and eighty vessels.

When they saw that the enemy 'carpeted the sea with warships', most of Olav's fleet fled, leaving him with a dozen vessels.[11] 'Haul down the sails,' he ordered the remainder. 'Never shall men of mine think of flight. I never fled from battle. Let God dispose of my life, but flight I shall never take.' He added that he was unafraid of 'soft Danes, for there is no bravery in them', nor of pagan Swedes, 'horse-eaters' who should have stayed at home 'licking their sacrificial bowls'. But he admitted that the exiled Norwegians were a different matter.

Both Snorri and *Fagrskinna* tell us the ensuing battle was among the bloodiest in Viking history. At first, it went in favour of Olav whose men boarded Sveinn Forkbeard's flagship, forcing him to flee to another vessel, but eventually sheer force of numbers prevailed and they were overwhelmed. In the end, only *The Long Serpent* remained unconquered, hemmed in by the enemy. Olav's hird grew so mad with rage that they tried to leap on board the hostile ships to get at the foe and kill them, but misjudging the distance sank beneath the waves under the weight of their armour. Jarl Eirík's Norwegians boarded, cutting down Olav's men until only the king and his marshal Kolbjorn the Red were left, driven back to the poop. Finally, Olav and Kolbjorn leapt into the sea, each from a different side, the king holding his shield over his head to ward off spears thrown by the men in the boats who surrounded the ship. Kolbjorn was captured but not Olav.

For years, rumours of King Olav Tryggvason's survival circulated, insisting that he had swum ashore and escaped, and was in Wendland or southern Europe, some even claiming that he had become a monk at Jerusalem. Yet no one ever saw the king again.

He had been genuinely popular and many mourned him. Oddr Snorrason tells how after Einar Tambarskjelve, the king's brother-in-law, was given quarter by the enemy he told Olav's dog, 'We have no master now, Vige', at which the hound growled, then gave a single, tremendous howl of anguish. Reaching the shore, he lay down on a mound, refused to eat and with tears running down his muzzle stayed there until he died.

Writing about 1190, Oddr hints that Olav might well have been another John the Baptist, in making Norway ready for his royal cousin. He says that Olav vanished at Svoldr in a flash of light, putting him in the same class as the prophet Elijah who prepared the way for Christ and went up to heaven in a whirlwind of fire. However, Adam of Bremen claimed that on the contrary Olav had not only patronised witches and had sorcerers among his bodyguard but that he had practised the black arts himself, divining the future from the flight of birds. Adam even implies that the king may have reverted to paganism.[12]

Snorri Sturluson's reading of Olav Tryggvason, as a convert who did not fully understand his new religion, is far more plausible, although even after his conversion the Norse gods remained very real to Olav, who believed that Odin visited him to win back a lost sheep for the pagan fold. Oddr Munkr relates how a one-eyed old man in a broad brimmed hat, strangely knowledgeable and eloquent to the point of garrulity, came to Olav when he was on his farm of Avaldsnes and, answering his question, told him that Avald had been a king who worshipped a cow and fell in a battle nearby. He also explained other events that had long been mysteries. Fascinated, Olav listened to him until late into the night until Bishop Sigurd, who sensed something wrong about the visitor, said the king must go to bed. However, the old man sat talking on the foot stool at the end of the bed, and as soon as he ended one tale Olav asked for another. Finally, the bishop persuaded the king to go to sleep.

When he awoke next morning, Olav immediately asked for the visitor but he had vanished. When the cook told him that he had left two fine pieces of beef for the royal table, the king found it was horse meat dressed as beef and ordered it to be burned. He now realised who the old man had been – Odin himself, and not just his ghost. Probably a dream that Olav described to his courtiers, it shows how strong a hold paganism kept on the Norse mind.[13]

In Snorri's view Olav Tryggvason had been a good Christian, if in his own way. He tells us the king detested the witches and warlocks who played a vital role in the old religion, describing with approval how he had left a band of warlocks roped together on a skerry at low tide so that they drowned as the sea came in, and how he had glowing coals placed on another's belly until it burst. When a notorious sorcerer chieftain named Raud the Strong refused to abandon his witchcraft and accept the new faith, the king made him swallow a live adder, forcing it to crawl through a horn tube down his throat – encouraged by a red-hot iron. We are told that the snake ate its way out through his left side and 'thus Raud perished'.

Norsemen remembered Olav Tryggvason as a great hero although his kingdom vanished with him, as did his work of evangelisation, many reverting to the old religion. Yet while he may not have been a second Elijah, one day his example would teach another man a good deal about how to become King of Norway. He had prepared the way for his cousin, Olav Haraldsson.

3

The Viking Olav Haraldsson

'like agile wolves [they] set out to rend the Lord's
sheep, pouring out human blood to their god Thor.'
William of Jumièges, *Gesta Normannorum Ducum*[1]

Snorri's saga tells us that Olav Haraldsson became a Viking in 1007 when only twelve, the career for which he had been born. For, as Sverre Bagge stresses, Norway was 'the Viking kingdom par excellence, as all its rulers between around 930 and 1066 had a Viking or mercenary background and most of them came directly from abroad to take power'.[2] Because of their country's long coastline and valuable merchandise Norwegians became a race of seamen and merchants – and of raiders and slavers.

In the second half of the twentieth century, historians began to 'rehabilitate' Vikings, stressing their role as merchants and explorers, playing down predatory aspects. 'Common sense' theories abounded about what drove them forth from Scandinavia, the most plausible being too few women. But in 2018 a revisionist historian, Tom Shippey, published a stimulating book, *Laughing Shall I Die*, in which, dismissing the 'not raiders' view held by academics whom he labels 'tender-hearted moderns', he argues that Vikings were driven by a death cult, as bizarre as it was ferocious.[3]

Heroism was defined by behaviour in defeat, not in victory, he believes. Since a man's life was so short and dying inevitable, there was little point in fearing death, as long as you made sure you died in the right way, which meant fighting to the bitter end and defying your killer with your last breath. This ensured admission to Valhalla with a seat at the table of the gods.

For over 250 years the Vikings raided England, Ireland, Scotland, the Netherlands, France, Italy, Spain, the Baltic lands and Russia, even their Scandinavian homelands. Victims were unable to appreciate their benevolent side, knowing only the accompanying bloodshed and ruin, and if they did not actually pray *A furore Normannorum, liberanos Domine* ('From Norsemen's fury, deliver us, O Lord') as tradition claims, the prayer tells us how they felt. To them, a Viking was a murderous predator who killed, raped, burned, plundered and enslaved. When they sighted his sail on the horizon they fled, although often he lowered his mast, using his oars – 'those oars that dip in blood' – and took them by surprise.

In contrast, everybody at home in Scandinavia admired a successful Viking, even when they themselves had suffered from his raids, since he had gained wealth and prestige. Besides a ship, he usually owned a large farmstead in which to house and entertain his crew. Having sown the spring crops he went raiding, returning shortly after midsummer for the reaping. When the harvest was in, he sailed on his autumn raid, coming home just before winter.

Admittedly though, many Vikings were merchants as well as raiders, who made their trading ventures in *knarrer*, tubby, half-decked cargo ships of up to sixty tons dependent on sail, but big enough to carry horses or livestock.[4] On the voyage out they took slaves, furs of polar bear, wolf, marten and otter, seal skins, reindeer hides, ropes of twisted whale hide, white falcons from Greenland or Iceland, goose and eider duck feathers, iron bars, soapstone and whetstones. The most valuable item was walrus tusk ivory, the only ivory available to northern Europe before elephant tusks began arriving from Africa.

They brought back French or German swords and armour, textiles, precious metals, gems, jewellery, gold and silver coins, glass beakers, pottery and wine from France or Spain, even Chinese silks. Friendly ports were available in lands settled by Vikings, but this did not stop

them from trading or selling and buying slaves in lands further from
home. On camel back, they even did business as far away as Baghdad.

Intrepid seamen, lacking compasses or astrolabes they navigated
by the pole star and the sun, using small wooden sundials; when the
sun was hidden by cloud, they found it with a crystal 'sun-stone'.
They also relied on their experience of currents, on prominent land-
marks, on how birds behaved, on smell. With these primitive aids
they sailed south to England and Ireland, to France and Spain, east
along the Baltic, and west into the unknown Atlantic as far as
Newfoundland and Labrador. If their navigation was at fault or they
were blown off course, they profited by finding new lands, colonising Iceland, the Faroes and Greenland.

Olav sailed on a *langskip* that, unlike a knarr, was a ship of war.
Designed for manoeuvrability and speed, with a resilient, clinker-
built hull of tarred, overlapping oak planks held together by iron
rivets over a very strong keel she stood up well to the pounding of
the waves and could weather high seas despite being low amid-
ships. Square-rigged, her single sail, of fine woven wool lightly
oiled and toughened by leather bands, might be as large as 1,000
square feet, and was raised and lowered by a windlass. Sometimes
the sail was striped red and white – 'blood and bone' to signify war
and death – or, still more threatening, black. Olav's flamboyant
half-brother Harald Hardrada preferred purple sails made in
Constantinople.

A longship usually had sixteen oarsmen a side whose light, narrow-
bladed oars were made of pine. The fastest vessel of her age, with a
fair wind in her sail she could reach twenty knots an hour over short
distances, while using oars alone she averaged from six to seven
knots.[5] Skilful use of the steering paddle (side rudder) mounted star-
board aft, together with co-ordination of the oars and the bast or
twisted whale-hide ropes working the sail, enabled her to turn in her
own length. When the steering paddle was pulled up, the hull's shallow draft allowed her to penetrate up rivers deep into enemy

territory. There was a big version, called a 'dragon-ship', and a smaller known as a *snekkja*. Olav Tryggvason's *Long Serpent* was so large that she needed 120 men to row her.

Undecked, these graceful vessels lacked any protection from wind, rain or sea spray, although in foul weather those on board might don oil-soaked woollen or leather clothing. The skald Sigvat Thordarson, who sang from experience, recalls how

> Down the fjord sweep wind and rain,
> Our ship's sail and tackle strain.
> Wet to the skin,
> We're sound within
> And gaily o'er the waves are dancing.[6]

At night while she rode at anchor, the crew slept under their oarsmen's benches in sleeping bags or wrapped in cloaks. Sometimes they rigged up an awning over the benches, using the sail.

The crewmen who hung along the gunnels their round, iron-bossed, iron-rimmed, lime-wood and leather shields, often painted red or white, were armed with bows, spears and above all with swords or battleaxes. In case he dropped his sword or his axe in the scrum at the shield-wall – all Viking battles meant fighting at close quarters – a long, single-edged, heavy bladed dagger hung from each man's belt, at an angle facilitating speedy withdrawal from its sheath.

In battle, the wealthy wore body armour, left off when rowing, that consisted of thigh-length byrnies of interlinked chain mail or of small metal plates fastened together with leather laces. They also had iron helmets, sometimes with a goggle-like guard for eyes and nose and a species of chain-mail veil to protect the throat and lower face that made them look nightmarish. Poorer men wore thickly padded leather coats with helmets of reinforced leather or even wood. (Contrary to the belief of nineteenth-century painters, the helmets never sported bulls' horns or eagles' wings.)

* * *

Vikings were fascinated by the sea and its enigma, as their sacred poetry shows. When Thor asks 'the all wise' dwarf Alvis what name he should give to the water on which men row in each and every world, he is told

'Sea it's called by men, and ever-lier by the gods,
the Vanir call it rolling one,
eel-land the giants, liquid-fundament the elves,
the dwarfs the deep ocean'.[7]

Yet however seaworthy a Viking boat might be, however tough and skilful those who sailed her, even the biggest longship or knarr was a tiny vessel too often overwhelmed by high seas, never to be heard of again. Out of twenty-five ships that Eric the Red took to colonise Greenland in 985, eleven were lost. The last moments of a doomed crew amid a howling gale that to their ears sounded like demon voices were made still more terrifying by their religion.

This taught that all who perished at sea, unless in a battle, must lie at the bottom for centuries, until summoned up to go on board *Naglfar*, a vast, rotting longship built from the fingernails of all drowned men and shrouded in green weed. When everyone had been packed aboard, some would man the oars and the sail while the dreadful god Loki would take the helm, steering them towards Ragnarök, where they would all fight – and die for ever. There were some fortunate exceptions, as the sea goddess Ran might trap drowned men in her great net of yarn, hauling them up into the home of her sea god husband, the giant Aegir, who like all giants lived in Jotunheim where there was good feasting and drinking. Sometimes their ghosts appeared to reassure their families. But they were a very small minority.

The voyages on which Vikings sailed were gambles, during which even the moaning of the waves might seem menacing. Yet the fatalism instilled by their religion gave them the resolve to embark. They called on Odin for help, remembering how he boasted that he could calm the wind that stirred up the waves and lull the sea to sleep.

In 1007 Olav's mother Åsta commissioned a longship for him, asking his foster-father Hrani, who was a veteran Viking, to command it and look after the boy. As skipper, Hrani was helmsman but, despite being called 'king' by the crew because of his royal lineage and in theory their leader in combat, Olav rowed with the oarsmen. Snorri and *Fagrskinna* describe his early adventures, with sparse detail and unrecognisable places names. Their sources were mainly Sigvat Thordarson's *Vikingarvísur* or the *Höfudlausn* of another skald, Ottar the Black. They tell us of Olav seeing hard-fought combats during raids along the Baltic coast and in England.

His first battle was with another Viking named Soto, a Swede, in some islands off the Swedish coast. Olav's men were outnumbered but had bigger ships. Anchoring amid a reef of sunken rocks, they made it impossible for the enemy to close and make use of superior numbers, dealing with them one by one, throwing grappling irons over their gunwhales, boarding and slaughtering their crews. In the end, the remainder fled. Sigvat writes, 'At Soto's rock, the wolves howl over their fresh food.'

During Olav's ensuing raid on Sweden, inspired by a wish to avenge his murdered father, he plundered the land around Sigtuna, besieging the recently founded royal town. Between modern Uppsala and Stockholm, near Lake Mälaren, this had a mint where Sweden's first coins were being hammered out, modelled on Anglo-Saxon pennies, with the words 'Olof, King in Sigtuna'. The town was the pride and joy of its founder, the avaricious Swedish monarch Olof Skötkonung (his name means 'tax king'), who rushed to defend it with a large army and trapped the Norwegians in Lake Mälaren, laying iron chains across the channel from the lake into the sea. Olav escaped by digging a new channel that, providentially, was suddenly flooded by heavy rain.

Then he sailed to Gotland, arriving in time for the harvest and forcing its inhabitants to pay him a heavy scatt. The beautiful island suited him so well that he spent several weeks there. After these attacks on Sigtuna and Gotland, Olof Skötkonung could never hear Olav's name mentioned without breaking into a rage.

For all his attempts to belittle Olav Haraldsson, Olof Skötkonung was far from being the all-powerful ruler he claimed. Despite his not very effective attempt to build a centralised, Christian monarchy, Sweden was still largely a land of semi-independent kinglets and most Swedes remained pagan. Although the kinglets acknowledged Olof as overlord, they were not under his direct rule, which was confined to the eastern areas.

Sometimes young Olav and his crew got a bloody nose, as in 1008 when he and his men landed on the Estonian island of Øsel (Saaremaa), demanding furs, food or amber – most prized of Baltic commodities. The Estonians, who were accustomed to Viking raids, responded by attacking in force, but the Norwegians managed to rout them.

In Finland, the locals vanished into the forest and, when evening came, ambushed Olav and his crew as they withdrew, attacking from all sides and inflicting heavy casualties. He and the rest of his men only just managed to escape to their ship. That night the Finns used witchcraft to whip up a terrible storm and high waves, but the king ordered the sail hoisted, then beat offshore all night, until the weather improved sufficiently for him to put out to sea. No doubt, Olav used magic of his own, praying to Odin who promised his worshippers he would come to their aid in battle:

I sing in the shields and in strength they go
Whole to the field of fight,
Whole from the field of fight,
And whole they come thence home.[8]

Usually, Olav (with Hrani behind him) was spectacularly successful in raid after raid, gathering substantial loot. In Kurland – part of Latvia – he slaughtered vast numbers of the natives when they refused to pay him tribute. He fought another battle with Vikings who seem to have been Danes off the Jutland coast of Denmark. Next, after lying offshore 'in dreadful weather', he attacked Friesland – North Holland. When he landed, the Frisians came down to the shore to fight, but he easily defeated them. Dutch sources record a raid by Vikings up the River Waal in 1009 during which they plundered and burned the town of Tiel. This sounds like Olav.

To be a Viking was to be a slaver, and they must have captured a fair number of sturdy men and pretty girls who would sell for their weight in gold in the slave market. Because of limited space on board a longship, these were trussed up with bast ropes and stowed like bundles under the rowing benches. There they would lie until they could be safely transferred to a knarr acting as support vessel which was waiting at an agreed rendezvous.

So prosperous a career earned Olav respect throughout the Scandinavian world. He was credited with an unusually positive *hamingja*, that inner spirit who brought good fortune. More and more Vikings joined him, eager to share in his astonishing run of luck. Soon he found himself commanding not just a single longship but a flotilla.

Snorri and *Fagrskinna* do not say where he spent the winters. The *Historia Norwegie* thought he did so at the far end of the Baltic in Viking Holmgard (Veliky Novgorod).[9] However, it is likely that he and his longships spent at least one winter in Norway, to sell or store booty, refitting and replacing casualties. Further cruises were out of the question during the winter months. They returned in mid-October, to reach home in time for the autumn ale drinking.

Having devastated the pagan shores of the Baltic in what a chronicler calls a 'prolonged bout of Viking ferocity', he looked for plunder elsewhere.

In September 1009 the Dane Thorkell Høye (the Tall) landed in England with forty-five ships. Many of his men were Jómsvikings, a brotherhood of dedicated warriors with tested combat skills, whose code forbade them to show fear even when captured and facing death or torture. If they lost their legs in battle, lying on their backs they went on shooting arrows at the enemy. Worshippers of Odin and Thor, these Jómsborgers, who had to be no younger than eighteen and no older than fifty, were forbidden to marry, living only for war and loot. They became so famous that a *Jómsvikinga saga* was written about them.[10]

They took their name from their base on the Baltic, at Jómsborg in Pomerania at the mouth of the River Oder, and in the land of the Wends – now Poland. Recently, the site of Jómsborg has been identified as Wiejkowo near Wolin. A supposedly impregnable fortress, it was defended by stone-throwing catapults that guarded a harbour with shelter for 360 longships. Despite paying an annual tribute to the Danish King Sveinn Forkbeard, who had close links with them, the Jómsborgers' loyalty was to their leaders alone.

Crack troops of this sort, superbly equipped and highly disciplined, with a reputation for inhuman ferocity, were more formidable than any of their Viking predecessors, infinitely superior to the local levies, half-trained, badly armed and poorly led, that made up the Anglo-Saxon *fyrd* (militia).

Olav had joined Thorkell in Denmark, bringing his own ships and men. Anglo-Saxon sources call him a 'host leader', implying he was second in command of the entire army. He must have been an unusually impressive young man for Thorkell and the Jómsvikings, who were mostly Danes, to accept him. Perhaps they saw him as a reincarnation of Olav Tryggvason.

Early sources differ in describing Olav's years in England. *Historia Norwegie* claims that throughout he worked in partnership with Knut, the son of King Sveinn Forkbeard of Denmark. However, I believe that *Fagrskinna* and Snorri are correct in saying that from the very start the two men were enemies and fought on opposing sides.[11]

Besides marvelling at England's wealth, Olav found himself at home since there were so many settlers in the eastern midlands and the north who spoke Norse as their first tongue. (As late as King John's reign, there were Norse speakers at Leicester.) But *The Saga of Gunnlaug Serpent-tongue*, written during the century after Olav, goes too far in claiming that 'in those days, the language in England was the same as that spoken in Norway and Denmark'.[12] However, Snorri tells us that Olav showed no reluctance to 'redden the hair of the English'.

Fortifying Greenwich as a base camp, Thorkell besieged 'Lundenburh' whose inhabitants defended it desperately. Hoping to cut off the *burh* of Southwark on the south bank from the 'castle' on the north – the Tower of London's forerunner – Olav offered to demolish London Bridge, which even then was so wide that two wagons could pass one another while crossing the Thames. It was fortified by breast-high wooden parapets and turrets.

Snorri says that Olav's men roofed their longships with timber torn down from huts in the area, tied together with hazel withies, for protection against the boulders, stones, spears and boiling oil or water that they anticipated (correctly) would be hurled down on them, taking care to make the roofs high enough to swing their swords and axes. Although many craft were driven back by the missiles, others succeeded in getting under the bridge where they tied chains to the oak piles that supported it, then rowed hard away downstream at a time of day when the current, at that period very strong, was in their favour. The bridge collapsed, spilling its defenders into the river.

In a verse from *Höfudlausn*, quoted by Snorri but probably rewritten by him, Ottar the Black declaims (in Samuel Laing's translation) that 'London Bridge is broken down'. It used to be thought that this was the origin of the old nursery rhyme, 'London Bridge is falling down', but recent criticism has shown that this is not the case. Even so, its destruction was a remarkable achievement and bears all the marks of Olav's ingenuity.

Contrary to Snorri's account, Thorkell failed to capture Southwark, so he collected horses, mounted his army and rode west where they sacked Oxford. Then, using the roads left by the Romans, plundering and burning towns and villages as they went, butchering every man, woman, child or beast they met, they returned to Greenwich in spring 1010. Embarking on their ships, instead of going home as the English expected, the entire host sailed round the coast to East Anglia. For three months they harried and looted, killing everything, even penetrating into the fens, defeating an English army at Ringmere Heath, and burning down Thetford and Cambridge. After this, they went back to Greenwich, perpetrating their customary atrocities with zest en route.

After this, Olav led the Viking army down to Kent.[13] Here he besieged Canterbury for nearly three weeks, storming and sacking the hallowed cathedral city in September 1011, 'colouring it red in the morning'. The *Anglo-Saxon Chronicle* says that he only broke through the walls because of the (unspecified) treachery of Abbot Aelfmar of St Augustine's.

In the tenth century Aethelweard, the scholarly ealdorman of Wessex and a member of the royal house of Cerdicing, described Vikings in his chronicle as 'the vilest of people' (*plebs spurcissima*). The English loathed them. It is revealing that the leather covering of the door of Hadstock church in Essex was long believed to be the skin of a Viking flayed alive. When in November 1002 King Ethelred ordered all 'Danes, who spring up like cockles amid the wheat', to be slain on St Brice's Day, thousands were slaughtered. Norsemen died too, no distinction being made between Dane or Norse. At Oxford a group were burned alive in a church where they had taken refuge. Others were murdered and buried in mass graves.

Written a century later, John of Worcester's record of what happened to Canterbury and its citizens after Olav's men stormed in helps to explain why they were so unloved. He tells how a quarter of the city went up in flames during the sack, how its defenders were thrown down from the ramparts or hung up by their private parts until they died. Matrons were dragged through the streets by the hair and pushed into the fires alive, younger women raped en masse. Babies were thrown up into the air, to be caught on spear points or crushed under cartwheels.[14]

Although the Vikings may have been settling the score for the St Brice's Day genocide, Olav's savagery was a carefully calculated terror tactic. In much the same way that Nazi troops used *schrecklichkeit* in the twentieth century, the aim was to strike fear into every Englishman and Englishwoman who heard about the sack of Canterbury. It would make them readier to pay Danegeld.

When the host left the city's smoking, corpse-strewn ruins, they took with them the saintly archbishop, Alphege (Aelfheah) as a hostage, dragging him along as 'a roped thing'. The *Anglo-Saxon Chronicle* mourned:

> Then was he a captive, he who had been
> The head of England and of Christendom.
> There might be seen wretchedness
> Where often bliss was seen before,
> In that unhappy city, whence came first to us
> Christendom, and heaven and earthly bliss.[15]

At Greenwich the next April, the archbishop refused to let himself be ransomed for the vast sum of £3,000. The reaction of the host, who were fighting drunk 'with wine from the south', was to hurl stones, ox bones and sheeps' heads at him or beat him with axe-handles. (Ironically, a punishment inflicted on cowards who deserted the shield-wall in battle.) Thorkell made repeated attempts to save Alphege's life but failed, despite offering to buy it with his ships. In the end, when the archbishop was half dead, a Christian Viking called Thrym, whom he had confirmed only the day before, put the old man out of his misery 'with compassionate impiety' by splitting his head with an axe. The Londoners took away the body and buried it at St Paul's.

What makes St Alphege's story still more poignant is that he had converted several Vikings to Christianity, notably King Sveinn Forkbeard in 994, and perhaps Thorkell the Tall. It has even been surmised that while a captive he discussed religion with Olav, but Snorri's statement that soon after Alphege's death Olav 'scoured the country', threatening massacre if the English refused to pay up, suggests otherwise. In *Vikingarvísur* Sigvat Thordarson explains what he was scouring for:

> Money, if money could be got –
> Goods, cattle, household gear if not.[16]

Olav's priority was not so much to terrify the population as to squeeze the last silver penny and handful of grain out of them.

Taking his share of the £48,000 of the Danegeld that King Ethelred paid Thorkell, Olav left England in summer 1012. We only know what he did next from Sigvat, as quoted by *Fagrskinna*, and by Snorri who are both unreliable for this period, but it looks as though he became a mercenary in the service of Duke Richard II of Normandy – a Norman chronicler says that 'Olav King of the Norsemen' captured Dol in Brittany for the duke.

He then went raiding in western France, in the wealthy region between Poitou and Touraine, besides burning down the town of Guérande in Brittany at the mouth of the Loire, campaigns made possible by his shallow-drafted ships' ability to sail up rivers. Then in autumn 1013 he went to Normandy with his men as mercenaries who once again were hired by Duke Richard to fight for him, this time in a quarrel with the Count of Chartres.

Unexpectedly, Richard and the count made peace. Olav decided that instead of returning to Norway he would spend the winter recuperating in Normandy.

4

Olav Abandons the Gods

friendly counsels,
and wisely composed,
seven I have imparted to thee:
consider thou them well,
and forget them never . . .

Songs of the Sun, Saemund Frodi[1]

Snorri Sturluson tells us that 'from Ganger Rolf descend the Earls of Rouen, who have long reckoned themselves to be of kin to the chiefs in Norway, and they hold them in such respect that they were always the friends of the Norsemen; and every Norseman found a friend in Normandy.'[2] Many people, including the modern Normans, are inclined to take this statement at face value.

Yet while we can believe Snorri when he says, 'To Normandy Olav came in autumn, and stayed all winter on the Seine in good peace and quiet,' the duchy had ceased to be a Scandinavian land despite its boundaries being little changed. Moreover, Ganger Rolf and his men had come from Denmark instead of Norway, and there is speculation that some may have been English-born Danes, recruited in the Danelaw.

After a thinly spread colonisation in a few areas, such as the north Cotentin, Caux and Roumois, especially on the coast, the leaders, who took over the estates of the French magnates and married French wives, had been easily assimilated. Lesser men who secured good farms and likewise married local women must have become French even sooner. There is little archaeological evidence for a Viking presence, merely a single burial and one or two swords. The only solid proofs are a scattering of place names in a few areas near the coast or on the banks of the Seine and the Orne, with some traces of Scandinavian law in the old Norman law code and a sprinkling of Scandinavian words in the French vocabulary.[3]

By the time Olav arrived, which was a century after the conquest, Ganger Rolf's language was dying out. When a boy Richard II, who was the present duke, had been sent to learn it at Bayeux where it was still spoken. People no longer understood it at Rouen, the duchy's capital. The former Viking colonists of every class now spoke French and looked like Frenchmen.

Even so, the Norman dukes and nobles were proud of their Viking origins (the Ganger's spear was presented to each duke at his investiture), while if it did not give birth to a new race, a dash of Norse blood produced a dynamic warrior elite that would conquer England, Ireland, southern Italy and Sicily. In the meantime, Normandy was becoming France's most powerful feudal state, its dukes lavishing money on arming their subjects. They could easily afford to do so, as their capital was growing richer and richer from the river-borne trade along the Seine to Paris.

Olav was made welcome, perhaps because of his value as a mercenary. During his stay, instead of smashing up medieval civilisation he saw it in working order. It is odd to think of a Viking from the sagas wandering peacefully through Rouen's prosperous streets, entering sumptuously decorated Romanesque churches, listening to the hypnotic Gregorian chant. He may have had the wonder of reading and writing explained to him and seen illuminated manuscripts gleaming with gold.

The chronicler William of Jumièges tells us that 'Urged by Archbishop Robert, King Olav, who had begun to find joy in Christianity, abandoned idolatry as did several of his men. Converting to the Christian faith, he was cleansed with baptism by the arch-bishop.' This took place at the cathedral in the winter of 1013–14. He would have worn a white robe for a week afterwards, as Ganger Rolf had done after his own baptism.

Archbishop Robert was Richard II's brother, so it is possible that the deeply religious duke, a Norse speaker, helped with his conversion. Another chronicler, Dudo of St Quentin, credits Richard with a temper not unlike that of the mature Olav – fond of clerics while crushing a peasants' revolt by removing its leaders' hands and feet. (Even Byzantium, the most 'advanced' European state of the time, seldom inflicted the death penalty but preferred to use mutilation.)

Some historians question Olav's conversion, arguing that he saw Christianity in purely political terms, a basis for 'a system of gift exchange' for asserting his rule more firmly over Norway when he became king. This, they argue, was why he became godfather to men who followed him in converting. 'Godparenthood was therefore perfect for reinforcing the relationship between a chieftain and his followers,' and Olav was seen '. . . as a warrior chieftain willing to use any means, including religion, to gain a greater following and more power.'[4]

Yet there is good reason to think Olav was sincere. A medieval man's life was so harsh that most men could not exist without the support of religion, and the old Norse faith was scarcely reassuring. Odin himself was going to die at Ragnarök while the world's entire land mass would be drowned by the sea. A tenth-century poem, *Völuspá* ('The Prophecy of the Seeress'), warns that

Brothers will fight and kill each other,
Sister children will defile kinship.
It is harsh in the world, whoredom rife –
An axe-age, a wolf-age – before the world goes headlong.
No man will have mercy on another.[5]

Although Christianity also foresaw a terrible end to the universe, it did at least offer hope.

Admittedly, it is unlikely that Olav fully understood his new religion at this early stage of his career. We can assume he was taught the basic foundations of belief, with the paternoster, Ave Maria and Creed in extemporary Norse translations. But he could not read the Bible which would have had to be translated from Latin and read to him, and lacked the mental equipment to grasp such concepts as the Trinity or what took place at Mass. No doubt as time went by he glimpsed more of Christianity's deeper meanings.

While at Rouen, Olav acquired a lasting admiration for 'St Charlemagne' – *Karolus Magnus* – the legendary Christian emperor and missionary who, as the skald Sigvat Thordarson sang to Olav when he was a king, 'had been the best man ever in the world'. Olav did not forget the tales, read to him from such chronicles as Einhard's *Vita Karoli Magni*, of Charlemagne's achievements, of how 200 years before he had created a great empire and tried to rebuild Roman civilisation.

He also heard how Charlemagne converted the heathen Saxons by force of arms, cowing them so that, in Einhard's words, 'they promised to abandon the worship of demons and submit themselves willingly to the Christian religion'. He heard, too, how the emperor decreed that should any Saxon 'scorn to come to baptism and wish to stay a pagan, then let him be punished by death'. In one day alone, he had beheaded 4,500 Saxons for rebelling against the new faith.

When Olav became king, his son was christened Magnus after the great emperor, while he named his mightiest longship the *Karl's Head*, which he adorned with a wooden figurehead of Charlemagne that he had carved himself. Nor did he forget the emperor's methods of conversion in his own missionary work.

Generally thought to date from as late as 1200, an Icelandic poem, the *Sólarljôd* (*Songs of the Sun*) gives an insight into what may have gone on in Olav's mind after he changed his faith. Some think it was written earlier, perhaps by the Icelander Saemund Frodi who died in

1133, a man so strangely learned that although a Christian he was credited with studying witchcraft. Almost a Norse *Pilgrim's Progress*, the poem consists of advice from beyond the grave by a father to his son, based on his own spiritual journey. The 'seven counsels' quoted at the start of this chapter were the Church's seven sacraments, yet the imagery is frequently that of Norse paganism with references to *Dísir* (ghost women who are every family's tutelary spirits), to Hel's ravens and even to Odin. The late date at which the poem was composed is a testimony to how long paganism survived.

Despite spending a week in a white baptismal robe, it took time for Olav's new beliefs to alter his behaviour. As soon as he left Normandy in 1014 he went raiding again in Viking style, in Spain, not before his conversion as Snorri says, but after. According to Sigvat he saw some hard fighting,

> Where Olav's honour seeking sword
> Gave the wild wolf's devouring teeth
> A feast of warriors doomed to death.[6]

Sailing south, he established a base camp at the mouth of the Miño from where he ravaged Christian Galicia with fire and sword, plundering and slaving, attacking Corunna and then Tuy which he burned to the ground. A charter of the following year records the declaration of a man selling land in the area; the Vikings had captured his three daughters, reducing him to poverty since he had been forced to pay a large sum in silver to save them from the slave market. Many others were enslaved or held to ransom, among them the Bishop of Tuy and his senior clergy who were made to pay in gold for their freedom.[7]

Going still further south, Olav is said to have attacked the Moorish city of Cádiz although no details survive. Snorri says that he planned to sail through the Straits of Gibraltar and 'on to the land of Jerusalem', but then had a dream in which 'a great and important man of terrible appearance', told him to give up his Viking life. 'Go back to your inalienable heritage,' he said. 'For you are destined to be king over Norway for ever.' He awoke convinced that the man had been his late cousin Olav Tryggvason, whose message was that he, Olav Haraldsson, was destined to be King of all Norway and that his heirs would wear the crown for centuries.

If he was to become king, he needed more money, but he knew where to find it. Sveinn Forkbeard had returned to England in 1013, bringing a large army and his nineteen-year-old younger son Knut. Determined to make himself king of the English, Sveinn set up a fortified camp at Gainsborough in Lindsey (Lincolnshire), a Norse-speaking town where Scandinavians had long been settled. The Norse settlers in the Five Boroughs who dominated the East Midlands and those in the rest of the Danelaw were quick to accept his rule.

Soon, all the English, even in the Cerdicing dynasty's Wessex heartland, recognised Sveinn as their king. Ethelred II took refuge on board the royal fleet which, fortunately for him, chanced to be at anchor in the Thames, and fled to Normandy with his Norman queen Lady Aelgifu (or Emma) who was the duke's sister. Very reluctantly, London submitted to Sveinn, giving hostages for its citizens' good behaviour. 'At this time nothing went right for this nation,' lamented the *Anglo-Saxon Chronicle*.[8]

Unexpectedly, after a reign that lasted only five weeks King Sveinn Forkbeard died in his bed at Gainsborough on 14 February 1014, apparently from a stroke. Snorri says the English thought he had been killed by 'Edmund the Saint' in the way that the Virgin had sent the holy Mercurius to kill the apostate Emperor Julius. England's patron saint – centuries would pass before he was superseded by St George – Edmund was the martyred King of East Anglia, tied to a tree by Vikings as a sacrifice to Odin and shot to death with arrows during an earlier Viking invasion. Although a convert to Christianity, Sveinn had only himself to blame, having threatened to pull down Edmund's shrine at Bury St Edmund's.

Knut Sveinsson was acclaimed as king by the Danelaw, but the English magnates thought differently. Inviting Ethelred the Unready to come home, they declared that every Danish king was an outlaw. When Ethelred returned, they greeted him with joy, despite his dismal record.

Snorri's story of Olav offering to drive the Danes out of England in return for Northumbria is one of his more glaring mistakes. Yet he may be right in stating that Olav sent Hrani across the Channel to find out what was happening. If so, when Hrani came back he would have reported that while some English magnates supported Knut because they thought a Viking was bound to win, far more of them disliked the prospect of being ruled by a Dane.

Olav met Ethelred II and his tough Norman consort at Rouen before they left for London. Tall and distinguished, the king was more impressive than his nickname suggests if we can believe John of Worcester. (In the *Saga of Gunnlaug Serpent-tongue* he emerges as a surprisingly likeable figure who tells Gunnlaug how to kill a famous berserker in a duel, giving him a special sword.)[9] Presumably after negotiating a hefty payment, Olav followed Ethelred to England early in 1015, bringing his veterans. It seemed an excellent investment. Thorkell the Tall had already gone over to the king while Ethelred's son and heir, the Atheling Edmund, was a brilliant soldier known as 'Ironside'.

A plausible guess is that Olav landed in the West Country, perhaps at Charmouth in Dorset, where for many years the haven had been used as an invasion point by Vikings and from where there was a good road north. Wherever they landed, he and his men made a forced march up to Lincolnshire where they joined Ethelred, who was at the head of an exceptionally strong and well-armed fyrd, accompanied by Thorkell the Tall and his Jómsborgers.

Taking Knut by surprise, before he could assemble his troops, Ethelred's army 'burned and slew every human being they could find' in Lindsey – presumably meaning the Norse settlers who supported Knut. Outnumbered, Knut withdrew to his fleet and sailed back to Denmark to find reinforcements, but not before cutting off the hands and ears and slitting the noses of the Londoners given to his father as hostages. As Ottar the Black said of Olav in *Höfudlausn*,

Landward, you brought back to his land
Ethelred and gave him his realm.
That close friend of warriors, strengthened
In power, there had your help.
Harsh was the strife . . .

Having kept his bargain with King Ethelred and received payment from him, Olav said goodbye and paid off most of his army.

He had got out just in time. Shortly after, Thorkell the Tall and his men who were mainly Danes, would change sides again and go over to Knut as soon as he returned with an adequate army, while Ethelred II would die in April 1016 at the ripe old age of fifty. The struggle for the English throne had only just begun.

Ethelred was succeeded by his son, King Edmund Ironside, one of Anglo-Saxon England's great heroes, who would fight four savage battles in almost as many months, during one of which he nearly succeeded in killing his rival in personal combat. But in October 1016 Edmund was decisively defeated by Knut at 'Assandun' – probably Ashingdon in Essex – where both sides suffered heavy casualties. The *Anglo-Saxon Chronicle* records dolefully that there 'all the flower of the English nation' lost their lives.[10]

Having fought each other to a standstill, the two kings met on the island of Olney where they partitioned England, agreeing that if one of them died the survivor should inherit his share, Knut taking Mercia and the north, Edmund Wessex. When Edmund died in November, many thought he had been murdered at Knut's prompting by his brother-in-law Eadric Streona, Ealdorman of Mercia, who more than once, bribed by the Danes, had deliberately spread panic among Edmund's army. ('Streona' means 'grasping'.) But while Knut used bribery, he did not admire traitors. A year later, at London during Christmas, summoning Eadric to his presence he ordered another ealdorman to 'pay this man what we owe him' – which was to behead him on the spot with an axe. Thrown over the city walls, Eadric's body was left to rot in a ditch.

'Knut the Great' was now undisputed ruler of all England, but his lengthy involvement in the struggle to defeat King Edmund and then establish his regime was a wonderful stroke of luck for Olav. So was the presence by his side of Jarl Eirík's son, who was a formidable soldier. Had these two been free, they would never have tolerated Olav's Norwegian ambitions.

Fabulously rich from years of loot, famous as an invincible leader in battle, Olav now set out to make himself King of Norway. In late summer 1015 he embarked from an unrecorded port, perhaps Norse Grimsby, taking with him a hird of 260 combat-hardened veterans, each of whom was equipped with an expensive mail shirt and an even more expensive steel helmet as well as the best weapons procurable. He also brought an English bishop named Grimkel (or Grimketel), with three other bishops and a team of priests.

They sailed in two knarrer. Tubby, unassuming merchantmen, these would attract less unwelcome attention than longships, while they had room in their holds for Olav's huge personal treasure of 'hack-silver' and silver coin. Every penny of it was going to be needed, to win over enemies and buy allies.

5

The Battle of Nesjar, 1016

'The king who o'er the sea
Steers to bloody victory'

Sigvat Thordarson, *Nesjavísur*

After weathering a fierce gale and high seas that almost sank them,
Olav Haraldsson and his knarrer made land at the tiny island of
Selje off the Stadlandet peninsula. Going ashore, his foot slipped
and he barely saved himself from falling. There could have been no
more alarming omen for the 'swinging of swords', as every Viking
knew. 'Foul is the sign if thy foot shall stumble as thou goest forth
to fight,' warned *The Lay of Regin*. 'Goddesses baneful at both thy
sides will see that wounds thou shalt get.'[1]

'The King falls!' Olav muttered ruefully.

'No!' said Hrani, who was standing next to him. 'You did not fall,
my lord, you were setting your mark firmly on the soil.'

The king laughed, saying, 'It may be so, if God wishes.'[2]

When Olav landed, there had been no King of Norway since Olav
Tryggvason's family governed most of the country: his son Jarl
Sveinn ruling the area around the Oslofjord with what is now
Swedish Bohuslän for Sweden, while his young grandson Jarl Hakon
ruled Trøndelag and much of the west coast for Denmark. Although
Christians, the two Lade jarls tolerated the old faith, leaving people

to worship whatever god they pleased, so that throughout the Upplands and the Trøndelag 'almost everything was heathen, but Christianity survived along the coast'.[3]

In other areas kinglets, some still pagan, were virtually independent. Among them were the five 'kings' in the Upplands, together with Einar Tambarskjelve who held 'great fiefs' in the southern Trøndelag and Erling Skjalgsson in the southwest. Almost everywhere, the old clan leaders and the rich bonder retained considerable authority.

Steering southward, Olav anchored in the Sauesund, off the island of Atløy. Here he was suddenly informed that, unaware of his presence, Jarl Hakon was about to enter the sound in a single longship. Quickly, Olav placed his two knarrer on each side of the narrow entrance channel with a cable running between them.

When the jarl, who assumed that the knarrer were harmless merchantmen, sailed into the channel and over the cable Olav's crews suddenly tautened it with their windlasses, right under the keel of his ship which capsized. Olav's hird then killed a fair number of his men as they were struggling in the sea. However, they pulled out Hakon with a few others, taking the jarl on board Olav's knarr.

Snorri Sturluson and *Fagrskinna* say that the seventeen-year-old Jarl Hakon was the most handsome man anybody had ever seen, his long hair fine as silk bound round his forehead by a gold band. Writing 200 years later, Snorri and *Fagrskinna* describe how Olav had the jarl brought to him at the prow. It was the first time that Olav had met a member of the Lade clan, who had been bitter enemies of Harald Fair Hair's descendants for nearly a century.

'It is true what people say about your family, that you are good-looking folk,' was Olav's greeting. 'But your luck has run out.'

'Success can always change, there is no luck about it,' answered Jarl Hakon. 'It is the same for your family as it is for mine – we take it in turns to be the winners. I am not much more than a boy but I and my men could easily have defended ourselves. However, we were not expecting an attack. It may work out better for us next time.'

'You do not seem to realise that you are in no position to look forward to either winning or losing,' Olav dryly reminded him.

'Only you can decide that,' replied Hakon.

'What would you give me, Jarl, if this time I let you go, unwounded and unharmed?' enquired Olav. When Hakon asked what precisely did he want, Olav's answer was, 'Nothing except that you leave this country, give up your earldom and swear never to fight against me.' Hakon took the oath whereupon Olav let him sail away in peace with those of his men who had survived the ambush.[4]

The jarl sailed to England where he was welcomed by King Knut, who was his mother's half-brother and soon after helped to instal him as ruler of what Scandinavians called the *Sudreyjar* or 'Southern Isles' – the Isle of Man and the Hebrides. Yet Olav was far from having heard the last of the jarl, who many years later would break his oath.

On reaching Hringerike, Olav's stepfather Sigurd entertained him and his men splendidly, 'giving them meat and ale every other day, alternating with bread and butter, with milk to drink', according to *Fagrskinna*.[5] Olav's mother, Åsta, who sounds as if she was still a disciple of Odin, gave him a more Viking welcome. After the feasting had gone on for several days, she told him, 'I would far rather that you were King of Norway even if you should stay king no longer than did Olav Tryggvason, rather than be so little a king as Sigurd Syr is, and die from old age.'

Olav then informed his stepfather, 'I intend to seek my patrimony with my battleaxe and my sword, and I shall do so with the help of my friends and kindred, and of anyone else who is ready to take my side.' Sigurd replied that of course he was going to help but only if the Uppland kings did so too, in which case he would use his influence with the local chieftains and country folk, besides lending him all his property.

'It grieves my heart,' added Sigurd, 'to think that the race and realm of Harald Fair Hair might end for ever, without trace.'

Together Olav and Sigurd went to see the five Uppland kings, who descended from Fair Hair and were his cousins, in order to ask for their support. King Hroerek, one of two brothers who ruled Hedmark, pointed out that once Olav Tryggvason had gained power, 'no man had been able to believe in whatever God he pleased'. He strongly advised letting things stay as they were. But his brother King Ring argued that it would be better for them to have a kinsman as King of Norway; if they helped Olav Haraldsson he would be sure to reward them richly. However, the real reason they decided to back him was that they thought a strong king would strengthen their hand in dealing with unruly chieftains and bonder reluctant to pay them scatt.

After Olav promised the five kings 'perfect friendship' and to obey and improve Norway's laws when he became king, they took an oath to support him. A lot more of Olav's silver must have changed hands.

Then he called a Thing at Trondheim, where he swore to drive out foreign rulers and let the bonder keep their ancient laws. One after another, the five Uppland kings spoke in his favour, until eventually the Thing acclaimed him as King of Norway with what appeared to be unanimity. Marching south, he found himself confronted by a large force of armed and hostile bonder, whom he invited to choose between fighting him or joining him. They chose to join him, swearing loyalty. Once again, silver must have worked its magic.

Olav planned to spend Yule at Nidaros, symbolically, because Olav Tryggvason had founded a town there that had fallen into ruin after his death. Collecting timber, he started to rebuild every dwelling as it had been in Tryggvason's time, which provided employment for men from miles around, while supplies of food and drink were brought up the River Nid (now Nidelva) in readiness for the festive season. He also acquired a skald, the young Icelander Sigvat Thordarson, whose verses pleased the king so much that he gave him a gold arm ring.

Knut's governor, Jarl Sveinn of Lade, was watching. Accompanied by his brother-in-law, Einar Tambarskjelve from Huseby in Orkdal

who was known as 'wobble belly' but also reputed to be 'the strongest man and best bowman in Norway', he took 2,000 troops and
attempted to take Olav by surprise at Nidaros. Luckily, at about
midnight mounted sentries posted on the town's outskirts spotted
them as they were approaching on foot and galloped back in time to
warn the king. Waking his hird, Olav ran with them through the icy
darkness to his boats in the River Nid, then escaped down the fjord
to Orkdal. Jarl Sveinn consoled himself by seizing all the Yule good
cheer, as well as burning the half-rebuilt town to the ground.

After marching south across Gudbrandsdal through the snow,
King Olav spent the remainder of the winter staying at 'guest quarters' in Hedmark – meaning that with his hird he billeted himself on
the homesteads of the richer landowners. When spring came, he
gathered further troops and went to Viken, where many other
bonder joined him with their armed followers. Even the normally
unadventurous Sigurd Syr sent a large contingent that he and his
friends had recruited.

Assembling a fleet of longships, the king prepared for what he
knew would be a decisive battle.

Although in his mid-forties, which then meant on the brink of old
age, Jarl Sveinn was still in his prime, an experienced leader fully
confident of his ability to deal with Olav Haraldsson. He was
strongly supported by many of Norway's leading magnates, notably
by Einar Tambarskjelve and Erling Skjalgsson. Rich, powerful noble-
men with many housecarls, these two saw any attempt to rebuild
Harald Fair Hair's monarchy as a threat to their independence.

While fitting out his longships, Sveinn had recruited every veteran
fighting man in the Trøndelag that he could find, helped by the
major landowners, who were also senior officers in his hird. (Only
the previous summer some of these men, together with more than a
few bonder, had solemnly pledged loyalty to Olav at the Trondheim
Thing.) Now that it was spring, Sveinn set sail towards the Oslofjord
in search of his opponent.

On the morning of 25 March 1016, Palm Sunday, Olav heard Mass after which he ordered everyone to eat a good meal in preparation for the combat ahead. (The *Legendary Saga* tells us that because it was such a holy day, he had asked Sveinn for a truce until after Easter but Sveinn had refused.) Then he went on board his great dragon ship, the *Karlhofdi* or 'Karl's Head', so called from its figurehead that he had personally carved. He steered her himself. Snorri tells us there were a hundred troops on board, who all wore more-or-less wound-proof armour – long 'cold shirts of ring-mail' – and strong, foreign-made helmets.

He says, too, that most of Olav's men carried white shields with crosses of gilt, red or blue, and that crosses were painted on their helmets. The king's white banner was less edifying, since it bore not a cross but a serpent – perhaps in imitation of Harald Fair Hair's old war banner.

Ordering the *lurs*, the great wooden war horns, to sound, he set sail to look for Jarl Sveinn's fleet, which he found lying at anchor at Nesjar in the Langesund inlet in Frierfjord. Lashing themselves together, taking down their masts, the ships of each fleet engaged the other prow to prow, in what in effect was a land battle on sea during which both sides would try to hack their way on board their enemies' vessels and wipe them out. Snorri says that while Sveinn had more men, Olav's were better armed – with better weapons and better armour.

Snorri also says that the king's tactics were to keep his ships in as tight a formation as possible and let his opponents attack first, waiting for them to exhaust their arrows, throwing spears and slingshot. Then he himself headed straight for Jarl Sveinn's ship and made it fast to his own with grappling hooks. As was to be expected from fighting at such close quarters, there were heavy casualties on both sides, with 'limb-lopping' and other terrible wounds. The sea grew red with blood, carpeted with floating corpses, some belly up, some face down, of over-confident Vikings who had led from the front to prove their bravery.

The wounded banner o'er the side
Falls shrieking in the blood-stained tide . . .
The war-birds now in blood may swim

sang young Sigvat Thordarson in *Nesjavísur*, which he composed the following summer as an eyewitness who had taken part, fighting for Olav. 'War-birds' were the Valkyries' ravens.[6]

Snorri's account of Nesjar, based largely on Sigvat's poem, is convincing. It tells us how Olav's men gradually got the better of Sveinn's until the jarl, deciding the battle was lost and that the time had come for him to leave as quickly as possible, ordered his crew to cut the ropes that joined his ship to other vessels. But as soon as this was done Olav's men came still closer alongside and cast grappling irons over his dragon figurehead. Jarl Sveinn had the figurehead hacked off in a desperate attempt to disengage, but was only saved by Einar Tambarskjelve who threw an anchor into his ship and towed him away. They were able to slip out of the fjord without being intercepted. The rest of Sveinn's fleet fled for their lives.

Sigurd Syr, normally so peaceable and unwarlike, urged Olav to pursue Jarl Sveinn and finish him off. However, Olav who knew that his enemy was thoroughly beaten stayed near Nesjar for several days, rewarding his troops with the booty. Sigvat the skald says that the pretty girls of Trondheim were given something to cry about when they saw their boyfriends come home as broken men. Although Sveinn was strongly advised by Erling Skjalgsson to sail north where he could find reinforcements and fight again, he went to Sweden.

Olav sailed along the coast with a large fleet, putting in at every major region and holding a Thing at each one where, besides discussing grievances, he had Christian laws read to the assembly. He also went inland, where he did the same. Thousands of men flocked to him to show their loyalty. Those in Viken and Agder recognised him as king. So did the Trønders, even the men of the inner Trøndelag and those of Hålogaland in the far north. For after his decisive victory over Jarl Sveinn at Nesjar, everyone in Norway could see that Olav's *hamingja*, his inherent good fortune, made it madness to think of resisting him. Snorri claims that 'people and commonalty ran together in crowds and would hear of nothing but that Olav should be king over all the country'. He was twenty-one years old.

The late Olav Tryggvason's brother-in-law, Erling Skjalgsson, who had fought at Nesjar for Jarl Sveinn with such skill and courage, was an exception to the general rejoicing. More or less independent ruler of a vast territory, Erling was the last magnate in Norway who might have resisted Olav, Einar Tambarskjelve having stayed in Sweden in self-imposed exile. Had Erling wanted to fight, he would have been no mean opponent.

However, after a fierce wrangle beneath a stone cross on the island of Kvitsøy, Erling reached an agreement with the new king. While he remained Norway's richest lendmann (great landowner), Olav refused to give him everything he wanted, so that he possessed less power than he had enjoyed under Jarl Sveinn, let alone Olav Tryggvason. Neither man trusted the other, which meant that one day there would be trouble. But under pressure from friends whom he knew he could rely on, Erling grudgingly accepted Olav as his king, leaving his son Skialg in Olav's hands as a hostage.

Now that Olav was King of Norway, he sent a message of friendship to all his new subjects. This, together with their tacit recognition, was the nearest he came to a coronation which would have been meaningless as none of them could have understood what it meant. But no doubt Bishop Grimkel gave him some sort of blessing. The bishop had reason to be thankful. A king's support was crucial for establishing the Christian Church – and eliminating paganism.

6

Building a Kingdom

The ale was drunk by the firelight

Snorri Sturluson[1]

Olav II is rightly seen as the founder of a united Norway. The kingdoms of his predecessors Harald Fair Hair, Hakon the Good and Olav Tryggvason, had broken up into separate territories and petty jurisdictions as soon as they died. However, despite lengthy periods of foreign occupation Olav Haraldsson's realm was going to endure for centuries.

The Norwegians who had most reservations about the new ruler, despite their leaders having sworn loyalty to him, were the inhabitants of Trøndelag and Hålogaland. The former was the fertile area in and around what is now Trondheim, the city on the northwest coast then known as Nidaros. Hålogaland was an adjoining region further up the coast and Norway's most northerly province, much of it lying in the Artic Circle.

The reason why the people of these areas disliked Olav was an inbred loyalty to the Lade jarls who ever since Harald Fair Hair's death had fought against any plans for a unified kingdom. After Sveinn's death, the current jarl was Hakon, whom Olav had trapped in 1015 and sent into exile. Northerners thought of him as their rightful ruler, almost a king over the water. As a result, 'Olav's dealings with Trøndelag largely had the character of an occupational regime, and this region also formed the centre of opposition against him,' says Sverre Bagge.[2]

Regardless of ill feeling – or perhaps because of it – Olav built a mead hall at Nidaros on the banks of the River Nid (Nidelva), where his ancestor Harald Fair Hair had first been acclaimed king and where Olav Tryggvason had tried and failed to found a town. It became Norway's first true city and during his reign developed into a great market centre. The hall was only one of several winter residences, however, because from spring until autumn the king travelled the length and breadth of his kingdom with his hird, spending weeks at a time as guests of the magnates. He made a point of avoiding western Norway, however, since he did not altogether trust Erling Skjalgsson.

The hall at Nidaros was in the northern part of what is now Trondheim. He took up residence here on three occasions, always at harvest time and remaining all winter. Snorri tells us that this was where King Olav dined with his court, afterwards drinking ale, 'ancient mead' or, more rarely, wine with them by the firelight. They would have drunk from gold, silver or hardwood cups, from bull, bison or auroch horns, from precious glass beakers made in the Rhineland. Alcohol-fuelled quarrels were speedily sorted out by the *stallere*, or marshal of the hird. ('Shun not the mead, but drink in measure' advises the High One, in *Hávamál*. 'For rudeness none shall rightly blame thee if soon thy bed thou seekest.') There must have been music to accompany the skalds when they recited their verses, but although archaeologists have unearthed bone flutes and tonal instruments no one will ever know what was played on them.

Long, tall and narrow, built of wood with a roof of wooden shingles instead of thatch or turf, the hall had walls that were probably painted white outside, to dazzle in the short summer months or the winter sun. Inside, except when the great doors at each end were open, it was very dark as to keep out the cold and there were no windows, only the smoke hole in the roof and a few small apertures high up. Other than a few foul-smelling tallow candles and the odd handheld lamp of cod-liver oil, the sole lighting came from the fire in the trench that ran along the centre of the room. It should be remembered that at Nidaros in midwinter the sun rises at 10 a.m., setting at 2.30 p.m.

However, the hall would also have been lit by the bright steel helmets, burnished mail coats and gold and silver hilted swords that the hird hung in rows on the walls, reflecting the firelight. Among them were the king's own gilded helmet, his byrnie (coat of mail) and a new sword, Hneitr ('Stinger') that for some unknown reason had replaced the once-beloved Baesing. They were supplemented by weapons and armour stripped from the bodies of enemies whom his hird had killed in battle.

> No other young ruler
> Can boast richer wall-hangings

sang the king's skald, Sigvat Thordarson in *Austrfaravísur* ('Verses on an Eastern Journey'), in which he calls Olav 'the giver of ocean's glitter' – meaning gold.

There would always have been a skald among the diners, who sang the king's praises to the company, to be rewarded with an unusually fine sword or a thick gold arm ring. Always Icelanders and highly articulate men, familiar with Olav's court, their verse provides invaluable information. Snorri stresses that they told the truth because everyone present knew if they were lying.

In winter, a hall made a welcome contrast to the snowy desolation outside. Everybody sat at a huge trestle table along the edge of the fire trench, on benches covered in furs or rugs. The table had a white cloth on which were gold and silver ornaments. Olav, who wore robes of furred and jewelled silk and drank from a great gold cup, presided from his high seat in the centre. Bishop Grimkel sat next to him, Bjorn the marshal opposite. High-ranking visitors were given a place of honour nearby. Then came the hird, including many of his councillors. The *gestir* (henchmen), who were seldom high-born, sat below the hird. Rewarded less generously, they acted as messengers, harbingers, provision gatherers, secret agents, tax collectors or hangmen.

There were other rough customers in the hird, men whose odd talents were prized by the king, the berserkers and *úlfhédnar*, specialists in breaking enemy morale at the start of a combat. The former were the 'bear warriors' in bearskin tunics who fought in a screaming, self-induced frenzy, bellowing and biting their shields. (Although they did not drug themselves with fly agaric mushrooms as once thought, they may sometimes have used black henbane as a hallucinogen, burning it and inhaling the smoke.) So too may the less well-known úlfhédnar or 'wolf warriors', who in action wore wolf skins and wolf heads and fought in a similar frenzy but howled like wolves as they charged. For all their value in battle, one guesses that these distinguished gentlemen, of whom there may have been a dozen or more, were seated fairly low down.[3]

Among many sizeable outbuildings were the king's bedroom and another large hall in which he held his council meetings. In addition there were rooms with beds for some sixty key household members, hird men and gestir. There were also bathhouses. Sixty servants staffed the royal palace of Nidaros, for that is what it was, together with a multitude of slaves who slept with the horses in the great stable.

As has been said, during his reign Olav only spent three winters at Nidaros.[4] During the other winters he and his court took up residence at Oppland or Borg in Viken, in southeastern Norway, where he seems to have been more popular with the locals, who unlike the Trønder had no nostalgic memories of the Lade jarls. In both places he built royal palaces, apparently on a similar scale to the hall at Nidaros.

An unexpected event overseas strengthened Olav's regime. In Sweden, the defeated Jarl Sveinn's brother-in-law, King Olof Skötkonung, who already loathed Olav and was driven to fury by his taking back Ranríki (Bohuslän) from Swedish rule, had offered to lend the jarl a large, well-equipped army with which to invade Norway. But Jarl Sveinn died shortly after the offer was made.

Unwisely, the two principal Swedish officers in Ranríki, Eilif Gautske in the north and Roa Skialge in the south, both of whom were wealthy local bonder, attempted to collect scatt, summoning a Thing. Olav sent seven henchmen to attend it, cloaks over their mail and hats over their helmets. When Eilif rose to urge loyalty to Olof Skötkonung, before he could utter a word he was decapitated with a sword. Roa fled. Olav also forbade the export of such essential commodities as herrings and salt from Viken to Swedish Gotland across the border.

Another incident angered the Swedish king. Olav had entered into partnership with a merchant who traded with Russia, asking him to buy court robes, sables and gold plate for the table. On the way home from Novgorod, the merchant was attacked and killed by a Swedish Viking who seized his goods, announcing that King Olav's articles must go to Olof Skötkonung as part of the Norwegian scatt due to him. However, off Sweden the Viking himself was attacked and killed by Eyvind Urarahorn, one of Olav's favourites, who recovered all the king's Russian valuables.

Anticipating trouble from the Swedes, Olav founded a town in Viken on a peninsula that jutted out into the River Glomma. He named it 'Borg', perhaps because he had seen towns of the same sort in England where it would have been called a *burh*. It was fortified on the landward side by a deep ditch behind which was a wall of turf and stone two metres high, with a palisade. The other sides were guarded by steep riverbanks and a waterfall. Inside were houses for the townsmen with the 'King's House' for Olav's use as a winter residence, and a church. Later, Borg was to become a thriving merchant city. Today, it is known as Sarpsborg.

The Danish king must have been no less angry than Olof Skötkonung at losing his Norwegian territory and scatt, but there was nothing he could do as his fighting men were abroad, helping his brother Knut to conquer England. Luckily for Olav, Knut was unable to spare the time or the troops to intervene. Wisely, the Danish officials withdrew without trying to collect the scatt and before Olav's henchmen could remove their heads.

Bishop Grimkel was clearly an exceptionally important influence on Olav who had very soon appointed him *hirdbiskop*, a household chaplain to his retinue. From his name, Grimkel (or Grimketel) may well have been of Scandinavian blood, perhaps born to Norse settlers in England. He became the king's spiritual adviser.

A genuinely majestic personality, dynamic and impressive, the king radiated the same sort of magnetism as Olav Tryggvason on whom, to at least some extent, he obviously modelled himself. 'A good, very gentle, man who was sparing of speech and generous, but too keen on money,' was how Snorri saw Olav Haraldsson in time of peace. In reality he had a violent temper that he kept under control only with difficulty and was not so much avaricious as desperate to fund the gifts that his lendmenn expected – he could no longer refill his coffers by plunder as he had done before becoming king. Although helped by his monopoly of the Sami trade and his shares in private merchant ventures, he never possessed the resources that would have bought unshakeable loyalty.

Snorri is more plausible when he says the king always attended the local Thing in every area he visited, ironing out disputes or helping to solve problems of public concern. He made a point of listening to men who, however humble, were obviously knowledgeable. Spokesmen read out for him the laws that Hakon the Good had unsuccessfully tried to promulgate sixty years before, of which he retained most, disregarding some he thought unnecessary and adding new ones.

While he let magnates such as Erling Skjalgsson and Einar Tambarskjelve (when he returned) keep most of their authority, he recruited new ones to act as counterweights. They came from the richer bonder, the *storbonder*, of the big farms who owned large estates and dominated the local Thing. Besides adding to their lands he paid them valuable retainers from the royal treasury, and they became *lendmenn*, landed men who swore to be loyal and send him armed men whenever he needed them. Using lavish gifts to sweeten his regular visits to their homesteads where he spent weeks at a time, he ironed out local disputes and feuds in their territories by diplomacy that often included arranging marriages.

Where Olav took over whole areas, as in the Upplands, he gave estates to reliable followers who joined the ranks of the lendmenn, making sure of their loyalty by allowing them to take over much of the old chieftains' powers. Old or new, however, there were never more than thirty lendmenn. Lesser landowners were given the job of administering law and order in their areas and collecting taxes. Overall, the system had a certain resemblance to the feudalism that Olav had seen in Normandy, lendmenn being roughly the equivalent of barons.

Ármenn, nominated by the king, ensured that taxes were collected and good law available to all. Men of humble background, even former thralls, they owed everything to Olav. Lendmenn resented these low-born and often arrogant officials whom they saw as spies, especially in the Trøndelag where, because he distrusted the Trønders' loyalty, Olav installed a large number. An unwelcome innovation, the ármenn were bound to cause trouble.

What concerned King Olav most was to make Norway a Christian country. Quite apart from his own personal beliefs, he was well aware that Denmark and much of Sweden were already Christian, and that there was no other way forward for Norwegians to acquire the magic gift of literacy and enter mainstream European civilisation.

There were of course other reasons. With no local power base apart from modest popularity in the southeast, he had every incentive to strengthen his regime by using the new faith to root out the pagan cult from which as *godi* the chieftains derived so much prestige and influence. This does not mean that he was driven by purely political considerations. 'There was no sharp distinction between the religious and the secular spheres in the early Middle Ages', writes Sverre Bagge, 'so that there was a strong connection between allegiance to a leader and allegiance to his gods.'[5]

Olav's priorities were to make the Norwegians accept baptism and to destroy paganism. It was going to be an uphill struggle because the old religion was so much a part of Norse life, one to which most people were deeply attached, and years would pass before the king and Bishop Grimkel felt ready to introduce a Christian law code. To appreciate how daunting were the obstacles that lay ahead of them, we need to know something about the Norse gods.

7

The Terrible One and Other Gods

Odin I am called now, Terrible One I was called before
Grimnir's Sayings[1]

No Viking could fully understand his religion, a collection of different traditions that was never codified, never possessed such things as creeds or sacred texts, and varied bewilderingly from place to place. It is still harder to understand for us who do not inhabit the same world. In 1964 the great Gabriel Turville-Petre began his masterly *Myth and Religion of the North* by saying, 'The Religion of the ancient Norsemen is one of the most difficult to describe,' which he attributed to their inability to express their thoughts in writing.

Even so, we know a certain amount about the Norse gods from the collection of verse named the *Poetic Edda*, which is preserved in a single surviving manuscript written down in the thirteenth century, known as the *Codex Regius* (or *Konungsbók*). This, with what Snorri tells us in his *Prose Edda*, has saved them from oblivion.

They were much the same as those of pre-Christian England or Germany but had often developed in different ways over the centuries, especially the lesser gods. They were divided into two heavily populated pantheons, the most powerful of whom were the great-hearted, warlike Aesir. The second were the wise, earthy Vanir, who were more concerned with fertility than with fighting, if far from entirely. On the whole, men tended to worship the Aesir. In contrast, women generally preferred the Vanir, as did every witch and warlock because the Vanir were such enthusiastic patrons of sorcery. During his boyhood Olav must have learned from his elders about the more important members of both pantheons, especially about the Aesir.

The Aesir's leader was Odin, a war god sometimes called 'Father of Victory' or 'Battle Screamer'. Among those whom he wished to charm or seduce – he was compulsively unfaithful to his beautiful consort Frigg – his face looked so handsome that it filled them with joy. But in combat it became ghastly beneath his golden helmet, paralysing enemies with fear when he charged on his eight-legged horse, hurling his spear Gungnir that never missed its aim. His memory lingered into Christian times as the leader of the *Odens Jakt*, the Troop of the Dead or Ghost Riders, who with their baying hounds gallop on a wild hunt through the night sky, especially during Yule.

Most complex and most sinister of all the gods, he had gone to ghoulish extremes in his thirst for knowledge. After bartering an eye for leave to drink from a magic well that bestowed wisdom, he sacrificed himself to gain still deeper understanding, by hanging on the World Tree Yggdrasil – in an unsettling echo of Christ's Passion:

> I know I hung on that windy Tree
> nine whole days and nights.
> Stabbed with a spear, offered to Odin,
> myself to mine own self given,
> high on that Tree of which none hath heard
> from what roots it rises to heaven.
>
> None refreshed me ever with food or drink,
> I peered right down in the depths[2]

Each day, two ravens, Hugin and Munin, kept him informed of what was happening throughout the world. In case they should miss anything, he carried with him the head of the dead Mimir, who answered every question he asked, or else he summoned up bodies from their graves for further information, which is why he was called Ghost Lord of the Mounds. He was also Lord of Hanged Men because if he saw a man swinging from a gibbet, he cast a spell with runes and the man would come down and tell him anything he wished to know.

A master of spells and incantations as well as runes, Odin was the inspirer of skalds. Loki (in *Loki's Quarrel*) accused him not only of practising witchcraft, but of dressing like a woman when he cast spells.[3] Able to change into an animal, a fish or even a worm, he often went about as a gentle old man with one eye, very tall, in a black cloak and a broad brimmed black hat, who carried a big staff. He was always followed by a black dog, sometimes two (in reality demon wolves). Living on wine, he never touched food, if we can believe *The Sayings of Grimnir* – 'On wine alone does the weapon-decked god Odin forever live.'[4] He made an exception when seducing the giantess Gunnlod in order to drink the 'marvellous mead' that gave the gift of poetry.

During his wanderings people often failed to recognise him in his disguise as a kindly ancient of years, an error that could bring disaster. 'He will probably sleep with your wife or, just possibly, your husband – a being of contradictions and seduction, unwise to trust,' is how a leading authority on Viking religion, the archaeologist historian Neil Price, sees him.[5] The *Edda* warns,

> Odin is ruler of every ill
> Who sunders kings with runes of spite.[6]

Among his many unsettling names were 'Evil Doer' and 'Oath Breaker'.

Olav must have been told how every thunderclap and lightning bolt came from another war god, Thor. This was Odin's red-bearded son by a giantess, who when not beating a huge anvil up in the sky with his mountain-smashing hammer Mjölnir was busy belabouring the giants despite his kinship with them. Although frequently swollen with rage, he was unusually bluff and straightforward for a Norse deity, credited with swinging Mjölnir to protect his devotees from storms, famines, plagues or blows in battle.

He had a clownish side that emerges in the poem *Thrymskvitha*. The giant Thrym, 'lord of ogres', steals Mjölnir, demanding the goddess Freyja as a bride in exchange for its return. To recover it, Thor impersonates Freyja, leaving off his iron gloves, putting on skirts, a bridal headdress and a glittering necklace – his embarrassment hidden behind a bridal veil. At the wedding breakfast he nearly gives himself away, eating an ox and eight salmon, which he washes down with three barrels of mead. However, Thrym is impressed by the performance, observing,

> I ne'er saw bride with a broader bite
> Nor a maiden who drank more mead than this.[7]

To bless the 'maiden', he orders that the mighty hammer be laid on her knee. Then, seizing Mjölnir, Thor leaps to his feet and gleefully batters to death Thrym and every giant within reach.

The tale did not affect his popularity. Nor did it discourage men from wearing small iron hammers around their necks, as Christians do the Cross, in the hope that Thor might help them. In the same way, when invoking the names of Odin and Thor at the seasonal sacrifices a priest made the sign of the hammer. Some longships bore a carving of Thor as a figurehead.

A god who would never help anybody, under any circumstances whatever, was Loki, the originator of all deceit, unremittingly nasty, who tricked the blind god Hodr into killing their brother Baldr, best looking and best natured of the Aesir. In reality an evil giant in the form of a god with a bizarre sense of humour, Loki was certainly the pantheon's strangest member and, as might be expected, begot fearsome offspring. During a masculine phase he sired the ravening Fenris Wolf on a giantess named Angrboda while in a feminine one (after eating the heart of a woman, roasted), changing into a mare he mated with a stallion and gave birth to Odin's eight-legged steed Sleipnir.

One of the Vanir, Frey, who had a reputation for amiability, was the nearest thing to a kindly Norse god yet he too could be dangerously fickle, even murderous. (Once, lacking a sword, he killed a giant with a deer's antler.) Renowned for virility, he had a weakness for giantesses – he married one – and a statuette dating from Olav's time, found in Sweden in 1904, shows him displaying his gigantic penis, ostentatiously erect. As he controlled sunshine and rain, men prayed to him for peace, a good harvest, a good voyage or good luck in general, while he was invoked in battle as 'shield god' or 'god of the helmet'. He always rode a golden boar.

Olav learned, too, about Frey's sister Freyja, the radiantly beautiful goddess of human fertility, copulation and sorcery, whose falcon-feather cloak enabled her to fly but who normally drove a chariot drawn by two lascivious cats. Occasionally, however, like her brother she rode a boar with golden bristles – in reality a berserker changed into a swine, affectionately known as 'Battle Hog'. Patroness of lovers, she had slept with every male god, not excepting brother Frey, as well as with all the elves and once with four dwarves in quick succession to get her hands on a wonderful gold necklace, Brisingamen, they had made in their cave. Loki, of all people, called her a whore – 'a witch much imbued with malice'.[8]

A mixture of nymph and earth mother, Freyja was revered by women in particular for bestowing the gift of children and because of her mastery of witchcraft in which she played a key role. At the same time, she was a war goddess who egged men on to fight each other, then rode over the battlefield choosing the best-looking corpses to take back to her hall in the sky, Folkvang, for 'dalliance'. Unsurprisingly, there was a strongly erotic side to her worship that included sexual orgies. No account of what took place has survived, but a horrified Adam of Bremen tells us that her rites were 'obscene', without going into detail.

*   *   *

The Vikings believed every mountain and valley, every field, wood, river and stream, was peopled – some might think overcrowded – with other worldly beings. They included giants, trolls, elves, dwarves, land wights and dragons such as the 'glittering worm' Fafnir. All were dangerous and needed careful handling, especially the trolls who rode on wolves with snakes for bridles, or the comparatively rare dragons although these kept to the mountains. A small animal might be an evil spirit, like Ratatoskr ('tooth drill'), the squirrel fiend who scampered up and down the world tree Yggdrasil, trying to stir up trouble between the great eagle above and the great serpent below. Ratatoskr also did his diabolical little best at setting men and giants against each other. In addition, there were the näken who drew men under a river or pool to drown them.

Everybody believed in spectres, ghosts and the uncanny in general. Not only phantoms of the night but the even more inexplicable daytime terrors were very real to them. They would have agreed with Milton in *Paradise Lost* that 'Millions of spiritual creatures walk the earth Unseen, both when we wake and when we sleep.'

Vikings who died in battle hoped that Valkyries would bear them to Valhalla, Odin's great drinking hall that was roofed with shields and supported by spear-shafts. There, so they fondly believed, they would spend the days honing their combat skills, feasting every night at the side of the gods. With them they would swill beakers of exquisite mead from the unfailing udders of the great nanny goat Heidrun and gorge on pork from the boar Saehrímnir whose delicious flesh renewed itself overnight. Other heroes preferred the prospect of being taken up to Folkvang, the hall of Freyja as 'chooser of the slain', whom they expected to entertain them in her own special way.

However, unheroic men and all women could expect a very different fate, although some courageous feminine souls aspired to 'join Freyja'. They would go down into Helheim which, Snorri tells us, was a dreadful place deep underground, its entrance guarded by the hound Garm. It was ruled by a spectacularly grim goddess, a daughter of Loki named Hel, half of whose once beautiful body had turned bright blue from putrefaction. Here they would pass a shadowy existence, awaiting annihilation.

This was an unremittingly bleak religion offering no long-term hope, despite a lavish provision of grave goods for the dear departed that suggests some sort of belief in a happy after life. Yet one day, three terrible years were going to follow each other, the *Fimbulvetr*, an unending winter when every crop would fail, when cattle and sheep would die in the fields, a conviction that originated in a folk memory of three ice-cold summers during the 530s that had brought starvation, followed by a pandemic in which half the population of Norway perished. After Fimbulvetr would come an apocalypse at Ragnarök, the Doom of the Gods.

Then Odin with his innumerable kindred, supported by the heroes from Valhalla and Folkvang, would fight to their foredoomed death in a last battle against the *Jotunn*, the fire and frost giants who with the Great Worm and Garm the Great Hound embodied evil and chaos. All were going to die without exception, gods and goddesses, giants and monsters, men and women, elves and trolls. Odin was to be eaten alive by Fenris Wolf, who would himself be slain. The sun would turn black, the stars lose their light and flames roar up into the skies, as the earth sank beneath the sea.[9]

Witchcraft, with its magical charms and spells, was an essential component of Norse religion, even of everyday life. The *Hávamál* advises that

> Earth prevails o'er drink, but fire o'er sickness,
> the oak o'er binding, the earcorn o'er witchcraft,
> the rye spur o'er rupture, the moon o'er rages,
> herb o'er cattle plagues, runes o'er harm.[10]

Snorri tells us that although Freyja rivalled him in expertise, Odin was the supreme master of the black arts of which there were many sorts, some borrowed from the Sami or the Finns. The highest form, *seidr*, enabled witches and warlocks to summon up spirits and see the future, to drive people so mad that they never stopped howling, to make them suffer from tormenting lust, unbearable depression or inexplicable terror, or to kill them. It did so by incantation, by the chanting called *galdrar* or by striking them with a metal staff. There were also shamanistic rituals to induce trances and visions, with frenzied drumming and dancing. A good deal of sexual activity seems to have been involved and it has been suggested that horse penises were dried and preserved, for use as ritual dildos.[11]

Apparently the sexual activity was so strenuous that after a few sessions many male practitioners developed strange physical and mental maladies, and most people thought that seidr was better left to 'spirit women'. Any man who persisted in practising it incurred 'a strange kind of dishonour and social rejection combining cowardice and general "unmanliness" with suggestions of homosexuality (against which Viking society held extremely strong prejudices)'.[12]

Yet if warlocks were regarded with uneasy dislike, there were many well respected witches who were sometimes known as hags or dusk riders. They enjoyed the power that the terror inspired by their calling gave them over the rest of the community, more than that possessed by any other women. But Odin knew how to deflect their spells, claiming that if he saw witches riding in the sky he could make them go out of their minds and even lose their bodies.

Everybody's destiny, human or divine, was woven by the Norns, three ghostly maiden spinners who sat beneath the world ash Yggdrasil, although some unknown power decided each person's ultimate fate. There was a vague philosophy of life, more a mix of gnomic utterance, folklore and plain common sense than philosophy, preserved in collections of verse such as *Hávamál* ('Song of the High One') or *Alvissmal* ('Sayings of the All Wise') in the *Poetic Edda*. Much of it merely states the obvious, *Hávamál* advising men not to trust 'a breaking bow or a burning flame, a ravening wolf or a croaking raven . . .'

For Vikings, virtues other than bravery, loyalty, hospitality or gift-giving counted for little. 'The one consistent feature [in their sagas] is fearlessness, or the appearance of it', argues Tom Shippey. 'The culture rated this as the highest virtue, superior to what we think of as morality.'[13] Psychopathic ferocity was a quality to be prized since they were entirely lacking in what Adolf Hitler would one day call 'the effeminate Judaeo-Christian pity ethic'. Predictably, inspired by their reading of Nietzsche and other baneful scriptures, members of Vidkun Quisling's Nasjonal Samling (Norway's version of the Nazi party) were going to draw inspiration from Norse paganism.

It is only fair to say that if the Norse deities were scarcely models of clean living or dependability, the heroes in the *Edda* displayed qualities that were genuinely noble. Their courage and their loyalty could be amazing. Their welcome to strangers was unbounded while their generosity knew no limits. It is heroes rather than gods who inspire Norway's modern pagans.

Nevertheless, Vikings attributed victory in war to the 'Battle Screamer' Odin, who made one's foes go blind or faint from terror, or blunted their weapons. When a Viking sent a 'death spear' through an enemy, he was sacrificing to Odin, Lord of the Spear, while a berserker in a combat trance was said to be possessed by him. A captured enemy might be offered up to Odin as a 'blood eagle', which meant cutting the man's ribs loose from his spine with a sword, then pulling his lungs out through slits cut in the flesh to rest on his back, so that he looked like a bird with red wings.

In danger, whether by land or sea, Vikings called on Odin, Thor or Frey, since they believed that where these three were, help might be near. After all, Odin claimed that

Winds o'er waves I can tame
And soothe all the ocean.[14]

Before setting out on a Viking cruise, it is likely that the youthful Olav had sacrificed to Odin, even offering him a human sacrifice

– some wretched thrall whom nobody would miss – and prayed to the Terrible One for good weather, and for plunder and slaves.

There was a curious lack of divinity about Norse gods, who were not even immortal and far from omnipotent, as well as all too human in their private lives, but perhaps that was part of their appeal. By the Norsemen's own account, from Odin down they were cruel and self-obsessed, despite a veneer of good will. Yet, catering to the most primitive instincts, they had an extraordinarily powerful allure that can be sensed in the *Poetic Edda*, especially in the haunting translations by Auden, Ursula Dronke or Carolyne Larrington.

We should never underestimate the Norse people's devotion to these deities, however fantastic and unreliable they may seem. Men forced to abandon their worship knew that they would lose Odin's support in battle or when facing shipwreck on a storm-tossed sea, women that they would forfeit the help of Freyja in conceiving children and giving birth or seeking her protection from male brutality. There was also the fear that the crops would fail. Adopting a new, untried faith meant a leap into the unknown that might bring reprisals by the betrayed gods of their fathers.

Only by realising the depth of the Norsemen's attachment to their old gods can we grasp the magnitude of the task that Olav had taken upon himself.

8

The New Religion

the shrine-destroyer piled up high corpse-heaps in many places; the ravens were often drawn to the blood of strife.

Hallfrod Ottarson, *Óláfsdrapa*[1]

As with Olav Tryggvason, the ancient gods must have haunted Olav Haraldsson, steeped as he was in their worship, and done so to a quite terrifying extent. He continued to believe firmly in their existence, but under Grimkel's tuition he now saw them as demons instead of gods, which was the Church's official definition. They were agents of the Devil, Grimkel told him, bent on dragging men and women down to Hell. Were he alive today, the bishop would no doubt describe them as anthropomorphic embodiments of dangerous, elemental forces that exist both inside and outside the human psyche.

Two hundred years later, Olav Snorri Sturluson, apparently still a believer in them as demons demoted from gods, was inclined to think they derived from forebears who had deified the earth and the stars. Or, alternatively, because of his patchy reading of the Latin Classics, that they might be memories of ancient heroes and their wives, perhaps even of refugee wizards from Troy. In reality, they came from the same Indo-European stable as the deities of ancient India or Greece, transformed by the unfettered unconscious of northern men amid the northern darkness.

Yet nothing deflected Olav Haraldsson from making his people Christian. He was helped by there being a network of people all along the coast who already belonged to the new faith because of the spadework done by Hakon the Good and Olav Tryggvason. According to Snorri, many in Viken (around the Oslofjord) were no strangers to it since Danish, English and German merchants visited them regularly. Others had been traders or gone on Viking expeditions, wintering in Christian lands. Tenth-century stone crosses and rune stones attest to the presence of converts.

Inland, it was a different story. Cut off from the sea and foreign contact by high mountains and dense forests, wholly dependent on their crops for survival, the inhabitants of these remote areas still believed that good harvests could only be ensured by sacrificing to the ancient gods.

While we know that sacrifices were offered in halls or in the open air, we also know that very occasionally they took place in wooden *hoffer* (temples), of which no good description survives. From archaeological evidence it seems improbable that the new faith took these over, except in a few rare instances. Yet it is hard not to believe that in some ways, such as using dragon-head gargoyles to ward off demons, the hoffer served as models because there were no other places of worship to copy. Like the hoffer, Olav's churches were built from logs and, just as the pagan hoffer had done, reflected a wooded landscape.

'The forests were God's first church and men took their first ideas of architecture from them,' wrote François-René de Chateaubriand. He was referring to France's Romanesque and Gothic churches but his words are no less applicable to Norway's early wooden churches. 'Ceilings carved with all kinds of foliage, buttresses propping up walls and ending abruptly, just like broken tree-trunks . . . the dark sanctuary, the dim twilight of the aisles, the secret passages, the low door-ways – everything that in a church makes for a sense of religious awe, of mystery and of God, calls to mind the hidden mazes in a wood.'[2]

Although there is some archaeological evidence, mainly foundations, we can only speculate what Olav's churches looked like. All we can say with certainty is that they were built of wood and forerunners of the 'stave churches' (of which less than thirty remain), dating from at least a hundred years after the king's death. Standing on flat stones, tree trunks supported a stave church's roof, covered by pinecone-like slats, with crockets, gables and dragon-head gargoyles. There was a nave for the congregation with a narrower, lower roofed chancel where the altar stood, usually in a semicircular apse. Everything was built of tarred timber, fastened together by wooden pegs and dovetails. Inside, it was very dark, with no windows.

In 2017 archaeologists excavated Olav's place of worship at Nidaros, St Clement's, that had stood next to the royal palace. A wooden church with stone foundations, single-aisled but big enough to hold the royal court, it was dedicated to the patron saint of seafarers, Clement, who took over from Odin and Frey. A screen separated the nave from the small chancel containing the altar. For those hearing Mass, there would have been standing room only, amid a reek of unwashed hirdsmen in coats of fur, sheepskin or undyed wadmal, mixed with the smell of tar and incense. One shudders to think what the cold was like during a Norwegian winter.

'It was King Olav's custom to rise in the morning, put on his clothes, wash his hands, then go to the church and hear Matins and the early morning Mass,' Snorri tells us. When in Trondheim Olav attended Mass at St Clement's every day, always at dawn, which meant he heard it in darkness except during the brief summer. The atmosphere was mysterious, altogether different from the bland togetherness of a modern Catholic or Lutheran Mass. Those outside, peering in through narrow slits in the walls, caught only glimpses of the priest, who was obscured by the chancel screen. There was almost no light in the church except in the chancel, and even those inside the church saw little of what was taking place on the altar.

In the chancel, lit by one or two guttering candles and a single hanging oil lamp, a silver dove containing the 'Body of God' was suspended on a chain over the altar beneath a large crucifix high up. On the wall behind were ghostly looking panels painted with pictures of the Virgin and the saints, hard to make out. The darkness deepened the mystery. Gleaming in a costly chasuble, tonsured and shaven but not yet necessarily celibate, at this date the priest was almost always a foreigner. A being apart, he said Mass with his back to a congregation whose adult males all wore long hair and beards.

He muttered rather than spoke the Mass in a strange language that he himself barely understood although the homily in which he explained the Gospel of the day in simple terms would have been in Norse. There was no elevation of the Host and the chalice at the consecration while Communion, with the wine drunk through a silver straw, was only given to the faithful at Easter. Instead, on Sundays or feast days, encased in a glass or crystal the Host (a conse-crated wafer) was passed from hand to hand for each worshipper to kiss.

The priest was one of several hundred whom Olav brought in during his reign, but we do not know how many or where they were recruited. Some must have been German since Norway fell under the archbishopric of Bremen's jurisdiction, while there was at least one Norman, Bishop Rodolf (who died as Abbot of Abingdon). However, it is likely that most were English, from Norse-speaking areas in the Danelaw. Importing these men in such numbers was the real turning point in establishing the new faith. It is also the most unsung of Olav's achievements.

Nothing could have been less like the old religion and not just because terrified horses or thralls were no longer hanged or because holy water instead of blood was sprinkled on the faithful. In contrast, the Mass and Christian discipline appeared cold and bleak, out of kilter with nature's rhythms. Many must have sighed for the sexual indulgence that had accompanied pagan sacrifices.

Nevertheless, *Hvitakristr* ('White Christ'), offered more than the old gods. However much you bowed and cringed before those strange deities, however often you sacrificed to them, they could not be trusted, if in dreams they sometimes seemed to talk sense and you might think you had won their favour. In contrast, White Christ promised not merely help in this life but happiness in the next, if only people would believe in him and do as he asked. Every woman, together with all those unmanly men who did not want to die in battle, could hope for something better than entombment in Helheim followed by extinction. Even the toughest warrior came to prefer the prospect of heaven to that of carousing with the gods in Valhalla or Freyja's exhausting embraces.

Moreover, the new religion incorporated pleasant customs from the old faith. The days of feasting and drinking in December survived, Christmas replacing the Yule *blót*, with toasts drunk to Christ, the Virgin and the saints in place of Odin and the gods. In place of the summer *blót* there was the *Jonsoknat* ('Wake of St John') when on St John's Eve the new ale was hallowed by the priest in the names of Christ and the Virgin, after which the local community celebrated with a lengthy drinking bout around a great bonfire. A harvest festival at *Mikkelsmess* (Michaelmas) took over from the autumn *blót* that had heralded the coming of winter.

Horse meat was strictly taboo, however. The priests cited St Paul's warning about eating the flesh of animals that had been sacrificed to idols; to have done so before conversion was no excuse, and anyone who did would end up in hell, because it was 'meat sacrificed to demons'.[3]

There was an uncompromising emphasis, later expressed in specific laws, 'on unacceptable pagan behaviour and practices, and not on the question of belief', comments Catharina Raudvere. She singles out as punishable, to use 'rituals in order to awaken the trolls, employ formulas and charms (*galdr*), perform divination or ride like a night-hag (a practice which was condemned and rejected, while treated as a possibility for evil-minded persons)'.[4]

It must have been hard for Norsemen to abandon the familiar, age-old gods of their fathers and to accept a Christian way of life. To be prevented from working on Sundays or saints' days was disruptive enough, but new standards of right and wrong were even more of a jolt, since the old religion had never developed a definitive moral code. No doubt, sexual taboos caused outrage, men arguing angrily with the priest when chided for sleeping with their slave girls. More than a few of the king's subjects despised his faith as a thin-blooded denial of their forefathers' savage virtues, 'White Christ' originating as a term of contempt.

Bewilderment as to what it was all about appears in *Faereyinga saga* when the Faroese chieftain Thrandur of Göta, an unwilling convert, teaches his foster-son to pray. Thrandur could say the paternoster, presumably in Norse, but his version of the Apostles' Creed was not so satisfactory. It ran:

> I go out not alone,
> following me are four,
> five of God's angels.
> I carry this prayer with me,
> this prayer to Christ.
> I sing seven psalms.
> May God be my rock.[5]

Priests did their best to explain it in a way that made sense to confused congregations. We catch a glimpse of what was one of their methods in *Heliand* ('The Saviour'), a German poem from the ninth century written to convert the pagan Saxons of northern and eastern Germany whose beliefs had been very like those of Viking Scandinavia. It retold the Gospel story in a way they could grasp. Christ, born in 'Nazarethburg', was a great chieftain who rewarded his war-band with heavy gold arm rings, while his Last Supper was in a mead hall at 'Jerusalemburg'. The banquet where Salome dances before Herod also takes place in a mead hall. Even the paternoster is written in runes.

No doubt, Bishop Grimkel used more sophisticated interpretations of the Gospel when preaching before Olav and his court, reading passages from the New Testament, then expounding what they meant, with the king making sure that everybody listened carefully. But most of early Christian Norway had to make do with simpler explanations and although it has not survived something like *Heliand* must almost certainly have been composed to win them over. Neil

Price believes this was the type of message brought to the Vikings by
the early missionaries, 'meshed with the ancestral stories of the
North'.[6]

To become a Christian meant no more than accepting baptism with
a promise to abandon the heathen gods, as to begin with there were
too few priests to explain the new religion. Bonder who saw it as an
untested form of magic must have asked, 'But what about the crops?'
Without police to enforce it people went on sacrificing in secret to
the old deities. Women in particular took care to placate the elves
and land wights, guardians of the soil who lived in every quiet corner
of the countryside, especially in deep woods or hidden valleys.

What may be a witness to the old religion's survival is carved on
top of a wooden column at the twelfth-century stave church of
Hegge in Valdres, a one-eyed face putting out its tongue derisively
and looking suspiciously like Odin. Similarly, the lovely church at
Urnes, also built over a century after Olav's time, has strange carv-
ings known as the 'Urnes Style', an intricate, swirling mass of writh-
ing, snarling, clawing creatures that has been called 'the swan song
of pagan animal-patterned ornamentation' – surely the work of a
heathen-minded artist.

When he realised the Norwegians' conversion was at best skin
deep, Olav resorted to force. The most detailed record of this
'missionary work' comes from Snorri, who is probably correct in the
broad outlines. As has been seen, after the battle of Nesjar in spring
1016 the king had sailed south from Trondheim with a fleet of
armed men, putting in at all major settlements. At each, he had
summoned a Thing where Christian laws and customs were
proclaimed. He had also threatened to take 'violent measures against
folk, great and small, who would not convert'.

What King Olav meant by 'violent measures' became all too clear
a year or two later when with a hird 300 strong he spent the entire
autumn in the Upplands north of Oslo, densely forested country
where the worship of the ancient gods had continued unabated.

Penetrating deep into the woods and up hidden valleys in the hills or along lonely lakes, wherever he found men who were still stubbornly pagan and refused to adopt his faith, he had their hands or feet chopped off, or had their eyes gouged out, or else had them hanged or put to the sword. 'No one was left unpunished who would not serve God.'[7]

There was a gratifyingly high conversion rate. The king still reckoned this by the numbers of those who came forward to be baptised, rather than of those who experienced a spiritual awakening. However, as even Snorri admits, it was a truism in the eleventh century that the religion they were taught as children retained the strongest hold over men if left to themselves. Naïvely, Olav had expected the baptised to refrain from reverting to the old heathen rites.

News of Olav's rampage against the forest pagans horrified the areas' magnates, especially those who privately sympathised with them. Snorri tells us that when the king took his hird to Raumarike, a local chieftain 'thought it a very bad business, men rich and poor coming every day to tell him of what was happening'. The chieftain complained to Hroerek, one of the five Uppland kinglets who only recently had helped Olav to defeat Jarl Sveinn.

The five met secretly at Ringsaker to discuss the situation. What upset them more than the violence was the threat to their status as leaders of the community who offered the sacrifices that ensured good harvests. Led by King Hroerek, a staunch but discreet pagan gifted with much cunning, and by King Güthroth, a strong personality who commanded great respect among his fellows, they decided that the only possible solution was to ambush and kill Olav Haraldsson at the first opportunity. 'And I can tell you this for certain,' Güthroth told his fellow kinglets. 'Our heads are never going to be safe so long as Olav lives.'

They were swiftly betrayed by a rich bonde, Ketel of Ringaness, who during the night after the meeting went secretly by boat down the fjord to warn Olav. On the following night Olav rowed through the darkness with 400 men, reaching Ringsaker before dawn, to surround the houses where the kings slept, each one of which was pointed out to him by Ketel. Having captured all five, he ordered Güthroth's tongue to be cut out and Hroerek to lose his eyes. The remaining three were spared mutilation but banished from Norway.

Olav confiscated the kinglets' lands, which meant a substantial acquisition of territory and authority. He also took hostages from the local lendermenn and leading bonder, to ensure their good behaviour.

> The giver of rings of gold
> The army leader bold,
> In vengeance springs
> On the Hedemark kings.
> Olav, the bold and great.
> Repays their foul deceit . . .
> He drives with steel-clad hand
> The small kings from the land.[8]

So sang the ingratiating Ottar the Black in the king's mead hall.

After the wounds healed Olav took Hroerek with him every-where, making the blind man sit by his side at dinner, taking him to church every day, as a warning for heathens. Several times Hroerek plotted to kill the king, trying to suborn anyone who would listen, but each time his plot was discovered or went wrong. Then, early one Ascension Day morning, just before Mass, Hroerek clapped his hand on Olav's shoulder in a friendly way, muttering, 'What fine clothes you are wearing today, kinsman!' The king told him that he was honouring Christ's ascension into heaven. 'I do not accept what you tell me about Christ,' replied Hroerek. 'I simply cannot believe it, even if some wonderful things may have happened in the olden times.'

At the end of Mass, aware from having felt Olav's shoulder that he was not wearing mail, the blind man tried to stab him with a dagger, but the king had suddenly knelt down in prayer and the blade only ripped his cloak. This time Olav's angry hirdmen urged him to put Hroerek to death. He refused. 'I do not want to spoil my victory over the Upplanders, when one morning, in just a single hour, I captured five kings and took all their lands without having to kill anyone,' he told them. 'Remember, they are all my kinsmen. I cannot see any need for killing Hroerek.'

In the end Olav sent him in safe custody to Iceland where, after spending three years on an isolated farm, he conveniently died 'from an illness'.[9]

Olav had triumphed over the five kings. Nevertheless, all over Norway sacrifices went on being offered to the gods, in secret. And he had other, absorbing concerns.

9

Olav's Empire

Der lived a king inta da aste,
Scowan ürla grün.[1]
Der lived a lady in da wast,
Whar giorten han grün oarlac.[2]

King Orfeo, a ballad

Olav must have envied Knut Sveinsson who after making himself
king of the English had inherited the kingdom of Denmark from his
brother, creating a northern empire. But there were lesser northern
lands over which Olav might become overlord. More than pride was
involved as the inhabitants would pay him scatt with which to refill
his coffers, the booty from his Viking days and his share of King
Ethelred's Danegeld having all been spent. In a world where gifts
were expected in return for loyalty, he needed money to reward his
followers.

Norsemen believed the name Orkneys meant 'seal islands'. They
had begun colonising them, together with the Shetlands, about the
year 800, leaving Norway because there were not enough good farms
to go round. By Olav's time there were about 2,000 men, women
and children living on nearly 400 farms in the Orkneys with another
1,200 on 200 Shetland farms. The islands stayed Norwegian until
1472, while 'Norn', the Orkney version of Norse, remained a written language until the reign of King James VI of Scots, lingering on
as a spoken tongue into the eighteenth century.

Early on, Orkney men began raiding the long coastline of their forebears' country, which caused anger all over Norway. Matters came to a head one summer about the year 875 when one of Harald Fair Hair's sons was killed on Ronaldsay and the king 'sailed west over the North Sea in order to teach a lesson to certain Vikings whose plunderings he could no longer tolerate', the *Orkneyinga saga* tells us.[3] From then on, or so Norwegians liked to believe, the Jarls of Orkney had held the islands as a fief of the King of Norway.

King Olav Tryggvason had succeeded in enforcing his authority over these tough islanders, insisting that they convert to Christianity. On his way back from England, he put in at Osmundswall with five longships and sent a messenger to Jarl Sigurd. 'I want you and all your subjects to be baptised,' he told the jarl. 'If you will not, then I shall have you killed and I swear that I will ravage every island here with fire and sword.'[4] Sigurd surrendered, agreeing to be baptised, handing his son and heir over to the king as a hostage. After this, 'all Orkney embraced the faith'.

After Olav Tryggvason vanished at Svoldr the Orkney men ceased to recognise Norwegian suzerainty. An invasion would have been too expensive so the only way for Olav Haraldsson to reassert it and make the islanders pay him scatt was diplomacy, of the most ruthless sort. In 1021 a dispute between two brothers of the ruling family over which of them should rule Orkney gave Olav the opportunity he needed. When they appealed to him to arbitrate, he forced them to accept not only his judgement but his overlordship. The *Orkneyinga saga* shows Olav during the negotiations at his shrewdest and most subtle.

'Ever since Harald Fair Hair's time, the Orkney jarls have held the islands as royal fiefs, never as their personal property,' he insisted when Jarl Brusi came to see him. 'Since I have inherited everything that was Olav Tryggvason's, these are the terms I offer. I shall let you have your part of the islands in fee, provided you become my man.' After pondering long, Brusi, a man who had a name for being unusually honest, agreed to become the king's vassal and swear fealty to him, but did so with obvious reluctance.

Then Brusi's brother arrived in turn to ask for Olav's help. Jarl Thorfinn was a big, ugly young man, very strongly built, with black hair and bushy black eyebrows, whose sharp features included a great, hooked nose. The king could see all too well that, as the *Orkneyinga saga* tells us, Thorfinn was 'forceful, greedy for fame and fortune'. He was said to be both clever and cruel, his excessive confidence buttressed by his maternal grandfather being Malcolm II, King of Scots.

Olav made the same demand he had made to Brusi. 'If ever you need my help against other kings, it shall be yours whenever you ask,' replied Thorfinn, smoothly. 'But I cannot swear fealty to you because I am already the King of Scots' man.'

'If you will not, then there is of course an alternative road for me to take,' countered Olav. 'I can give any man whom I choose full power over the Orkneys. I merely want you to swear that you will never lay claim to any more land in the isles, and that you will never disagree about whoever I may decide to put in charge.' The king was hinting that he might appoint Brusi.

Thorfinn asked for time to consider. Would Olav let him go home and come back next summer, so that he could consult his friends? 'All my advisers are over there and I am only an inexperienced young man.' The king told him he must make up his mind up at once. Shortly afterwards, Olav sent one of his men to whisper into the jarl's ear that he was completely in the king's hands and that, whatever he might be planning, he would take a most dangerous risk if he tried to depart without reaching an agreement. Realising he had no option, with apparent cheerfulness Thorfinn agreed to swear fealty as Brusi had done.

Whoever wrote the *Orkneyinga saga* gives us a fascinating glimpse into the workings of Olav's mind. Brusi had accepted with obvious reluctance, and Thorfinn happily without trying to bargain or make reservations. From this the king concluded that he could rely on Brusi to keep his word but could never trust Thorfinn.

He ordered the wooden horns to sound and summon a meeting, to which he invited the two jarls. Then he gave his verdict. Brusi and

Thorfinn were given in fee the third of the Orkneys that each of them already held, but the king claimed for himself the third that had belonged to their murdered brother Einar in recompense for Einar having killed Eyvind Auroch's-Horn, a royal hirdsman.

Thorfinn left for home as soon as he could, but Brusi took his time. Suddenly, when on the point of leaving port, he was summoned to an audience. 'I have decided that it makes sense for me to appoint you my governor in the west, Jarl Brusi,' Olav told him.

'I should like you to keep the two-thirds that you have already been governing, so that you will be no less important and powerful now you are my liegeman than you were before. However, as a guarantee of my trust in you, you must leave your son Jarl Rognvald here. I am confident that with my backing and controlling two-thirds of the islands you can easily hold your own against your brother Jarl Thorfinn.' The king also offered to become the ten-year-old Rognvald's foster-father. Brusi was only too glad to accept, staying for some weeks longer.

It says a lot for Olav's personality that Rognvald, one day to be Jarl of Orkney, who stayed as a hostage, grew devoted to him. Growing into a giant as shrewd and courteous as he was tall, Rognvald was a fine man who later shared the king's exile and fought by his side in his last battle. (He himself would lose his life by refusing to abandon his dog when pursued by murderers.)

Jarl Thorfinn spent little time in the Orkneys during Olav's reign, more interested in consolidating his rule over Caithness and Sutherland, where the King of Scots had appointed him *mormaer*, or jarl. (Norsemen had settled along the coast and in the northeast here, making Norse the main language.) Ignoring Brusi's complaints and despite levying harsh taxes, he did nothing to help defend his homeland against raids by Danish Vikings, who regularly carried off the farmers' cattle. Nor would he fight for Olav in his hour of need.

King Olav saw his assertion of power over the Orkneys as a triumph. Sensing this, Ottar the Black composed a flattering poem:

No commander so courageous
in all the eastlands, as you
the overlord of Orkney.[5]

It is also possible that Olav fell in love with an Orkney girl, although it is hard to see where or how he could have met her. Despite telling Sigvat Thordarson that he did not understand the 'skald's craft', he wrote mediocre verses (quoted in the *Legendary Saga*) in praise of an unknown lady, in which he declares that when he first saw her, he felt as if flames had suddenly shot out of the floor, that no other woman could carry herself so proudly and that she had rendered him speechless.

From the kenning (word play), this spellbinding lady has been tentatively identified as Ingibjörg Finnsdóttir, wife of Jarl Thorfinn. Olav's infatuation seems to have gone no further than poetry, but if Thorfinn the Black knew that his overlord felt like this it is unlikely to have inspired him with loyalty. Could the old Northern Isles' ballad of *King Orfeo* (which is also known in Norway) with its Norn refrain have been inspired by a confused memory of King Olav's passion for Ingibjörg? Pure speculation, yet not entirely without reason.

Olav was less successful in his dealings with the wily inhabitants of the Faroe Islands. Although there were comparatively few of them, as with the Orkneys a military expedition was out of the question. It would have been difficult to approach the islands undetected while choppy surf at every possible landing place hindered longships from putting men ashore.

The Faroes were an archipelago of eighteen islands west of Norway, far out in the Atlantic Ocean, between Iceland and the Orkneys, wet, windy and treeless. The only cereal that could be grown was barley which because of the short summer had to be reaped green and dried over a peat fire.[6] Yet there was superlative grazing for sheep whom the climate allowed to stay out all winter with no need to shelter in folds. During the second half of the twelfth century, the *Historia Norwegie* says that 'the peasants there have a rich, abundant flock and some of them own thousands'.[7] Unsurprisingly, the Faroes' other name was 'The Islands of Sheep'.

There was also excellent fishing and 'wild fowling' – which meant harvesting seabirds and their eggs. Another resource was whaling, the communal *Grindadráp*. At an agreed date during summer all the adult male population assembled their fishing boats to combine in herding the animals, who were mainly pilot whales, into shallow water where they speared them to death with harpoons. Shared out, whale meat, whale blubber, whale oil, whale hide and whalebone were crucial for the islanders' survival.

Norsemen had begun settling here during the ninth century, according to tradition refugees from Harald Fair Hair's regime. In Olav's time the population was under 3,000 souls, who lived in isolated farmhouses scattered throughout the islands, but the archipelago was far from remote. Between Iceland and the Orkneys, on one of the sailing routes from Scandinavia to Britain, it was ideally placed for trade, even if the Faroese had little other than wool to sell to visiting ships.

Although so few, they were a self-reliant race who had developed a strong sense of national identity and they saw no reason for Norwegians to interfere in their affairs. Their government consisted of the *Løgthing*, a miniature parliament that met every summer on the biggest island, Streymoy, where it decided disputes and tried anybody accused of a serious crime. However, real power lay firmly in the hands of one or two wealthy chieftains.

When Olav became king, the man who had dominated the Faroes for many years was Tróndur í Gøtu, who took his name from the farmstead where he lived on the island of Eysturoy. Fiercely opposed to Norwegian interference or to paying scatt, he was tough, shrewd and manipulative, ready to kill if needs be, a man who nearly always succeeded in destroying his enemies. He was also unusually rich for an islander, having bought a knarr in Norway for his trading ventures.

Tróndur was an Odin worshipper who could raise the dead. *Faereyinga saga* describes how he did this to learn if Sigmundur Brestirsson had been murdered. The séance took place in a 'fire-room', a farmhouse's living room. First, he told spectators to keep their mouths shut, to prevent demons from entering into them. Then, having lit a large ritual fire to attract spirits, four metal baskets, each holding a smaller fire, were placed to form a square, after which he marked nine concentric circles on the earth floor around the square – nine being a number sacred to Odin. Finally, he sat on a stool between the big fire and the circles, not unlike Odin in *Grimnirsmal* (one of the poems in the *Poetic Edda*), who sat between two fires. Three men materialised, the last of whom, covered in blood, held his severed head in his hands. It was Sigmundur and the séance led to his killers' hanging.[8]

Ironically, Sigmundur Brestirsson had been an enemy of Tróndur, a protégé of Hakon the Evil, who tried to exploit the rivalry between the two in order to impose his authority on the Faroes. In 989 after the exiled Sigmundur became a member of Hakon's hird, the jarl sent him back to govern the islands as a fief of Norway.

Before Sigmundur had set out, Hakon took him to his temple to beg his protectress Thorgerd Shine Bright for help. Standing in a forest clearing, the temple which must have been the Lade jarls' temple to Frey was lit by windows in the roof and decorated with gold and silver. Inside stood many idols. The one before whom Hakon tearfully fell on his knees was that of a richly dressed woman, seemingly made of flesh and blood. This was Thorgerd. Having given her some silver coins, he pulled a heavy gold ring off her finger, which he presented to Sigmundur, saying it would always bring him good luck. (One day he was to be murdered for it.)[9]

For some years after, Sigmundur was supreme in the Faroes, annually collecting the scatt which he sent to Jarl Hakon as tribute. Perhaps surprisingly, Sigmundur was popular with the islanders, although not with his enemy Tróndur who bided his time.

When Olav Tryggvason became king, Sigmundur remained as governor of the Faroes, ingratiating himself with Olav by converting to Christianity, while continuing to wear Thorgerd's gold ring. In 998 he persuaded the islanders to be baptised, forcing even Tróndur to do so and making him swear allegiance to Olav. But Tróndur refused to visit Olav whom he knew had no illusions about his conversion or his allegiance. The king called him 'the vilest man who ever lived in the northern countries'.[10]

The Faroes ceased to pay scatt after Olav Tryggvason's disappearance at Svoldr while Sigmundur was long dead by the time Olav Haraldsson made himself King of Norway. However, increasingly short of money, Olav was eager for them to resume payment. Unluckily for him, Tróndur í Gøtu was still very much alive and had no intention of handing over a single coin. He had abandoned Christianity, saying it made him miserable.

In 1024, at Olav's request a Faroese delegation paid him a formal visit. It was significant that Tróndur, who had been specifically invited, should ostentatiously prepare his ship for a voyage and then at the last moment announce he was staying at home. As soon as the Faroese arrived at Nidaros, they were summoned to King Olav's presence. He announced that he wished their islands to obey his laws and pay scatt. After several bad-tempered meetings, the king bullied them into accepting and in token of good will took two into his service. Despite it being late in the year, he had a ship fitted out which he sent to the Faroes to collect the scatt.

'All that is to be told is that they did not come back, and no scatt either,' says Snorri succinctly. 'For no man had come to the Faroe Islands, and no man demanded scatt there.' Next summer, Olav sent another ship to collect the scatt. As little was heard of this vessel as of the first.

In the summer of 1026, Olav sent yet another ship, with a message demanding that one of the island's officials come and see him. The Faroese realised immediately that it was to explain what had happened to the two lost vessels and their crews. A certain Thoralf agreed to go, but was killed by neighbours before he even set out, 'his head cloven down to the shoulders'.

When the news reached the king, he declared that Thoralf must have been killed because he would have supplied information about 'the murders, which I suspect is how my messengers died'. In summer the following year, Olav held a House Thing in the Herøy Islands, on the northwestern coast of Norway, where he announced that the scatt which the Faroese had promised him had never arrived and he needed men to collect it. His hird refused to carry out such a dangerous mission.

Then a fine-looking man in a red coat with a helmet on his head, a sword at his belt and an axe in his hand stood up, rebuking the assembly for failing to help their 'noble king'. 'I am Karl Maerske,' he said. A veteran Viking, he was also a notorious robber whom Olav had long wanted to hang, but he was so pleased by his words that he asked him if he would accept the mission. When Karl agreed, the king pardoned his crimes and gave him a ship with twenty armed men.

Karl landed at Tórshavn on Streymoy where he summoned a Thing and told the Faroese why he had come. Some agreed to pay scatt. As he sat in a tent, guarded by a ring of Norwegians and counting coins into his helmet, a Faroese named Gautur the Red suddenly rushed at the group, aiming blows at them with a small axe which he sank into Karl's head. Karl was not yet dead, so Thorthur the Short hit the axehead with a staff, driving it through his brain.

When Karl's ship returned to Norway and its crew informed King Olav of his death, Snorri tells us he 'was in no pleasant humour and threatened speedy vengeance'. But by then he was in no position to do anything about it because of events nearer home. Tróndur í Gøtu, who had almost certainly organised the killing – Thorthur was his foster-son – outlived Olav, dying in his bed as a Christian.[11]

Ironically, in the twenty-first century the national holiday of the Faroese Islanders, who remain as independent minded as ever, is the *Olavsøka* – Olav's Wake.

*   *   *

There was another Norse archipelago, the Lofoten, inside the Artic Circle. Despite mountains and frowning cliffs, its islands had some good farmland, with a flourishing little capital, Vågan. Its biggest asset was the cod that came in huge shoals to spawn in the surrounding waters, which were harvested and dried, to be sold at Bergen as stockfish, while its worst feature was the maelstrom Mockstraumen, a group of fearsome whirlpools. Olav never visited the Lofoten, but the archipelago appears to have recognised his suzerainty and its people may even have paid him scatt. He had no links with Greenland, another farmers' republic, perhaps because it was so difficult of access.

But the biggest territory coveted by Olav was Iceland, which was over 900 miles away, out in the Atlantic 'on the edge of the world'. It was very different from Norway, a country not only of mountains and moorland, but of lava slopes, of rushing torrents and waterfalls, of glaciers and geysers, and of new, volcanic islands that suddenly emerged from the sea.

Discovered by accident in about 825, it was not colonised for nearly fifty years. The first Scandinavian explorers were amazed by the contrast between winters harsh even by their standards and summers during which bright sunshine, rain and fog occurred in a single day in quick succession. They also reported that the fields were covered in rich green grass ideal for sheep and horses. Norwegians began settling there, originally to escape from King Harald Fair Hair.

Iceland has always produced talented men and women in numbers out of all proportion to its small size, with 'ice and fire' in their veins. In Olav's time when the population was about 10,000, besides Vikings they produced the skalds on whose verse every Scandinavian king and chieftain relied to make him famous.[12] Olav never visited the island and it would have been from the skalds that he learned about the country and its people. In the *Saga of Bjorn, Champion of the Hitardal People* we find 'some account of the Icelanders who lived in the days of King Olav Haraldsson, and became his intimate friends'.[13]

One of these was Thord Kolbeinsson who, learning that his mother's brother, a rich Dane named Hroi the Wealthy had died leaving all his goods to him, fitted out a ship to go to Denmark and claim his inheritance. Putting in at Trondheim, he asked for an audience with Olav at which he explained the reason for his voyage. The king responded by ordering a letter of recommendation be written for him to give to powerful friends in Denmark that he sealed with his personal seal. In gratitude, Thord composed verses in praise of Olav that he chanted in his presence, to be rewarded with a gold ring, a silk tunic and a fine sword.

No doubt Olav hoped that news of a welcome like this would make the Icelanders think well of him. Knowing it was a land without trees, he sent them timber for a church and also bells. Yet they were never tempted to accept his overlordship. They had built an entirely new society with its own 'Grey Goose' law code, and were quite content with their government.

The 'Old Commonwealth' was a republic, in which the supreme authority was the annual Althing, 'the oldest parliament in the world', where laws were made and disputes settled, even if it had become an oligarchy dominated by a score of rich families. Only when these families fell out seriously among themselves would there be any chance for a Norwegian king to establish his rule, and it was not going to happen for another two centuries.

Olav was undeterred. He may even have felt he had a duty to add Iceland to his domains, as it was a land where Christianity, recently established, was laxly observed. Sigvat Thordarson and other Icelanders told him that horse meat was still being eaten there, and that unwanted babies were left out to die. They also gave him detailed information about the country's leading personalities, such as the much respected 'lawspeaker' Skopte Thoraddsson.

Although not of high birth, an Icelander called Thorarinn Nefiolfsson who possessed polished manners as well as plenty of common sense became Olav's personal envoy. His level head and eloquence compensated for remarkable ugliness and a shambling walk due to one foot lacking a big toe. (When he showed him his feet, Olav joked that the whole one was the more hideous since it had five toes while the other had only four.) But Thorarinn owned his own ship, going home regularly and the king had already used him for confidential missions, such as deporting the blind King Hroerek to Iceland.

In 1024 the king sent him with a message for the Althing when it met on the Law Hill at Thingvellir. After the usual disputes and lawsuits had been settled, Thorarinn rose and told the assembly he brought greetings from Olav, 'God almighty's salutation and his own'. Then he added, 'If you will become his subjects, he will be your king, so that you and he can become truly firm friends, working together for the common good.' The assembly replied that they would certainly like to be King Olav's friends if he wanted to be a friend to their country – implying that they had no desire to be his subjects.

Thorarinn rose again, to say that Olav would feel even more friendly towards the people of the north part of Iceland, if they let him have the island of Grimsö at the mouth of Eyjafjord, which was uninhabited and twenty-five miles out into the sea. In return, he would send them anything they might want from Norway. He was addressing this message to Gudmund Eyolfsson of Modrovald in particular, because he knew that Gudmund had great influence in the north.

The Althing adjourned to discuss the request. Gudmund wanted to let Olav have the island, which seemed a cheap price for his goodwill, but his brother Einar differed, saying that by giving Grimsö to the king they would end up having to pay the same heavy scatt that he was extorting from the Norwegians. If they really wanted to keep their freedom, it would be most unwise to let him have the slightest piece of territory, in particular Grimsö which could feed an entire army. 'Were foreigners with longships there, the bonder would soon find trouble on their doorstep.' However, he thought it advisable to send Olav presents, such as Iceland falcons, horses, tents or sails, to stay on good terms. But under no circumstances must he be allowed to occupy Grimsö.

On learning that the Icelanders would reject Olav's request, Thorarinn went back to the Law Hill where he invited all the leading bonder, including the *lagman* (lawspeaker) Skopte, to visit Norway as honoured guests of the king. 'Do not refuse his invitation if you set the slightest value on his friendship,' he added. Suspecting that the invitation was part of another plot to gain control of Iceland, after much private discussion they politely declined, but promised to send men who represented them.

No doubt it was on Thorarinn's advice that the king tried to obtain Grimsö, as a military base from where his men could bring the Icelanders to heel. The episode shows the same cunning that characterised Olav's dealings with the Orkney jarls when asserting his overlordship. But in the jarls' case he had been negotiating from a position of strength.

Unwisely, some leading Icelanders sent their sons to Norway in response to the king's invitation. They included Gelle Thorkellson whose father was an important chieftain, and Stein Skoptason, who was the lagman's son. All were welcomed and entertained lavishly, but when after spending several months at Olav's court they asked for permission to go home, the king prevaricated. Finally, he summoned them, saying that Gelle might go if he took a message from him to the Althing. The others must stay until he received an answer.

Gelle sailed home next summer and delivered the message. It was a demand for all Icelanders to adopt the laws of Norway forthwith and to pay King Olav thane-tax as their overlord, as well as a nose-tax of a penny from every Icelander – so called because non-payment was punished by cutting off the nose. If they accepted, he would be their good friend. Otherwise, he would avenge himself. When the message was debated at the Althing, it refused unanimously to pay Olav taxes, let alone to accept he had a right to make himself overlord of Iceland. In the autumn Gelle rashly sailed back to Norway, bringing the Althing's refusal. Furious, Olav reacted by placing Gelle and his friends under house arrest with no prospect of ever seeing their homes again.

The hostage – for that is what they had become – whom Olav considered most valuable was Stein Skoptason. A handsome young man, a skald as well as a notable warrior, navigator and athlete who dressed magnificently, he was very conscious of his worth. His father had composed a flattering poem about Olav but, resenting his treatment, Stein composed an extremely insulting one of his own about the king that he often quoted to his friends. When he went to Olav and asked if he would like to listen to the lagman's verses, the king said angrily, 'Read your own first.'

'I haven't composed any,' answered Stein. 'If I had done so, they could never have done you justice.' He realised Olav knew about his poem and that he was in danger. Soon after, he left Nidaros secretly, with a single serving boy.

That evening, reaching a royal farm in nearby Orkdal he asked the bailiff Thorgeir to lend him a horse and cart. 'I don't know the reason for your journey or if you have the king's permission,' answered Thorgeir, who had been present at Olav's angry meeting with Stein. 'The conversation between you and the king the other day was not exactly amiable.'

'I may not be my own master where the king is concerned, but I am not going to be treated like this by a slave,' retorted Stein, who drew his sword and killed the bailiff. Then he appropriated the horse and cart.

Pretending to be king's officers, Stein and his serving boy always managed to find food and shelter. Eventually they came to the homestead of a rich bonde called Thorberg Arnason. When Thorberg's wife Ragnhild had been near death during a difficult pregnancy, Stein had fetched a priest to baptise the child and hear her confession, and she had told him he must come to her for refuge if ever he was in trouble. He explained how he had angered Olav and she promised to do all she could to help him.

When her husband, who had been away, returned he wanted to be rid of Stein as soon as possible, explaining that after the bailiff's murder Olav had held a Thing outlawing him. 'I've too much sense to infuriate the king by standing up for some foreigner.' His wife retorted that if he was so frightened of Olav, he should send him to her father Erling Skjalgsson, but Thorberg said it would make the king angrier still with Erling, who was already under a cloud. Only after Ragnhild threatened to go home to her father, did he allow Stein to stay for the winter.

Olav was furious when he heard that Thorberg had sheltered Stein, but forgave him. However, he refused to pardon Stein although he let him leave Norway. It was not surprising that the young Icelander then went to England and entered the service of King Knut, whom everybody knew to be Olav's greatest enemy.[14]

As with the Faroes, matters elsewhere prevented King Olav from continuing with his attempts to bring Iceland under his rule. Yet even if he failed, there were always Icelanders at his court and in his hird, especially skalds, some of whom were genuinely devoted to him. Several wrote sagas that provide the earliest evidence for his career. The most notable being Sigvat Thordarson.

Born in Iceland about the year 1000, he was the son of a chieftain, Thord Sigvaldson, who had himself led an adventurous life, first as a merchant, then serving with the Jómsvikings as skald to Thorkell the Tall. After this, he had taken part in Olav's Viking raids along the Baltic. He had also accompanied him on his campaign to become King of Norway.

Sigvat joined his father and Olav's army in the Trøndelag in winter 1015, fighting at Nesjar, after which he wrote *Nesjavísur* ('Nesjar Stanzas') the only contemporary account of the battle that we have. He had already written *Vikingarvísur*, the story of Olav's thirteen battles as a Viking, based on information obtained from his father. He went on to be a trusted member of the hird and then *stallare*, or court marshal. This career was interrupted by a spell with Knut in England and Denmark from 1025 to 1026 when he wrote *Knútsdrápa* in praise of the Dane, but neither king nor skald took to each other

– perhaps Knut tried to worm secrets about his former employer out of him – and he returned to Norway where Olav accepted him back into the hird.

Over 150 verses from Sigvat's poems survive, many preserved only by Snorri who relied on him as a source. Other skalds did not rate Sigvat too highly, since he made sparing use of the kennings they admired and did not include enough references to the old gods. But from the historians' point of view, as a fervent Christian who knew Olav really well and, as he showed in poems after the king's death, an unshakeably loyal friend, Sigvat's verse is an invaluable testimony to the king's life.[15]

Olav Haraldsson may have failed to add Iceland to his domains, but he owes a huge debt to the Icelandic skalds who kept his memory green. There were many others besides Sigvat Thordarson. Three of them would fight to the death for him at his last battle.

10

Olav and the Swedish Princesses

Tell me, herdsman, sitting on the hill,
and watching all the ways,
how I may win a word with the maid,
Past the hounds of Gymir here?

Are you doomed to die or already dead,
Thou horseman that ridest hither?
Barred from speech shalt thou ever be
With Gymir's daughter good.

Skirnir's Journey[1]

Everybody knew how Queen Sigurd the Haughty had burned
Harald Grenski to death and plotted Olav Tryggvason's destruction,
so we might expect Olav Haraldsson to have distrusted all royal
ladies who came from Sweden. Yet he became obsessed with marrying Olof Skötkonung's daughter Ingegerd without ever even seeing
her, developing a true 'princesse lointaine' complex. Snorri gives a
long account of this ill-starred romance that played such an important part in Olav's life, and of the politics and clash of personalities
that doomed it.

It all started with King Olav's wish for a reconciliation with Olof
Skötkonung, which plainly was not going to be easy. The border-
lands of Norwegian Viken and Swedish Gotland were in a perma-
nent state of undeclared war because of the enmity between their

kings, Olof Skötkonung bitterly resenting the loss of his territories in Norway. Under any circumstances, he was a tricky man to deal with. Although the first Swedish king who stayed a Christian all his life, dying as one, his religion did nothing to improve his arrogance or his bad temper.

In 1016 he had sent his bailiff Asgaut into Verdal to collect the dues as formerly, but the bonder refused to pay, as did all those in other once-Swedish districts. Asgaut went to Olav and complained. The king told him they were quite right to refuse.

'It is not surprising you are called Olav the Thick, when you answer a royal message in such a way and cannot see how hard it will be for you to survive our king's wrath, as bigger men than you have found out,' retorted Asgaut. (He was referring to Olof's part in destroying Olav Tryggvason at Svoldr.) 'If you want to keep your kingdom, you had better hurry up and accept his overlordship, in which case we might perhaps beg him to let you keep it as a fief.'

'Look, Asgaut, here is a little advice in return,' said Olav, gently. 'Go back east to your king and tell him that next spring I plan to travel eastward to the boundary that used to divide Norway from Sweden. Then, if he wants to, we can make peace and keep the lands each of us has inherited.'

Instead of going home, Asgaut went to Möre with a dozen men, demanding taxes in the name of his king. This time Olav was not so restrained, hanging bailiff Asgaut and his tax collectors on a hilltop gallows by the seashore where their bodies could be seen from every passing ship. Next year King Olof Skötkonung forced Roa Skialge to go on a similar mission. Together with his men poor Roa, who had only saved his life during a previous attempt by running away, was quickly hunted down and killed. After this, the Swedish king's hatred for Olav grew so venomous that no one dared to speak of 'King Olav' in his presence, referring instead to 'The Thick Man'.

Swedish Västergötland on the border bore the brunt of the hostilities and its jarl, Ragnvald Ulfsson, begged Olav to make peace. His Norwegian wife Ingeborg, Olav Tryggvason's sister, who always did her best to help her cousin Olav Haraldsson, had persuaded her husband to go and meet him, and both men agreed that there must be a reconciliation. In the meantime the Swedes retaliated, plundering and burning.

The bonder of Viken lobbied Bjorn the Marshal, leader of Olav's hird, imploring him to tell the king of their misery. He informed Olav that an increasing number of people were being killed on both sides without deciding anything. 'Your lendmenn, your bonders and many others want an end to this strife,' he warned, advising him to send an embassy to Sweden and make peace. 'The Swedish king's courtiers will welcome the proposal because everybody would gain.'

Anticipating trouble from Knut of Denmark after he had subdued England, King Olav was too shrewd not to see the wisdom of this. Somewhat callously, he told Bjorn that as it was his own idea it was only fitting he should lead the embassy, even though it meant risking his life. 'If any danger is involved, you will only have yourself to blame,' added the king.

Hialte Skeggesson, an Icelander much liked by Olav because he was a strong Christian, had recently arrived at Trondheim and as an honoured guest sat next to Bjorn the Marshal in the hall. The pair had struck up a strong friendship. The day after Olav appointed Bjorn to lead the embassy, Hialte saw that the marshal looked unusually glum and asked him, 'What's the matter with you, man? Have you fallen ill or do you hate somebody?'

Bjorn explained that Olav had given him a very dangerous mission. When the Icelander tried to cheer him up, the marshal replied, 'You can come too, if you think it's all that easy.'

'Yes, I will come,' said Hialte. 'It is unlikely I shall ever again run into such a good comrade.'

When the embassy reached Jarl Ragnvald's house, Bjorn presented the jarl with a gold arm ring given to him by Olav for a token and the pair were well entertained. Then the marshal explained his mission to Ragnvald, who was horrified. 'What have you done, Bjorn, for the king to send you to your death? You cannot succeed.

I do not think any man alive could talk like that to our king without enraging him.' Ingeborg interrupted, telling her husband the message must reach Olof whatever the cost and Bjorn should stay with them until they worked out the best way to deliver it.

Then Hialte offered to go to Olof Skötkonung. 'I am not a man of Norway so the Swedes will not be able to find anything wrong with me,' he said. 'And there are Icelanders in the king's household who know me well, the skalds Gizur and Ottar the Black.'

When Hialte reached the Swedish court, the two skalds sang his praises and the king asked to see him. As he was presented, Hialte poured a stream of silver into the lap of Gizur, who was standing next to the king, and explained that this was the tax Icelanders paid on arriving in Norway, saying, 'I know you have the best right to power in Norway so I hasten to pay it to you.' It was a large sum, which made an excellent impression on the 'Tax King', always greedy for money. Hialte now stood high in royal favour.

Olof appears to have enjoyed his conversations with this engaging young Icelander. He himself was a lazy, boastful, bullying windbag who, save for the Svoldr campaign and a solitary raid on Wendland, had never done anything except hunt, hawk and drink. He was also a dangerous man to cross, quick to take offence and bear a grudge.

The skalds then took Hialte to Princess Ingegerd in her house 'where she sat at the drinking table with many men'. She received him in a most kindly way, 'and they sat there till late in the day, drinking'. He repeated his visits, until eventually he asked her if there was any chance of her father being reconciled with his master. Ingegerd Olofsdotter's answer was not encouraging. 'The king is so furious with him that he can never bear to hear his name mentioned.'

The Icelander refused to give up. 'One day he was sitting with the king and talking to him, the king being very merry and very drunk,' relates Snorri. 'Splendour and grandeur have I seen here,' Hialte began, 'seeing with my own eyes that which I have often heard spoken of. No monarch in the north can be so magnificent,' Hialte went on to complain how sad it was that his fellow Icelanders dared not visit Sweden because the Norwegians were so hostile to anybody on their way to that beautiful land.

'Cannot someone try and make peace with King Olav the Thick?' he continued. 'People say he wants to marry your daughter, Princess Ingegerd, which should certainly help. I have heard well informed men say that he is a most distinguished person.'

'You must not talk like that, Hialte, but I cannot blame you this time as you do not know that everybody here is forbidden to say such things,' replied Olof Skötkonung, who then launched into a drunken rant. 'That fat fellow is never going to be called "king" by my household and he has none of the qualities that people say. You can see for yourself what a bad son-in-law he would make.' He, Olof, was king of a great power, whereas miserable Norway with its few, scattered folk was not even a proper kingdom. When Olav Tryggvason set himself up as a king, he and Sveinn Forkbeard had cut him down to size and taken over the entire country.

'You are a clever man and surely you do not think that I would give Norway away to such a fat fool?' continued Olof. 'I am amazed he does not remember how he only just escaped when we had him trapped in Lake Mälaren. He may have saved his life that time, but if he wants to survive, then he will have to think of something more sensible than challenging us Swedes.' The king ended, 'Hialte, never dare to speak to me on that subject ever again.'

Later, the Icelander persuaded Ingegerd to try. 'People are complaining about losing their property and having relations killed because of all this strife,' she told her father when she found him in an unusually good mood. 'It would be a very bad idea for you to try and rule Norway. It is a poor country, hard to get at, and with very tough people, who would prefer any king rather than you. Why not try and conquer some other country, on the Baltic?'

'So you are telling me to give up Norway and let thick Olav have you in marriage, are you?' shouted back her infuriated father. 'Next winter I shall call a Thing at Uppsala and issue a royal proclamation. All must board their ships before the ice is off the sea, and I shall go with them to Norway and lay that land to waste with fire and sword,

burning everything, to punish them for not keeping faith with me.'
He was so mad with rage that nobody present dared to say a word.

When Ingegerd told Hialte his quest was hopeless, he asked if he
might tell her what was in his mind. 'Speak freely,' she said, 'but so
nobody else can hear.'

'What would you say if Olav, King of Norway, should send envoys
to you with a proposal of marriage?'

She blushed, then replied, 'I have not yet decided what answer I
shall give, but if Olav is as you say, then I could not wish for any
other husband – unless your description is too complimentary.'

Begging him to be discreet, she sent letters to Jarl Ragnvald and
his wife, informing them of her wish to marry Olav Haraldsson.

Hialte then left Olof Skötkonung's court. Saying farewell to the
king, he repeated that never, anywhere, had he encountered such
splendour and magnificence. 'You are an unusually intelligent man,'
replied Olof.

After receiving Ingegerd's letter, Jarl Ragnvald visited her at one of
her farms, staying for several days. Hialte was there too. The jarl
asked her how she would react if Olav of Norway wooed her. 'My
father has the right to arrange my marriage,' she answered. 'But of
all my relations, you are the one whose advice I depend on. Do you
think it would be a good idea?' Ragnvald said it was an excellent
idea, then praised Olav, telling her how he had once taken five kings
prisoner in a single morning. Above all, such a marriage would mean
lasting peace between Norway and Sweden. They agreed that while
very difficult to arrange it would be a most suitable match.

Accompanied by Bjorn the Marshal, the jarl went to enlist the
help of his foster-father, the lagman Thorgny, who lived in a great
mansion, waited on by a host of servants. Bjorn and Ragnvald had
never beheld such a fat old man, with a beard so long and so thick
that it covered his entire chest and reached down to his knees. Even
so, the lawman was surprisingly lively and high spirited. It was also
clear that he was exceptionally shrewd. Pointing out that the jarl

would risk his neck by going against Olof Skötkonung's wishes, he nonetheless promised to help him if he proposed the marriage at the Uppsala Thing.

At the Thing, King Olof sat on a stool in the centre, Ragnvald and the lawman sharing a stool opposite him, surrounded by a vast crowd. When the ordinary business was settled, Bjorn the Marshal rose. 'King Olav has sent me here to say that he offers peace to the Swedish king with the old frontiers,' he announced. When he heard this, Olof Skötkonung jumped to his feet, shouting for him to shut up. 'Speeches like that are worth nothing!' So Bjorn sat down.

Jarl Ragnvald stood up, welcoming Olav the Thick's offer and his proposal for peace. He told the assembly how the West Gotlanders were suffering because of the war, how they had to do without all sorts of essential goods from Norway. They were also very frightened of being left defenceless if the Norwegian king attacked them. Then he announced that Olav had sent envoys to ask for the hand of Ingegerd Olofsdotter.

When Ragnvald sat down, Olof Skötkonung jumped to his feet. He was not going to listen to any more peace proposals, he shouted. He said he utterly condemned the jarl for making friends with 'that thick fellow' – Ragnvald deserved to be driven out of Sweden for rank treason. He must have been bullied by his wife into behaving so disgracefully and it was his own stupid fault for having married such a wicked woman. Throughout his speech, the king cursed Olav the Thick, over and over again. When he finished, there was dead silence.

Then the old lagman Thorgny stood up, everyone crowding closer to hear him. 'Swedish kings are different from what they used to be,' he said. He recalled how his grandfather had campaigned with King Eirík Eymundsson in raiding successfully all over the Baltic. His father had remembered how prosperous Sweden was under King Bjorn. In his youth he himself had been on war expeditions with King Eirík the Victorious, who enlarged the country's borders. It had always been easy for anybody to talk to him.

'But this king we have today will never let any man dare to speak unless he is going to say what he wants to hear. This is the only use that he ever makes of his high position while he lets his scatt lands in other countries be taken away from him, through sheer weakness and laziness. Now he wants to rule Norway, which no Swedish king before him has ever wanted to do, and as a result he will bring war and distress upon many men.

'Now it is our will, we bonders, that you, Olof Skötkonung, make peace with the King of Norway and that you marry your daughter Ingegerd to him. If you intend to reconquer the kingdoms to the east that your kindred and ancestors ruled, we will certainly follow you to war. But if you do not do as we wish, then we will seize you and put you to death, because we can no longer put up with chaos instead of law and order. That is what our forefathers did when at the Mórathing they drowned five kings who had been full of the same insufferable pride that you have shown towards us. Tell us at once, what you intend to do.'

The air rang with shouts of approval, men banging their swords against their shields. King Olof stood up again, replying that he would do whatever the bonder wanted. 'All Swedish kings have always done so and have let the bonder decide everything.'

With the country's leading men he drew up a peace treaty on the King of Norway's terms. They agreed that Ingegerd Olofsdotter should marry Olav Haraldsson, Jarl Ragnvald being given full powers to arrange the wedding, which he and Ingegerd then discussed in detail. Meanwhile, Ingegerd sent Olav a cloak of the finest material, sown with gold and with silk ribbons. Bjorn the Marshal returned to Norway in triumph to announce the success of his mission.

A fleet took King Olav and Norway's leading men to Sweden for his marriage to Princess Ingegerd. But when they arrived at Konghelle, the appointed venue for the wedding, there was no sign of Olof Skötkonung or of his daughter. No one knew where they were. The jilted king went home a laughing stock.

What had happened was that, bitterly resenting his humiliation at the Uppsala Thing, the Swedish king was more determined than ever that his daughter should not marry the Norseman, saying nothing for months, but declining to make any preparations for a wedding. Ingegerd took it very much to heart, growing sad and melancholy. Although desperate to know her father's intentions, she dared not ask him, while suspecting that he would never keep the promise he had made at Uppsala.

One morning, he came home in an excellent mood from a hawking expedition, delighted at having brought down five blackgame. 'Did you ever hear of any king catching so many in so short a time?' he asked her.

'No one can say that is not a good morning's hawking to have caught five blackcock, but it was a much finer morning when King Olav of Norway captured five kings and took over all their kingdoms,' she answered.

Her father's amiability turned to fury. 'It is time, Ingegerd, for you to realise that however much you may love this man, you are never going to have him nor will he ever have you,' he shouted, jumping down from his horse. 'I shall marry you to some chieftain with whom I can be friends. I could not possibly be a friend to a man who has stolen my kingdom and done me so much harm by robbing and killing all over my lands.'

Ingegerd then sent messengers to Jarl Ragnvald, warning him that her father had gone back on his word. There would be no peace with Olav and West Gotland should prepare for further hostilities. In turn the jarl warned King Olav, saying he hoped that they would stay friends even so, and begging him not to inflict still more misery on his people. After Olav had received Ragnvald's message nobody could get a word out of him for several days.

Finally Olav held a House Thing, a species of privy council where Bjorn explained the situation to the assembly, emphasising that King Olav had wanted peace and Jarl Ragnvald had shown himself a true friend. It was the Swedish king who was their enemy. Should the Norwegians invade Gotland?

The House Thing decided that for the moment there should be no war. But when Olav announced that next summer all the realm's fighting men must be ready to invade Sweden and punish Olof Skötkonung for breaking his word, everyone applauded. That autumn, 1018, the king went to Viken with his hird, to spend the winter there in his hall at Sarpsborg near the border, in preparation for all-out war.

Then everything changed. The skald Sigvat Thordarson had visited his 'great friend' Jarl Ragnvald in order to spy on the Swedes. It was early winter and his journey was so gruelling that afterwards he wrote 'Verses on an Eastern Journey' (*Austrfaravísur*), in which he recalls 'joyless weather, wind, rain, and pinching cold, feet in pain, sleep, fatigue and hunger, no songs and no rest'. At one farmhouse, significantly called Hof ('temple'), the bonder's wife refused to give them shelter, shouting, 'Come not in, accursed fellow, any further. I fear Odin's anger and we are heathens.' Sigvat explains that the 'hateful hag who drove me off like a wolf' was busy sacrificing to the elves.[2]

But all turned out much better than Sigvat can ever have expected. He was given a splendid welcome by Ragnvald who presented him with a gold arm ring. At first the news was bad, the jarl announced that he had received a letter from Ingegerd to say Grand Prince Yaroslav of Rus had sent envoys to King Olof asking for her hand in marriage, and it very much looked as though Olof would accept the offer.

However, Ragnvald then added that Olof possessed another daughter, by a Slav concubine captured during his raid on Vendland (either modern Holstein or Mecklenburg), whom men called 'the king's slave girl', although her father was a Vendland jarl. By chance, this royal thrall's daughter, Astrid, came to Ragnvald's hall during Sigvat's visit. 'Why should not your Olav marry Astrid?' the jarl asked Sigvat. 'I do not think we need her father's consent.' The skald agreed. So did Astrid.

On Sigvat Thordarson's return to Norway, he first of all informed King Olav of Ingegerd's betrothal to Yaroslav. The king was grief-stricken, saying that he had always expected evil from her father and that one day he would repay him in a way he should never forget. After Olav had grown calmer, Sigvat told him more about his visit to Jarl Ragnvald, declaring that he was a true friend. Then he spoke about the wonderful girl he had seen there, just as attractive as her half-sister. He was not exaggerating. In Snorri's words, Astrid 'was a very lovely girl: her words came well in her conversation; she was merry, but modest, and very generous. When she was grown up she was often in her father's house and every man thought well of her.'³

When he saw that Olav was listening intently, Sigvat told him he had already discussed the possibility of his marrying Astrid with her and that she had looked most enthusiastic. 'The King of Sweden will never believe I could dare to marry one of his daughters without his permission,' laughed Olav, who immediately sent a message to Jarl Ragnvald, telling him to bring her to Sarpsborg without further delay. The jarl and Astrid set out at once, in secret but with a large, well-armed escort, arriving on Candlemas Day (2 February) 1019.

There was a magnificent wedding at Sarpsborg, to which all Norway's lendmenn were invited, Jarl Ragnvald receiving many presents from a grateful King Olav. After a few days, while the feasting still went on, the jarl drew up a marriage contract with the same dowry that had been proposed for Ingegerd and the same 'bride gifts' from Olav. The king accepted the contract without hesitation. When the jarl left for home, he and Olav parted the best of friends 'which', says Snorri, 'they continued to be for as long as they lived'.

Queen Astrid never gave her husband a male child although in 1024 she bore a daughter, Ulfhild. In the same year, an English thrall named Alfhild, 'usually called the king's handmaiden although of good descent', suddenly went into labour and nearly died, as did her prematurely born son by Olav.⁴ Hastily baptised, he was given the name Magnus after the Emperor Charlemagne 'as the best man that had ever been in the world' by Sigvat Thordarson, who had not dared to disobey the king's orders that he was never to be woken.

When awoken next morning, Olav was overjoyed to find that he had an heir whose very existence was a vitally important political asset. He also accepted the name bestowed by Sigvat. Queen Astrid brought the boy up as though he were her own child.

Meanwhile, Olof Skötkonung ordered Ingegerd to marry Grand Prince Yaroslav. As her Russian marriage settlement, she asked for the town and jarldom of Ladoga. She also asked that 'my kinsman Ragnvald' should escort her to Kiev. Angrily, Olof told her, 'I shall reward the jarl in another way, for treason against his master in going to Norway with my daughter and trying to give her to that thick fellow whom he knows is my worst enemy – I shall hang him this summer.' But Ingegerd insisted so stubbornly that he yielded, and when she reached Russia she presented Ragnvald with Ladoga, for him to rule as its jarl.

Olof Skötkonung's troubles however were far from over. The West Gotland bonder, who were sorry to lose so fair-minded a jarl as Ragnvald, were in despair at the never-ending Norwegian raids. After his departure they held a Thing to discuss what could be done, then thirty of them led by their lagman Emund went to Olof. A subtle negotiator, he spoke to the king mysteriously about an obscure law case. After Emund left, a puzzled Olof asked his courtiers to tell him what the lagman had really been saying. Nervously, they explained that Emund was referring to a 'Retribution Thing', summoned to depose him. His only chance of survival was to call an alternative Thing at Lake Mälaren as quickly as possible, where he must 'offer every man the laws and rights of old'.

When this met, the Swedish bonder declared they could no longer recognise Olof as their king because of his blatant disregard for the law and stubborn refusal to accept advice. After much wrangling, a compromise was agreed. Olof's twelve-year-old son Anund Jacob became joint king, while Olof remained king on condition that he made peace with Norway.

Hastily, Olof arranged a meeting with Olav at Konghelle, where the two rulers made a lasting peace. 'The Swedish king was remarkably mild in manner and agreeable to talk to.' When a vexatious question was raised, of whether a farm on the Gotland border belonged to Sweden or Norway, they diced for it and Olav won. The pair parted amiably and Olav was to have no more trouble from the man who had been his most bitter enemy – and was soon to die of natural causes.

Yet despite having left Scandinavia for ever, and despite her marriage, Ingegerd Olofsdotter would one day play a crucial role in the life of Olav Haraldsson.

The face of the Viking pirate and slaver who demolished London Bridge. Later Olav Haraldsson became a Christian, mutilating or blinding those who refused to convert. Yet he was also a hero king, inspiring deep loyalty among his friends and followers. (Photo: Lennart Karlsson, Swedish History Museum/SHM (CC BY))

The Gokstad ship, formerly thought to be the burial place of King Olav Geierstadalf, Olav's adopted ancestor, who also fell in battle and whose beautiful sword, Baesing, taken from his burial mound, facilitated Olav's birth. (warasit phothisuk/Shutterstock)

A Viking longship under sail. Essentially a war ship, designed for raiding and piracy, she was the fastest vessel of her day. Using oars as well as her sail, with a strong wind a longship was capable of reaching speeds of up to 20 knots over short distances.

Freyja, goddess of fertility, copulation and witchcraft, whose chariot was drawn by two lascivious cats. She flew over the battlefields looking for handsome corpses to take back for her entertainment to her sky home Folkvang, the alternative to Valhalla. (The Picture Art Collection/Alamy Stock Photo)

Odin's red-bearded son Thor, wielder of the mountain-smashing hammer Mjolnir, whose blows can be heard in every clap of thunder and lightning. Another war god, his devotees wore small iron hammers round their necks. (Heritage Image Partnership Ltd/Alamy Stock Photo)

Above. The great sea battle of Nesjar in 1016, where Olav won a decisive victory that enabled him to become King of Norway. His young skald Sigvat Thordarson, who was present, recalled how mortally wounded men fell shrieking into the blood-stained sea.

Left. Knut, King of Denmark, England and later Norway, the megalomaniac who drove out Olav. Besides bribery, his agents spread the belief that Knut possessed such huge resources that he was bound to win, turning the Norwegian magnates against their king.
(German Vizulis/Shutterstock)

Above. A church at Borgund in Sogn. None of Norway's stave churches is earlier than a century after Olav's death, but they developed from the small wooden churches of his day that reflected the design of the pagan temples, using their dragon gargoyles to ward off demons.

(robertharding/Alamy Stock Photo)

Right. Ingigerd Olofsdotter, the Swede whom Olav hoped and failed to marry, consort of Grand Prince Yaroslav of Kiev. The couple sheltered Olav during his exile. An ikon after her canonisation as St Anna, the Wonder Worker of Novgorod. (Album/Alamy Stock Photo)

Above. The Golden Gate of the Kiev kremlin through which Olav must have passed during his exile in 'Rus', as the guest of Yaroslav and Ingegerd, reconstructed by the Soviet government in 1982. (robertharding/Alamy Stock Photo)

Left. The fatal battle of Stiklestad in 1030, in which the outnumbered Olav was defeated and killed by an army of his own Norwegian subjects, led by resentful magnates. His overeager troops abandoned a well-chosen defensive position to charge the enemy.

A fifteenth-century painting of 'Sanctus Olofius' with his axe at the church of Barton Turf, Norfolk. Venerated for his powers of healing, during the Middle Ages many English men and women went on pilgrimage to the king's shrine at Nidaros in hope of a cure. (Ashley Taylor, Push Creativity)

A War on Demons

The houses burning,
All people mourning;
Who could not fly
Hung on gallows high

Arnórr Jarlaskáld Thordarson, Haraldsdrápa

In recounting the life of King Olav's half-brother Harald Hardrada, Snorri quotes Arnórr, one of the greatest Icelandic skalds, who recalls Olav's 'mission' in the inner Trøndelag and the Upplands. Hagiographers gloss over Olav's ways of converting men to Christianity, while even Snorri is reticent about the brutality and devastation inflicted.[1] To understand why the king used such extreme methods, we must try and understand Olav himself. Any attempt to get inside his mind must take his religion into account, both the old and the new faith.

It is reasonable to suspect he was tormented by an overriding fear that the old faith might suddenly return to Norway in a pagan revival. He reacted in a way verging on paranoia whenever told that in secret his people were still 'sacrificing to demons' – to the old gods who, driven by the Devil, were wandering through the Norse world for the ruin of souls.

He may well have felt he was being targeted by four of these demons in particular. All early sources agree that the king was a great dreamer and one guesses that his nights were made terrible by dreams of those whom he had rejected for the White Christ – Odin, Thor, Frey and Freyja. Although this is speculation, it would certainly explain why he showed such little mercy to anyone who continued to worship such diabolical beings.

The synod held in about 1024 – the date is debatable – on the island of Moster, at the entrance to the beautiful Hardangerfjord where Olav Tryggvason had built a church, may have given him a fleeting sense of making progress. This approved a code of Christian law drawn up by Bishop Grimkel, assisted by Bishop Sigurd with 'other learned priests', that incorporated many of King Hakon's laws and was also modelled on Anglo-Saxon precedents. We know of its provisions from a codex later written down in the Gulathing Laws.

There is insufficient space to go into detail, but they included a strict injunction to observe the Church's major feast days, which must be kept holy in the same way as Sundays, by fasting and refraining from work. No meat could be eaten on Fridays or during the seven weeks of Lent, while eating horse flesh was outlawed. Marriage between close cousins was forbidden. So was 'out bringing', leaving unwanted children to die (the fate Olav himself had nearly suffered), except in instances of severe deformity, such as a child's face being where its neck ought to be, in which case it must be christened, then left at the church to die. Slavery remained, but slave owners were asked to free at least one thrall every year. Laymen must pay for the upkeep of priests and churches.

There were striking omissions. Clerical celibacy was not mentioned and it would be another 200 years before Norway's priests were forbidden to marry. Nor was there a ban on laymen keeping concubines. Such a deprivation would have been considered too cruel for men who had so long been accustomed to polygamy.

In 1956 the curator of the Vitenskapsmuseet at Trondheim was the first person in modern times to notice a runic inscription on the other side of a stone in the museum's collection that included a cross. It came from the island of Kuløy off Nordmøre. Deciphered, the runes read 'Thorir and Hallvard raised this stone for Ulfjótr . . .

twelve years had Christendom been in Norway'. Dated by dendro-chronology to the mid 1030s from timbers close by, the *Kulisteinen* seems to refer to the Synod of Moster and is sometimes called 'Norway's certificate of baptism'.

Yet much of Norway remained far from Christian. Late in 1020, well before the synod, Olav had been informed that a large number of the bonder in the inner Trøndelag had met at Maere at the top of the Trondheimsfjord and celebrated a winter-day's *blót* in the ancient way. 'It was told to the king that all the remembrance-cups to the Aesir, or old gods, were blessed according to the old forms; and it was added that cattle and horses were slain and the altars sprinkled with their blood, and the sacrifices accompanied with the prayer to obtain good seasons.' He also heard that the bonder were now plan-ning to offer a Yule *blót*.

It is unlikely that Olav did not know of the recent history of Maere, the place where King Hakon the Good had been forced to eat horse meat. So holy to pagans that formerly nothing except live-stock might be killed there, before its destruction by Olav Tryggvason the temple there had contained the idols of many gods, the biggest being Thor who, made of gold and silver, sat in the centre. The shrine had also been a species of Norse Delphi where, according to Theodoricus Monachus, 'oracular voices' answered questions put by the faithful.[2]

The rumour added that the Trønder – presumably tipped off by the oracle – 'saw clearly that the gods were offended by the Hålogaland people turning Christian'. Nothing could have been better calcu-lated to enrage Olav than the revival of an important pagan shrine such as Maere. However, his agents encountered a wall of silence whenever they tried to find out if there was any truth behind what might be pure fantasy.

Learning of his suspicions, the Maere folk sent an envoy to him, a rich, smooth-talking bonde, Olvir Griotgardsson of Egge, who told the king that the bonder were indeed planning to meet together in the neighbourhood of Maere, but merely for some seasonal drink-ing in company. Suspecting that the man was lying, Olav growled,

'Sooner or later, I shall find out what you are hiding from me, and in a way that will make it impossible for you to go on denying it. Whatever is behind all this, don't do it again.'

Shortly after Olvir left, a man named Thorald who was bailiff of a royal farm in nearby Verdal, suddenly asked for a private meeting with the king. Having requested armed protection for himself, his wife and his children, he told Olav what was really afoot. 'Throughout the inner Trondheim land almost everybody is still heathen in religion, even though some have been baptised,' he explained. 'They offer the same sacrifices they always did, at autumn, midwinter and summer ... There are twelve who preside over these feasts, and Olvir, a leading organiser, is responsible for preparing the one at Maere and bringing everything necessary.'

Despite heavy snow and ice, the king promptly took five ships with 300 hirdsmen on board and set off for Maere, sailing up the Trondheimsfjord with a strong wind in his sails. Arriving in the winter darkness, he surrounded Olvir's house and had him dragged out and killed with his fellow organisers, arresting other leading bonder as hostages. Besides confiscating provisions stored for the Yule feast, which as well as ale and meat included fine clothes, he ordered his hird to plunder the organisers' farmhouses.

Next, he summoned all the richer bonder of the inner Trøndelag to a Thing at Maere. Because he had so many of their relatives or friends in his custody, they dared not protest when he sentenced all those who had been in any way involved in organising the abortive sacrifice to be executed, maimed, banished or heavily fined. He also arranged for Olvir's widow to marry a member of the hird, Kalv Arnason, who was given his lands at Egge and made a lendmann.

Before leaving, the king gave instructions for building churches and installing priests. Unusually, the Maere temple seems to have been converted into a Christian place of worship. Today's medieval (stone) church stands on the site.[3]

*   *   *

In 1021, in the summer following the Maere incident, Olav heard that pagan communities still remained in the south, all over the remote Upplands to the north of modern Oslo. Men who consorted with demons deserved no mercy and, ready as ever to take violent measures, he went to Lesje and Dovre. He was accompanied by Bishop Sigurd, an Englishman who had come with Grimkel (like him in possessing a Norse name). Sigurd brought his mitre and crozier. When the king arrived, he summoned all the local leading men to Things in each region, offering them a choice between death or Christian baptism. All chose baptism. Then he demolished their temples and idols, taking hostages to ensure they would stay faithful to the new faith and installing priests.

After this, Olav marched high up into the hills with his hird, to the top of Gudbrandsdal, a mountain valley. 'A river runs along the valley which is called the Otta,' Snorri tells us, 'and on both sides of the river lies a most beautiful hamlet named Lóar, from where the king could see far down over the whole neighbourhood.' According to Snorri, the prospect deeply moved Olav, who sighed, 'What a pity that such a lovely hamlet will have to be burned!'[4] He spent the next five days at Lóar but spared it, since although some of its inhabitants fled all the rest submitted to him, promising to become Christians, besides surrendering their sons as hostages to prove they intended to keep their word.

Today, Lóar (now known as Lom) beneath the Jotunheim mountains, the highest in northern Europe, remains a place of marvellous beauty because of its setting. A log cabin where the king is said to have spent the night, the St Olavs-stuggu, is still shown to visitors. The finely restored stave church here dates only from the mid-twelfth century, but postholes beneath it show that an earlier church must have been built on the site soon after the king's visit.

Some lines by that very strange twentieth-century poet Tor Jonsson, who was born at Lom, recapture something of how his pagan forbears had felt:

The timeless mountains rise and soar,
red rays from a constant sun pour

over peak and crest.
And those to whom I raised my spear
are born of the same blood and fear,
and have the same unrest.[5]

Olav went on to find that other bonder in Gudbrandsdal, further
south, were a much more difficult proposition, even for a determined king who brought a heavily armed hird.

'A man named Olav has come to Lóar and wants to force us into
believing a new religion in place of our fine old one, as well as smashing all our gods to pieces,' grumbled Dale Gudbrand, a rich chieftain getting on in years whom Snorri says was like a king in the area
even if he did not have the title. He quotes Sigvat the skald, who
claimed that Gudbrand was almost as wealthy as Erling Skjalgsson,
Norway's richest man. A devoted worshipper of Thor, he was also
the pagan priest of Gudbrandsdal.

Gudbrand was addressing a meeting that assembled after he had
sent round the war arrow on learning of the havoc wreaked by Olav
further up the valley. 'He claims he has a more powerful god and it
is a wonder that the earth does not give way beneath him or that our
god does not punish him at once when he dares to say such things,'
he continued. 'I know this for certain, that if we carry our Thor, who
has always stood by us, out of our temple on this farm, Olav's god
will melt away, and he and his men will turn into nothing as soon as
Thor looks at them.'

He was cheered to the echo by the bonder, who shouted that if
Olav dared to threaten them, then he would never leave their valley
alive.

Led by Gudbrand's son, 700 bonder took up arms and marched
off to meet the king. They found his hird drawn up in battle order,
with Olav in front, wearing mail and mounted on a horse. Riding
over, he invited them to become Christians. 'We'll give you something else to do today, instead of making fun of us,' they yelled back,
banging their swords on their shields. The hird responded by charging, throwing spears as they ran, whereupon the bonder bolted.

Taken prisoner, Gudbrand's son was sent home to tell his father the king would soon be with him. Pointing out that they had only 200 bonder left, he begged him not to fight. Gudbrand called him a coward.

However, that night Gudbrand had a nightmare in which a terrifying man surrounded by dazzling light warned him not to give battle. 'If you do, you and your people are all going to die, and wolves will drag away your bodies, torn in strips by ravens.' When he told his neighbour, old Thord Istromaga ('Pot Belly'), Thord replied that he had had exactly the same dream, and strongly advised him to talk things over with Olav at a Thing.

Gudbrand agreed. The Thing met beneath pouring rain where Olav told them that all the neighbouring villages had become Christian and that their people now believed in the god who had made heaven and earth. 'We don't know what you're talking about. Why do you call someone God whom neither you nor anybody else can see?' answered Gudbrand. 'Here we have a god who can be seen at any time, even if he has not come out today because it is too wet. When he does, you will find him terrible, awe-inspiring. I think you are going to be frozen with fear. Since you say your own god is so great, ask him to arrange for a cloudy but dry day tomorrow, and let us meet again.'

That night Olav asked Gudbrand's son, whom he had taken back as a hostage, to tell him about their god. He answered that he looked like Thor, carried a hammer in his hand, and although very tall was hollow inside. (He would also have possessed an enormous phallus.) Whenever he went out, he was carried on a big litter. 'He has plenty of gold and silver on him and every day he is fed with four cakes of bread and other food.'

The king had a trusted henchman, Kolbein the Strong, a giant of a man from the Fjords' district, who always carried a big club and was employed by Olav on unusually secret and dangerous errands. He ordered Kolbein to take men and, when it was dark so that no one could see them, to bore holes below the waterline in the boats that had brought the bonder up the river to the Thing. He also instructed him to go to all the farms where their horses were stabled, and let them loose. The king spent the rest of the night in prayer.

Next morning there was cloudy but dry weather. Wearing his episcopal robes, Bishop Sigurd (whom Thord Pot Belly, the bonders' other spokesman, wonderingly described as 'that horned man with a staff in his hand, crooked at the top like a ram's horn') preached a lengthy sermon to the Thing on the Christian god and his religion. When he had finished, the pot-bellied one, still unconvinced, asked Olav to come back again next morning, when the sun was expected to shine so that he would be able to see their Thor in full glory.

Shortly after dawn on the following day, the king and Bishop Sigurd went to the Thing again, where they saw a crowd approaching, carrying 'the image of a huge man that was gleaming with gold and silver', on a litter they put down on the Thing field. Telling everybody to look to the east where the sun was rising, Olav announced, 'Behold our god is advancing, in great light.' When they did so, Kolbein gave the idol such a terrific blow with his club that it broke in pieces at once, and mice 'as big as cats' came running out, accompanied by toads and snakes.

Terrified, the bonder rushed to their boats, which promptly sank beneath them. Others ran to the stables, only to find that their horses had vanished. King Olav rose to his feet. 'Pick up those gold ornaments that are lying all over the grass and give them to your wives and daughters, but do not ever dare to hang them up on wood or on stone again,' he told the few bonder who had not fled. 'I make only two conditions. Either you become Christians or fight us. The victory will go to those to whom the god we worship gives it.'[6]

Amazed that Olav had not been struck down by a thunderbolt, Dale Gudbrand answered, 'Our god has been overthrown and, since he seems to be incapable of helping us, we are forced to believe in the same god in which you believe.' He and the king who had begun as enemies parted as firm friends, and soon afterwards Gudbrand built a church.

As has been suggested, King Olav's frenetic zeal in rooting out pagans came largely from an inbred dread of the ancient gods whom he had once worshipped himself, and who despite all his efforts continued to haunt the Norwegian landscape. Like many converts, he must also have felt an occasional twinge of nostalgia for the old faith, even irrational guilt at abandoning it. Such feelings could only be dispelled by an ever more extreme commitment to the new religion.

At the same time, we may credit him with a conviction that night and day Odin, as wily as he was evil, and that vixen Freyja, together with the less subtle Frey and so many others, not excepting elves, draugr, barrow wights, trolls and water spirits, aided by ghosts and phantoms, were all working against him to undermine everything he had so far achieved and thwart his future plans. He suspected they were striving to reassert their authority, paving the way for great Thor to come roaring back to life and batter down the Cross.

Nor is it fanciful to suppose that a vendetta had begun in Olav's mind between himself and the old gods. Something like this had existed in the mind of the skald Hallfred Vandraedaskald ('Troublesome Poet'), a reluctant convert who was ordered to change his religion by King Olav Tryggvason. At first he writes that he tries to be neutral, telling heroes to worship Odin, 'priest of the raven-king', even though Odin repays praise with fraud. Later, however, when Hallfred has committed himself, he says nervously that Frey, Freyja and Thor 'will bear fury against me' because he has turned against them, while only demons ask for mercy from Grimnir (Odin). Finally, the Troublesome Poet declares:

All mankind casts Odin's words
to the winds. Now I am forced
to foresake Freyja's kin
and pray to Christ.[7]

Since his own conversion, the king would have thought in such a way, certain he could see the four as they really were, evil spirits who to appeal to human beings had taken on semi-human form. It was an insight that in his eyes transformed great Odin into no more than a trickster, mighty Thor into a dangerous buffoon, amiable Frey into a liar who never kept his word and sweet Freyja into a raddled old whore. If they came to him in dreams, his nights must have been hideous, their memory when he awoke only partly soothed by Grimkel.

Olav's realisation of how widespread was the secret resistance to his faith must have come as a profound shock. With real bitterness he saw that most of the neophytes had accepted baptism to save their lives in this world, not the next. They were still in thrall to the terrible demons to whom he himself had once belonged. And behind each of the four, as Grimkel would have warned him, quoting the Scriptures, was mankind's untiring enemy the devil, who 'goeth about roaring like a lion and seeking for men whom he might devour'.[8]

Snorri tells us that after leaving Gudbrandsdal, Olav went on to Hedmark, to discover how far the new faith had progressed. (A more likely date is summer 1022.) This was the region where King Hroerek, whom the king blinded, had reigned and, realizing he might be none too popular with the locals, Olav had kept away from ever since his coup. When he found that only a small part of Hedmark was baptised, he went all over the region, consecrating churches and installing priests.

Although he had no trouble with Hringerike, in Raumarike (once the kingdom of Ragnar Lodbrok) he was attacked at the River Nid by a bonder army, but his hird proved more than a match for them and they ran, soon giving in and meekly accepting the new faith. Olav did not leave until he felt confident that Christianity had been firmly established. Then he went east to Solør, where he baptised the entire neighbourhood. Next year, he did so in remote Voss, which even today is wild country. Again there was armed defiance and again he overcame it without much difficulty.

Olav then met with potentially serious opposition in Valdres, where both freemen and unfreemen took up their swords, axes, spears and shields, assembling in large numbers to resist him on the shore of Lake Vasetvatnet. However, he easily outwitted them by sailing with his hird to the far side of the lake where he burned and plundered their houses, the flames making every man in the bonder army run back to his home. Then he did the same on the other side.

They quickly surrendered, throwing down their weapons and begging the king to have mercy. 'He gave every man peace who truly wanted it, restoring all his goods to him,' according to Snorri. 'And nobody refused to become a Christian' – meaning that nobody dared. After overseeing their baptism, Olav took many hostages. He stayed in the area for over a month, building churches and leaving behind priests to staff them and instruct the people.

The old gods were far from beaten, however, still haunting the Norse mind. Those who continued to believe in them attended Mass ostentatiously on Sunday, keeping their real opinions to themselves. The sacrifices still went on in secret, as no doubt did discreet orgies in honour of Freyja under cover of darkness.

Even so, the methodical demolition of pagan shrines and smashing of idols into pieces never provoked the slightest retaliation from any of the Aesir or the Vanir. Nor was a single thunderbolt hurled down on Olav. Slowly the Norwegian people came to believe that the White Christ must be stronger than all their former deities put together.

In language they could understand, Olav claimed to have a spiritual hird fighting by his side. These were the saints, who were led by such awe-inspiring archangels as the warrior Michael, that scourge of the devil and all demons, however much worshippers might see him as a substitute for Thor or even Odin. No doubt, the priests enlisted each man's *hamingja*, explaining that it was his guardian angel to whom he must pray for good fortune. Churchgoing on Sundays and Holy Days meant being present at the Mass, which if at first baffling and incomprehensible, played a vital role in planting new beliefs in place of the old. Bells sounding across the fjords and mountains, and through the woods, became part of the landscape, every peal proclaiming the Christian faith.

To us, Olav's missionary methods sound like those of a psychopath, yet most medieval men would have approved and not just Snorri. 'Pagans are wrong and Christians are right' is how their attitude was defined in the twelfth-century *Chanson de Roland*, whose other hero Charlemagne massacred thousands of unbelievers. During the next century the crusader king St Louis said that the best way of arguing with an infidel was to thrust six inches of steel into his belly while the Teutonic Knights were even less gentle in their mission to the Baltic pagans of Prussia and Lithuania.

Nevertheless, a rune stick dated to as late as 1200 has been found at Bergen which is inscribed, 'May you be in good health and spirits. Thor receive you, Odin possess you.'[9] This hints that sacrifices to Odin and Thor, and no doubt to Frey and Freyja, went on in secret for long after Olav's time. We can guess that they would not be entirely abandoned for generations to come.

The Killing of Asbjorn Slayer of Seal

When men of power saw the king gave equal judgement
to great and small, they began to be ill-pleased.

Fagrskinna[1]

Olav's rule seemed firmly established. In 1022 Einar Tambarskjelve
finally submitted, coming home from years of exile in Sweden to be
given back the Trøndelag estates that had been his wife's dowry as a
sister of Olav Tryggvason. The following year Erling Skjalgsson
reached a better understanding with the king. Recognition by
Norway's two greatest magnates gave his regime an appearance of
solidity. So did the devotion of fine men such as Jarl Rognvald of
Orkney, Bjorn the Marshal and Kalv Arnason's brother, Finn, with
that of many others who were ready to fight to the death for him.

Yet this solidity was an illusion. Many lendmenn and rich bonder,
especially in the Trøndelag, thought Olav was a tyrant. Some alleged
that he was 'hard, overbearing, severe, spiteful, mean, avaricious,
ferocious, quarrelsome, haughty and proud'. Surprisingly, the catalogue comes from the hagiographic *Legendary Saga of St Olav*,
although whoever wrote the saga dismissed such allegations as vile
slanders. Yet it may well have been the real opinion of those who had
always disliked him, even of some of his supporters. Certainly, he
could be a difficult man to deal with, prone to react violently.

More and more of Norway's ruling class resented Olav's growing
power over their lives and what they saw as his harsh rule. In the old

days their sons had sailed on Viking expeditions or plundered neighbours as a matter of course, in the way that Olav had done himself when he was a boy. But now he was king, he forbade raids on Christians, whether at home or abroad. Anybody who broke the law was sentenced to death or mutilation. Nothing could save those found guilty, however rich and powerful their relations might be, however much money was offered to spare them. As Snorri saw, Olav had banned the Viking way of life, a prohibition that played a role in his downfall.

Sverre Bagge argues that there are no examples of the king coming into conflict with the magnates because of banning robbery or Viking expeditions.[2] But if Snorri does not record specific instances, he quotes some lines by the skald Sigvat Thordarson:

> They who on Viking cruises drove
> With gifts of red gold often strove
> To buy their safety – but our chief
> Had no compassion for the thief.

Detailing the gruesome penalty they suffered, the skald adds,

> Good king, who for the people's sake
> Set hands and feet upon a stake,
> When plunderers of great name and bold
> Harried the country as of old . . .[3]

'He punished great and small with equal severity,' comments Snorri. 'This was the origin of the hostility of the country's great men to King Olav.' In Snorri's view, one reason why people came to dislike him was that his punishments were so severe. He does not mention another grudge of the rich and powerful, which was losing their prestige as pagan priests.

Above all, lendmenn of ancient family who had been chieftains resented losing their independence, and the appointment of new lendmenn to strengthen Olav's control over them. It was clear they were never going to recover their old powers under such a king. They did not consider the possibility that they might have even less independence if they replaced him by someone so autocratic as Knut.

Their anger grew during a series of bad harvests, severe enough in southern Norway but calamitous in the north, the worst being that of 1024. Many must have blamed the crops' failure on the new religion and ending the sacrifices to the old gods, although no one dared say so to the king, who made matters worse for the north by decreeing that landowners in the south could not sell corn or malt to northerners. Lendmenn were infuriated by the officious way his inspectors, the ármenn, generally men of humble origin, enforced the rules.

The story of young Asbjorn Slayer of Seal, who was a substantial northern landowner from Trondenes up in Hålogaland, not far from modern Tromsø, tells us a lot about the reasons behind the lendmenn's hostile attitude towards Olav. It also helps to explain their hatred of the ármenn.

Although Asbjorn's late father had adopted Christianity, he had gone on holding the old feasts three times a year, not centred around sacrifices but as 'great friendly entertainments', days of banqueting over which he presided. These brought respect and status. Asbjorn, an eighteen-year-old lendmann, who had only recently entered upon his inheritance, was eager to follow in his father's footsteps. Drinking ale in vast quantities was an essential part of the festivities, but you need grain to brew ale. 'Without grain to give parties, Asbjorn is nothing,' Sverre Bagge points out with his usual clarity. 'Admittedly, people like the young lendmann had slaves and tenants whom they could command, but to become leaders of larger areas, they had to win adherents by generosity.'[4]

In 1022 Asbjorn sailed south in a small ship to Nord-Jæren, on the coast near modern Stavanger, where his mighty uncle Erling Skjalgsson had a great homestead. As soon as he arrived, he asked

Erling to sell him some grain. At first Erling refused, saying, 'I know no man here who has the courage to go against the king's order, and I find it difficult [enough] to keep well with the king, so many are trying to break our friendship.'

Asbjorn retorted that he was surprised to learn that Erling could not do as he pleased with his own grain for fear of upsetting 'the king's thralls', by which he meant the ármenn who enforced Olav's laws. He was implying that Erling lacked the courage to do so. Erling replied grimly, 'You Hålogalanders know less of the king's power than we do here.' However, next day he relented, suggesting that his nephew should buy the corn from his thralls. 'They are not subject to law or land regulation like other men.'

Sailing home, Asbjorn anchored in the Kormt Sound near Avaldsnes, to shelter for the night. A royal bailiff lived here, Thore Seal or Slayer of Seal (so named because of his skill in hunting seals) who, uninvited, came on board. 'Thore was a man of low birth, but he had swung himself up in the world,' Snorri tells us. 'He was polite in speech, showy in clothes and fond of distinction, not apt to give way to others.' Slave-born on both sides, Thore typified the ármenn who so infuriated the old ruling class.

Learning of Asbjorn's cargo and where he had bought it, Thore summoned a hundred armed men to overawe the crew, who were only twenty all told, and placed an embargo on the ship. 'Erling is doing what he usually does, despising the king's orders,' he remarked. 'He is unwearied in opposing him in all things – it is wonderful that the king suffers it.' Then he told Asbjorn, 'You can either go on shore or we will throw you overboard, for we do not want to be troubled with you while we are unloading the cargo.' Finally, he added insult to the injury by having Asbjorn's expensive new sail hauled down and replaced with the tattered old sail of his own boat.

Asbjorn reached home safely, but reports of how Thore Seal had humiliated the young lendmann circulated throughout Norway, making him a laughing stock. He was so ashamed that he declined an invitation to attend a Yule feast with his mother Sigrid from his father's brother Thorir Hound, who sneered, 'he thinks there may be a Thore Seal in his way on every holm'. Asbjorn could not face the jokes at the drinking table. (In Sverre Bagge's words, 'the drinking table is the great tribunal, where a man's deeds are evaluated'.)[5] He never left his farm all winter, brooding over his humiliation.

Next year, Asbjorn fitted out a longship, a snekkja of twenty oars with a crew of ninety, all of whom were heavily armed. Shortly after Easter, as secretly as possible and avoiding the usual routes, he sailed to Kormt Island to look for Thore Seal. Landing in a lonely area, he set up tents for his men, then disguised himself as a thrall in ragged clothes and a broad-brimmed hat, carrying a pitchfork in his hand. His sword hidden beneath his cloak, he went on alone to spy on his enemy at Avaldsnes.

There he found that King Olav had arrived and was dining with Thore. Because of his shabby clothing he was able to go unnoticed into the dining hall and listen to the conversation. Here he heard a man ask Thore, 'How did Asbjorn behave when you unloaded his vessel?'

'When we were taking out the cargo he bore it tolerably but not well,' answered Thore. 'When we took the sail from him, he fairly wept.'

At this, Asbjorn drew his sword (no doubt a prized family heirloom) and, rushing forward, struck at Thore. 'The stroke took him in the neck, so that the head fell upon the table before the king, and the body at his feet, soiling the table-cloth with blood from top to bottom.' Almost speechless with anger, which was usual when he was in a fury, Olav ordered his men to arrest Asbjorn and put him in chains.

Skialg Erlingsson, who was a son of Erling Skjalgsson, jumped to his feet, offering to pay whatever price the king asked for his cousin's life, however great. A little tactlessly, he added that it was a shame Olav disapproved of what had been done, because in many ways it was a fine piece of work. 'Is it not a matter of death, Skialg, that a man should break the Easter peace and kill a man in the king's lodging?' shouted the enraged Olav. 'And what about using my feet as a chopping block?' With heavy sarcasm, he added, 'But this may appear a small matter to you and your father.'

Despite their oaths of loyalty to Olav, even his hird sympathised with young Asbjorn and did their best to save his life, making all sorts of excuse to postpone his execution, regardless of the king's anger. They despised the late Thore Seal as a low-born member of the ármenn, a 'king's thrall' who had treated his betters disgracefully. In their view, he had deserved to die.

Alerted by his son, Erling Skjalgsson suddenly arrived at Avaldsnes, accompanied by 1,500 armed men who released Asbjorn, breaking his chains while the king was hearing Mass. Erling then drew up his men on each side of the path from the church and the hall. When it was over, Olav and his hird had to walk back to the hall in single file between two threatening ranks. He showed no trace of fear.

In the hall, 'red as blood in the face', Erling told King Olav that he wanted to stay on good terms with him, or 'we shall never meet again', making it clear that the price for continued co-existence was sparing his young nephew's life. There was a tense moment until Bishop Sigurd intervened, begging the king to accept Erling's plea. Aware that Erling's war band was many times bigger than his hird, Olav gave way. Not only did he reprieve Asbjorn, but in token of forgiveness he appointed him as his bailiff in Thore's place with the duty of managing the royal estates at Avaldsnes.

In the event, Asbjorn, who was henceforward known as 'Slayer of Seal' on account of killing Thore Seal, did not live long. Returning to Trondenes, he went on as he had always done and, in a foolhardy gesture of contempt for Olav's magnanimity, never bothered to take up his post as the royal bailiff at Avaldsnes. The king could not be expected to tolerate such an insult.

A year later, when Asbjorn was coming home from the great fish market at Vaage on a large knarr painted red and white and unmistakable, a longship drew alongside. On board was one of the royal sheriffs of Hålogaland, Asmund Grankelson. As soon as his crew identified Asbjorn as the man in a blue cloak at the helm, Asmund said, 'I shall make his blue cloak red', and hurled a light spear with such force that it went right through his body and stuck fast in the stern post – 'and Asbjorn fell down dead at the helm'.

The spear, a valuable weapon with a gold-mounted socket beneath the blade, was retrieved and given with Asbjorn's corpse to his mother Sigrid. After preparing the body for burial, she ran to her brother-in-law Thorir Hound as he was boarding his ship and shouted, 'Here is the spear that went through Asbjorn my son, and there is still blood on it, to remind you that it fits the wound you can see on the corpse of your brother's son.' She added that it would be a most honourable deed if he sent it through King Olav's own body. 'This I can tell you for certain, that you will be named coward in every man's mouth if you do not avenge Asbjorn.'

Although Thorir had held a poor opinion of his late nephew, he was so upset that he could not utter a word in reply, nearly falling off the gangplank into the sea. He knew that he had to avenge Asbjorn or face all Norway's contempt.

Furthermore, that Asmund Grankelson was never punished for murdering Asbjorn and stayed in office as a royal sheriff spoke volumes for Olav's complicity. In consequence, the king had a family blood feud on his hands, a complication he could ill afford at a time when he was threatened by an exceptionally dangerous foe. Asbjorn's killing marked the end of his years of success, the moment when everything began to go wrong.

13

The Shadow of Knut the Great

I will defend Norway with battleaxe and sword as long as life is
given me

Olav Haraldsson to Knut's ambassadors[1]

'Knut, King of all England, Denmark and Norway and of some of
the Swedes', as he proudly styled himself in official documents, had
always been a more powerful ruler than Olav. Although his reign
over England had been established by conquest, during which he
presided over systematic slaughter and murder, the English remembered his later years as a time of unusual peace and prosperity. This
was largely because he made them observe their traditional laws, and
did so himself – when it suited him.

According to Timothy Bolton, his latest biographer, he was 'an
intelligent and pragmatic diplomatist, an energetic and active ruler,
a cunning and resourceful military leader, and most probably a
devout Christian'.[2] This glowing portrait needs qualification. A
Victorian historian wrote, 'His craftiness is abundantly proved by
his intrigues in Norway, and the natural cruelty and violence of his
temper surely need no special proofs.'[3] Olav never faced a more
formidable opponent.

Eager to expand his 'northern empire' still further, it was only to
be expected that Knut the Mighty should want to take over Norway.
In any case, he was 'a man who hungered after the possessions of
others'.[4] He also believed the kingdom to be his by right since his

grandfather Harald Blue Tooth had been its overlord. So had his father Sveinn, after Olav Tryggvason's overthrow. The Jarl Hakon driven out in 1016 was his sister's son and had Knut not been so busy conquering England, Olav Haraldsson would never have become king.

Ever since Knut established his rule over England, especially after inheriting Denmark from his brother, Norwegian magnates who looked back nostalgically to the days of Danish overlordship when they were kinglets, had been visiting him discreetly. They came to complain of a tyrannical regime at home, making it clear that they wanted to return to rule by Lade jarls under a Danish sovereign. They received a flattering welcome from Knut who as ruler of two of the richest lands in northern Europe could afford to give visitors rich presents, and they rarely left his court empty-handed – the great among them receiving gold arm rings or fine swords, the less distin-guished bags of silver pence. He made them aware beyond any ques-tion that he, Knut Sveinsson, was going to offer himself as an alter-native to Olav.

In the summer of 1025 Knut sent ambassadors to King Olav, who grew noticeably uneasy as soon as he heard they were on their way. When they arrived, magnificently dressed and armed, they read out a letter to him. This declared:

> King Knut considers all Norway as his property, and insists that his forefathers before him have possessed that kingdom; but as King Knut offers peace to all countries, he will also offer peace to all here, if it can be so settled, and will not invade Norway with his army if it can be avoided. Now if King Olav Haraldsson wishes to remain King of Norway, he will come to King Knut, and receive his kingdom as a fief from him, become his vassal, and pay the scatt which the earls [the Lade jarls] before him formerly paid.

Olav's response to the letter was equally blunt, telling the ambassadors:

> I have heard say, by old stories, that the Danish king Gorm [Harald Blue Tooth, Knut's grandfather] was considered a fine and powerful king, yet he ruled only Denmark, but the kings who succeeded him thought that too little. It has since come so far that King Knut rules over Denmark and England, and has conquered for himself a great part of Scotland. Now he claims my paternal heritage too. Does he wish to rule over all the countries of the north? Will he eat up all the kail in England? He will have to do so, and reduce that country to a desert, before I lay my head in his hands, or show him any other kind of vassalage.
>
> You shall tell him that these are my words – I will defend Norway with battleaxe and sword as long as life is given me, and will pay scatt to no man for my kingdom.

When the ambassadors delivered Olav's reply to Knut, the Dane commented, 'King Olav guesses wrong, if he thinks I shall eat up all the kail in England; for I will let him see that there is something other than kail under my ribs, and cold kail it shall be for him.'[5]

Shortly after the ambassadors' return to England, Olav was informed by merchants who had been there recently that Knut was assembling an army and a fleet of warships. This meant only one thing – an Anglo-Danish invasion of Norway was imminent. Olav made ready to summon a *leidang* as soon as he should receive definite news that Knut was about to attack. (A leidang was a levy of all Norwegian longships, with every able-bodied lendmann and bonder.)[6] He also posted spies in Denmark to give warning of Knut's arrival.

In autumn 1025 he sent an embassy to the new Swedish king, his young brother-in-law Anund Jacob. His message was that Anund Jacob would not stay king for long should Knut conquer Norway and that if he wanted to survive he should make a treaty of defence with Olav, 'and then we will be strong enough to hold out against Knut'. Anund Jacob agreed, telling the Norwegian envoys to inform their king he would ally with him and that each should go to the help of whoever was attacked first. He, too, was apprehensive about Knut's intentions. There was no sea barrier between Sweden and Denmark since the Danes had annexed fertile Skåne (southernmost Sweden) during the previous century, and he was more than justified in suspecting that a predator like Knut would want to take over still more territory.

To persuade Anund Jacob not to ally with Olav, Knut, who was by now in Denmark with his army, sent an embassy to the Swedish king, with lavish gifts and promises of friendship. A letter delivered by his ambassadors contained an eloquent request for the Swedes to stay neutral. 'For you, Anund Jacob, and your kingdom shall be in peace so far as I am concerned,' Knut assured him. But the ambassadors could see from Anund Jacob's cold reaction that he did not trust their king's promises and preferred an alliance with Olav.

That winter Anund Jacob rode with 3,000 men to Sarpsborg where Olav was in residence. Confirming their alliance, they agreed to meet again in spring 1026 at Konghelle, but postponed their second meeting until they had more information about Knut's movements. Then they received news that Knut had taken his army back to England, but realised that Knut had only postponed his onslaught. Next summer they held another meeting at Konghelle. Here they held long discussions that were clearly deep and wide ranging, although few people knew what they talked about. When they left Konghelle the pair parted as firm friends, giving each other rich presents.

Olav might have made a new ally abroad, but he had formidable enemies at home, if for the moment most of them tried to remain secret. Thorir Hound, the late Asbjorn Slayer of Seal's uncle, a lend-mann from Bjarkøy (an island in Hålogaland in the far north, off the coast from Tromsø, was particularly dangerous. 'I need not be reminded of my injuries to be roused to vengeance on King Olav,' he later explained. 'I remember well my heavy loss when King Olav slew four men, all distinguished both by birth and personal qualities; namely my brother's son Asbjorn, my sister's sons Thore and Griotgard, and their father Olvir.'[7]

Despite the approaching crisis, Olav had found time to invest in a trading venture to 'Bjarmeland', a remote country on the southern shore of the White Sea near modern Archangel that was inhabited by a pagan Finnish people. To begin with, the venture consisted of a single, small ship skippered by a man from the island of Lango, a member of the hird named Karli, who would share the profits with the king. Karli was accompanied by his brother Gunstein.

Thorir Hound, who had already led successful raids on Bjarmeland, offered to join them. Karli welcomed the proposal by such an experienced Viking and Thorir brought his own, much bigger longship, which was manned by eighty well-armed men, far more than Karli's crew of twenty-five. Reaching a Bjarmeland port at the mouth of the River Dvina without incident, they traded very satisfactorily, buying valuable furs such as beaver and sable, as well as many wolf skins.

When they put out to sea again, Thorir held what he termed a 'seamen's council' on board his ship. An Odin worshipper with no time for other religions, he suggested to both crews that they should go back at night and plunder the burial mounds of the Bjarmelanders' ancestors, which were packed with treasure. The crews responded enthusiastically to this enticing proposal, ignoring his warning that it might involve considerable danger. After digging up quantities of loot from several howes without retaliation by the undead, they went on to despoil the idol of the local god, Jómali, stealing past the guards posted outside his shrine. Thorir took a silver bowl filled to the brim with silver coins from the idol's lap while Karli used his axe to hack off a heavy gold necklace from around its neck. But in doing so he hit Jómali's metal head so hard that it rang out loudly.

Alerted, the shrine guards sounded the alarm and the Bjarmelanders chased the raiders 'with shouts and dreadful yells'.

However, two of Thorir Hound's men had brought a sack from which he took out what looked like ashes, scattering handfuls behind him on the path as they ran. Powerful magic, it prevented the Bjarmelanders from seeing them and they boarded their ships, sailing off without hindrance.

When they reached a safe haven, they landed and pitched their tents. Thorir suggested they should divide up the loot at once, but Karli and Gunstein insisted that this must wait until they reached home. Thorir then asked if he could speak with Karli alone. Karli agreed, whereupon Thorir thrust a spear through him and he fell down dead. 'There, now you have learned to know a Bjarkøy man,' laughed his murderer. 'I thought you should feel Asbjorn's spear.'

Gunstein and their crew fled, hastily putting out to sea. When Thorir's ship nearly overtook them, they made for the closest shore, jumping out and running for their lives. Thorir and his men boarded the brothers' boat and removed all valuable goods, including the furs, the loot from burial mounds and the idol's necklace. Then they piled heavy rocks and stones in place of the cargo, cut a hole in the bottom, and scuttled her.

Such wolfish behaviour was only to be expected from a man like Thorir Hound, a brother-in-law of the late Olvir Griotgardsson, the 'martyr' of Maere. An unreconstructed Viking of the traditional sort, predatory and bloodthirsty, Thorir detested Olav's war on the old gods that had eroded his power and prestige, and no doubt he went on offering the sacrifices in secret. Able to keep the old ways because of the remoteness of his northern lair where there were kindred spirits, he despised men such as Karli and Gunstein as lily-livered followers of the White Christ.

Gunstein escaped with difficulty – saved by the intervention of a friendly witch, it was rumoured – and reported to Olav what had happened. 'Ill pleased', the king told Gunstein to stay with the hird, promising to help him obtain justice when he had an opportunity. Olav realised this was not just robbery but revenge for Asbjorn Slayer of Seal's death – the murder of Karli, a member of the hird, and the theft of his goods including the king's was calculated defiance. Normally he would not have rested until Thorir had been hunted down and killed. However, these were not normal times.[8]

In 1025 Olav sent Finn Arnason, Kalv's brother, up to Hålogaland to raise men and ships for the defence of the realm against King Knut's invasion, expected to come in the following year. A lend-mann who owed his rank and wealth entirely to Olav, Finn – one of the king's closest friends and a man whose loyalty was never in doubt – had no trouble with the bonder in the southern part of the region. Then he went further north, where he summoned a Thing. Seeing Thorir Hound among the assembly, he asked him what *mulct* (fine) he proposed to pay for murdering Karli on the Bjarmeland expedition and the theft of the king's goods.

Hemmed in by armed, hostile men, among whom were the late Karli's brother Gunstein with many friends, all shouting threats, Thorir saw that if he wanted to live he must pay. He asked Finn Arnason to refer the amount to the king's decision. As Olav's representative, Finn decreed that Thorir should pay ten marks of gold to the king, ten to Gunstein and to Karli's family another ten as compensation for the lost goods. All must be paid on the spot.

The Hound growled that it was a very heavy fine indeed and he must go home to find such a vast sum. Finn, who was no fool and did not trust the man, refused to let him leave, demanding he hand over the gold necklace stolen by Karli from the idol Jómali. When Thorir denied ever having had such a thing, Finn put the point of his spear on his chest and shouted at him to produce it, where upon Thorir surrendered the necklace, which was hanging round his neck. Despite Finn breathing menaces and flourishing his spear as if he meant to use it, Thorir took so long to count out the fine, handing the money over in small packets wrapped in knotted rags, that by late evening he had paid only a third. Reluctantly, Finn told him he could pay the rest later.

'Good will is not wanting to pay this debt,' said Thorir, smugly and untruthfully. Then he set sail, ostensibly bound for home to collect the rest of the fine. Instead, he went straight to England where he was very well received by King Knut. 'Better to have him at a distance than near us,' was Olav's dry comment.[9]

Norway contained other revengeful enemies besides Thorir Hound, if more secret, who hated Olav with equal fervour. As Sverre Bagge emphasises, the opposition to him was not a conflict between monarch and aristocracy, but the result of a series of conflicts with individual members of the aristocracy.[10]

14

War with Knut

The wolf did not miss prey
Nor the raven, on that day

Ottar the Black, *Knútsdrápa*[1]

In spring 1026, Olav summoned a full-scale levy of Norway's armed men and longships, in readiness for an invasion. He intended to sail on board the newly built *Bison*, a huge dragon ship with a gilded bison's head at the prow that was easy for the rest of his fleet to identify in battle.

Discouragingly, his most powerful subject, Einar Skjalgsson, did not join the levy, but sailed to England with his sons where he joined King Knut. Einar was not the only magnate who did so. Even so, Olav had an excellent army of hand-picked, well-armed veterans, having sent home any second-rate men, while despite the desertions it included most of Norway's lendmenn.

Snorri stresses how closely Olav and Anund Jacob co-operated. They were encouraged by news of a plot by Knut's brother-in-law Jarl Ulf, who had been his right-hand man for many years, to seize control of Denmark and instal one of Knut's sons as king, eight-year-old Hardeknut (Harthicanute), with himself as regent and the real power. Ulf was supported by several leading Danish nobles.

Aware that even together they would be heavily outnumbered, Olav and Anund Jacob attacked first, Olav sailing to the Danish island of Zealand where his men plundered and burned, killing or dragging off to slavery any Dane who did not flee. Anund Jacob harried Skåne, then part of Denmark, before marching to the coast and joining forces with him. When they met, they announced their intention of conquering Denmark, asking its people to join them, as they hoped for support from the Danes involved in Jarl Ulf's plot. 'Wheresoever they went they laid the country all round in subjection to them, and laid waste all with fire and sword,' records Snorri. Their object was to force Knut to give battle. They calculated that while they did not have enough strength to defeat him in a full-scale confrontation they might do so with the right tactics.

As soon as Knut heard that his enemies had invaded Denmark and of Jarl Ulf's plot, he gathered an army that besides Danes included Englishmen and a small force of Norwegian exiles under Jarl Hakon. He had a large fleet that contained some impressive vessels, his dragon ship being the biggest ever built in Scandinavia with sixty benches of rowers, while if smaller with only forty benches Hakon's was equally fine in her own way. Their hulls were painted in bright colours, with sails striped blue, red and green, and a gilt figurehead at the prows. The army on board consisted of veterans armed with the best weaponry available. Knut always insisted that his bodyguard should carry gold adorned axes and richly hilted swords, presumably with blades of the finest steel.

Learning that Knut was on his way, Olav and Anund Jacob joined forces in Skåne and intensified their ravaging and burning, killing everybody they caught. There was no more hope of Danish support as Jarl Ulf's plot had collapsed at the news of Knut's imminent arrival. The jarl had hastened to make peace with his terrible brother-in-law, bringing ships to join his fleet.

Together, Olav and Anund Jacob went east along the coast, anchoring in the estuary of a river 'called Helge-aa'. Nobody can be absolutely sure where the battle of Helgeå, or the Holy River, was fought. Snorri says that it took place at the 'Helge River', which the

Anglo-Saxon Chronicle calls 'the Holy River', without explaining why. Several sites have been suggested, each of them plausible, but the estuary of the Helge in eastern Skåne, then Danish territory, seems the most likely.

Aware that Knut's fleet was approaching, they held a council at which Olav proposed a means of defeating their enemy. Remembering how ingeniously Olav had trapped Jarl Hakon years before, and the *Historia Norwegie*'s claim that he was 'a great expert in the science of warfare', the scheme sounds as though it was his brainchild.[2] It was he who put it into action, supervising the minutely planned and laborious work involved.

Taking his men up to the big lake in the forest where the Helge had its source, the king dammed the river at its head with a great dam of trees and turf. At the same time, he dug a deep ditch through which he channelled other streams into the lake so that it became still deeper. He also raised the level of the Helge by laying large tree trunks in the riverbed, which were intended as missiles that, hopefully, would wreak havoc on the Danish ships.

The work took him many days. Anund Jacob was left in command of the rest of the army on board their fleet, which lay at anchor in the estuary of the Helge. He posted lookouts to give immediate notice of King Knut's arrival.

Enraged when he heard of the damage done to his homeland, as his enemies hoped Knut sailed towards them with his entire fleet. Early one evening Anund Jacob's lookouts sighted the Anglo-Danish ships, whereupon the Swedish king ordered the wooden war horns to sound, warning his men who hastily struck their tents and went on board their own ships. He also sent a message to Olav, informing him that the crisis was at hand. Leaving a demolition party at the lake, with instructions to demolish the dam at a specified time, Olav and his men returned to the coast, rejoining Anund Jacob. Then the two kings sailed their combined fleet out of the estuary, to a hidden anchorage on the coast nearby.

Knut arrived when it was too dark to give battle. Seeing that his enemies had obligingly vacated the estuary, he anchored with part of his fleet in this seemingly secure haven. At dawn next morning many of his men went on shore to chat with other crews. But during the night the dam upstream had been destroyed at the time specified by Olav. Suddenly, the Helge River burst upon them 'like a waterfall', flooding all the fields and drowning everybody in its way.

A large number died in the estuary where a substantial part of the fleet was sunk by the huge tree trunks Olav had placed upstream that came careering down with the flood, battering rams that smashed into the Danish ships, holing them below the waterline. A few skippers reacted quickly enough to escape, cutting their anchor cables, but though their vessels survived they were scattered far and wide across the sea. 'Many men perished on King Knut's side, both Danes and Englishmen', laconically records the *Anglo-Saxon Chronicle*.[3]

Out of control, Knut's great dragon ship was driven straight into Olav and Anund Jacob's fleet by what appeared to be a tidal wave. The Norwegians and Swedes tried to board her from both sides but her hull was exceptionally high, 'as if it were a castle', and difficult to climb, while once they recovered from their shock Danish bowmen shot down on them from above. Meanwhile, the majority of Knut's ships, prevented from anchoring in the estuary because his fleet was so large, had survived while Jarl Ulf soon arrived to rescue him.

Knut's surviving vessels came together again fairly soon. Aware that they 'had got all the victory that fate would permit them to gain', Olav and Anund Jacob ordered their fleet to cut loose from Knut's dragon ship and withdraw. Still dazed, their enemy did not attempt to pursue, more concerned with reassembling his own battered craft.

Yet despite the Danes and their English friends suffering such heavy losses in ships and men, and despite a spectacular tactical defeat, King Knut had 'kept the field'. In strategic terms, he was the clear winner. He still possessed enough ships to blockade the Øresund between Skåne and mainland Denmark, which prevented Olav's fleet from sailing back to Norway

Although few of Olav and Anund Jacob's men had been killed, they knew that their combined forces would never be strong enough to defeat Knut in a straightforward confrontation. Unable to fight their way through the Øresund, they set sail for Sweden. When they arrived, many Swedes deserted and went home. King Anund Jacob then called a House Thing.

'We have forayed wide around in Denmark, and have gained much booty, but no land,' he told Olav. 'I had 350 vessels, and now have not above 100 remaining with me . . . Now I will offer you, King Olav, to come with me, and we shall remain assembled during the winter,' he continued. 'Take as much of my kingdom as you will, so that you and the men who follow you may support yourself well.' Then they could decide what it would be best to do when spring came.

Thanking him, Olav agreed that it would be wise to keep their armies together. He, too, had had 350 ships before leaving Norway, but had weeded-out less warlike men from the levy, leaving only enough to man the sixty ships he had brought with him, which was why there were still sixty of them. Had Anund Jacob done the same, he would have kept all his ships. Even so, Anund Jacob's best troops and chieftains, who were just as good as the Norwegians, had stayed with him. 'We have picked men and fine ships, and we can lie all winter in our ships, as is the Viking custom.'

In Olav's view, it was difficult for Knut to maintain his offensive. If he came in pursuit, they could easily escape and their peoples would rally to them, while if Knut stayed in harbour, his men would desert. After being so harried by Swedes and Norwegians, the bonder of Skåne and Zealand were going to think twice about staying loyal to him, as Knut knew very well. His army would be so widely scattered that no one could tell who would win.

Olav's speech was applauded by the House Thing, who unanimously agreed to follow his advice. Spies were sent to infiltrate

Knut's army and report on his movements while during the early months of the winter Olav and Anund Jacob remained where they were with their armies. They were too optimistic.

Admittedly, King Knut, who stayed in Skåne with his fleet until the harvest was in, must have been far from happy with the situation. The tsunami engineered by Olav had given him real cause to worry. He may even have attributed it to seidr, good old-fashioned, pagan witchcraft, even perhaps to the intervention of Odin, regardless of Olav's reputation as a Christian.

We can see that Knut's nerves were in a bad state from the savagery with which he disposed of Jarl Ulf. Although Ulf had rescued him at the Helge, despite a seeming reconciliation he had not forgotten his abortive plot. Towards the end of the year the Danish king and his court rode to Roskilde, where the jarl, who was understandably anxious to placate him, had prepared a splendid entertainment for them during Yule.

From the first day the king remained silent and sullen, despite Ulf making every effort to be agreeable. However, on Christmas Eve he thawed, consenting to a game of chess. Soon he made a false move and the jarl took a knight from him. Knut refused to accept its loss, replacing it on the chessboard. At this, Jarl Ulf, who was famously hot-tempered, threw the board on the floor and stormed out. As he was leaving the room, Knut shouted, 'Run away, Ulf the Fearful!' The jarl turned, snarling, 'You would have run much further at the Helge River if you had come to grips with the enemy. You did not call me Ulf the Fearful when the Swedes were beating you like a dog.'

Waking early on Christmas morning, the king summoned a housecarl who was a Norwegian and not a Dane, and ordered him to kill Jarl Ulf at once, even though the 'Wolf' was at church where Roskilde Cathedral now stands, hearing Matins. When the man returned and showed him his sword covered in blood, Knut asked, a little unnecessarily, 'Have you killed the jarl?'

'I have killed him,' was the answer.
'You have done well,' said the king.

If King Knut was more taken aback by the Battle of the Holy River than he cared to admit, realising that Olav Haraldsson was an opponent of a type he had never encountered before, he soon regained confidence. When all was said and done, Olav had been driven off the sea. Despite his assured speech to the House Thing, his ships must stay bottled up in Sweden for so long as Knut's fleet blockaded the Øresund, wide as it was. Olav knew that his men did not have enough food to see them through the winter. They faced starvation.

Olav may also have guessed that, far more serious, the Danish king had identified his greatest weakness. This was the enmity of Norway's lendmenn, especially in the Trøndelag where too many of the hated ármenn were at work. Nor was resentment of Olav's regime confined to the Trøndelag. Lendmenn in the Upplands and along the west coast had never fully accepted him. *Fagrskinna* records that Knut's agents came back reporting how 'powerful men had sworn oaths that they would accept Knut as king over all Norway if he came to the country'.[4] Olav did his best to conciliate them, but without success. Words from the *Songs of the Sun* are only too applicable:

> Peace to them he granted
> with heart sincere:
> they in turn promised him gold,
> feigned themselves friends.[5]

Explaining Knut's success in outwitting the heroic King Edmund Ironside in their desperate struggle for the English throne, Timothy Bolton says that the duel between the two had been that of 'a cunning and intelligent man versus a more straightforward warrior, with Knut using more underhand methods such as securing the support of a core of English collaborators to tip the balance'.[6] The Dane employed the same methods in Norway, and Olav soon found that matters were going from bad to worse.

Olav must have hoped that the battle in the estuary would settle matters one way or the other, as at Svoldr or Nesjar. But it had settled nothing. In fact it made Olav's position worse, and not only because his men failed to bring home the loot that might have been theirs had they been victorious. After the confrontation at the Helge River, Norway's magnates realised that Knut was bound to win. His shadow dominated all Norway. As Sigvat Thordarson sang:

The base traitors ply
with purses of gold,
Wanting to buy
What is not to be sold –
The king's life and throne
Wanting to buy . . .[7]

There were increasing signs of open disaffection, unmistakable, ominous and alarming. By now, Olav knew that he had all too many foes among the magnates and bonder, as well as some who were not so secret. Visiting Knut discreetly or sending messages, they promised to help establish his rule as soon as he led an invasion.

Luckily for Olav, King Knut gave him another respite by making a pilgrimage to Rome – on foot with a staff and a pack on his back, if *Fagrskinna* can be believed, where in March 1027 he watched Pope John XIX crown the Holy Roman Emperor Conrad II at St Peter's.[8] Knut's object in going to the Holy City was to secure privileges for the Church on the Danish border and in England, which he obtained. But never for one moment did he forget about Norway, instructing his agents to continue their work of undermining Olav.

After spending the last months of 1026 in his ships with his men, who besides running short of food had no better roof to keep out the cold than sailcloth covered in brushwood, early in the New Year Olav left his fleet in the Swedish king's care, manned by skeleton crews, and marched home across the mountains despite the winter weather. Travelling through Småland and West Gotland, his army stowed their baggage on packhorses, save for their weapons, to march faster through the snow. Presumably they carried food in their backpacks, but even if wrapped in furs and equipped with skis or snowshoes, many must have been crippled or killed by frostbite.

Reaching his town of Sarpsborg, Olav spent the rest of the winter there in comfortable quarters at the King's House. As soon as the weather improved, he sent home those of the army who had survived. He kept his hird with him, together with his more dependable lend-menn and their housecarls. He was encouraged by the arrival at Sarpsborg of his former skald Sigvat Thordarson, who after going to England and becoming King Knut's skald, had decided that he much preferred Olav's employment, which he explained in a highly flatter-ing poem. This clearly soothed Olav's ego since the king told Sigvat to take his old seat in the dining hall. Within a short time he was once again high in Olav's favour, reinstated as marshal of the court.

During Yule the skald was among a small group of courtiers who accompanied the king on a visit to a house where he kept his most prized possessions, to look for seasonal presents. These included many gold-mounted, blue-bladed swords and Sigvat sang hopefully:

> The swords stand there,
> All bright and fair –
> Those oars that dip in blood:
> If I in favour stood,
> I too might have a share.
> A sword the skald would gladly take
> And use it for his master's sake.[9]

King Olav responded by giving him a particularly beautiful sword.

*   *   *

Meanwhile, Knut stepped up his efforts to bring down Olav from within. Knowing that many in the Trøndelag remembered the Lade jarls with affection, the Dane promised publicly to reinstate the banished Hakon as viceroy. He also gave valuable presents to the lendmenn or rich bonder whom his spies had identified as discontented, assuring them that when he was King of Norway they would regain all their old independence.

Olav and those genuinely loyal to him knew that the situation was deteriorating every day. There was bitter talk of Jarl Hakon, who was reported as being ready to break his solemn oath of never taking up arms against the king. It looks as though the steadily increasing but secret menace from within induced a state of mind in Olav verging on paranoia – recaptured in the lines by Ottar the Black quoted at the start of this chapter. The king grew feverishly suspicious, seeing secret enemies all around him – and not without reason.

Thorir Olvirsson of Egge from the inner Trøndelag, whose father had been executed by Olav as a stubborn pagan, was a typical example of Sigvat's 'base traitors'. Eighteen years old, he was a big, handsome young bonde whom everybody liked. Rich and well connected, he had recently increased his wealth by marrying an heiress from Hedmark and was famous for his lavish hospitality. He then invited Olav and his hird to visit his farmstead, impressing them by his entertainment, 'the best that could be got'. The king and his men did not know what to admire most, relates Snorri, 'whether Thorir's house outside, or the furniture inside, the table service or the liquors, or the host who gave them such a feast'.

Yet Olav did not quite trust Thorir Olvirsson, remembering how he had ordered the killing of the young man's father. Or it may be that he recalled the advice of the High One in *Hávamál*:

Within the gates ere a man shall go,
Full warily let him watch,
Full long let him look about him;
For little he knows where a foe may lurk,
And sit in the seats within.[10]

Shortly after the first banquet at Thorir's house, King Olav went for a quiet walk outside with Dag Raudsson, a man whom he knew to be as honest as he was well informed. He asked him to say in confidence what he knew about Thorir. In response, Dag began by saying that in his personal view Thorir was too fond of money.

'Is he a thief or a robber?' enquired the king.

'Neither,' replied Dag.

'What is he then?'

'He is a traitor to his sovereign,' Dag answered bluntly. 'He has taken money from Knut the Great for your head.'

'What proof have you of this?' asked Olav.

'He has upon his right arm, above the elbow, a thick gold ring that Knut gave him, and which he lets no man see,' replied Dag. That appears to have been all he said, but it was sufficient to enrage the king.

Olav returned to the house. During the banquet that evening Thorir went round the hall to see that everyone was being properly served and enjoying the entertainment. When he came to the table in front of the king, Olav asked him how old he was. 'I am eighteen,' replied Thorir.

'A big man you are for your years, and you have been very fortunate,' said the king. Then he took his right hand and felt Thorir's arm up towards his elbow.

'Take care,' said Thorir, 'for I have a boil on my arm.'

'Have you not heard that I am a physician?' replied Olav, which was true enough. 'Let me see the boil.'

Realising that it was no use trying to hide it any longer, Thorir took off the ring and laid it on the table. Then the king asked him if the ring was a gift from King Knut. When the young man said he could not deny it, Olav ordered him to be put in irons.

Kalv Arnason, who was his stepfather having married Olvir's widow, repeatedly begged the king to be merciful, offering to buy Thorir's life, as did many others present. However, the king was so angry that nobody could get in a word. 'Thorir shall suffer the same doom that he planned for me!' he said and gave orders for the young man's immediate execution.

On hearing of Thorir's death, his elder brother Griotgard Olvirsson, who lived nearby, began to attack the royal estates in the area, killing all the king's men that he could find. Between raids, he hid deep in the forest or in safe houses. Eventually, learning that he had taken refuge at a lonely farm, Olav and his hird surrounded it during the night. Awoken and told that the king was outside with troops, waiting for him to emerge, Griotgard came out fighting, sword in hand with his shield over his head. Defiantly, he shouted, 'I am not a man who begs for mercy.'

However, it was still only just dawn and in the dim light he could not see clearly. He lunged at Olav, but a hird man called Arnbiorn Arnason (Kalv's brother) put himself in the way, taking the sword thrust meant for the king in his stomach, below his mail – 'which was Arnbiorn's death wound'. The other hird men soon rallied, killing Griotgard with most of his followers.

All this mayhem badly damaged King Olav. Both Thorir and Griotgard were nephews of the exiled Thorir Hound, who was already eager to avenge their cousin Asbjorn Slayer of Seal. More fateful still was Kalv Arnason's reaction. Until now he had been one of the king's most trusted henchmen, owing him his estate at Egge and rank as lendmann, even his rich wife. Yet he never forgave Olav for what he saw as the murder of his beloved stepson. Thorir Olvirsson's killing turned Kalv from being the king's devoted friend into a sworn if still secret foe. Others too were alienated by such harshness.

The knowledge that anyone who cared to stand up against Olav could always find unlimited support from King Knut began a breakdown in his authority that was going to end in the complete collapse of his regime. How Knut secretly fanned the flames can be glimpsed in the case of Harek of Thjotta.

Off Hålogaland there lay an island, little more than a rock but of considerable value as a fishing ground, and also for seal and bird catching as well as for harvesting birds' eggs. For many years it had been owned by the family of Asmund Grankelson, the man who had killed Asbjorn Slayer of Seal. Recently, however, a local magnate had laid claim to it.

The magnate was Harek of Thjotta, lord of a much larger island nearby from where he had evicted all the small bonder. While belonging to the old aristocracy as a descendant of Harald Fair Hair, he had begun life as a poor man, but since then had grown rich by ingratiating himself with Olav who had made him royal agent for the highly profitable trade with Lapland and for collecting the Sami people's annual tribute to the king of furs, ivory and falcons. By now elderly, he was one of the Hålogaland's most respected figures.

Even so, Asmund and his father Grankel thought there was a good chance of recovering the little island in view of Asmund's position as royal sheriff of Hålogaland and record of service to the king. However, Harek warned him that although he might enjoy the king's favour and have killed several chieftains without being fined, he should go carefully in this matter. 'You are far from being my equal,' he growled, making clear his contempt for his opponent as a 'new man'.

'Harek, in dealing with you many people have suffered because you are friends with great men and as a result you have acquired so much power that they have lost their property,' was Asmund's answer. 'But now you are going to have to look elsewhere, instead of threatening us with your usual violence. You must stop defying the law.' Asmund meant that he had King Olav on his side.

Harek reacted by sending a boat with a dozen of his servants to the rock to take anything they could find there that was worth taking. But as they were about to set sail for home, they were pounced on by Grankel's men who cudgelled them and then threw them into the sea, confiscating all they had taken. 'Never before has it happened that my people have been beaten like this,' said old Harek when they told him.

Next year he went in person to appeal to the king. Without hesitation, Olav found in favour of Grankel when Asmund produced witnesses who swore that Grankel had always been the rock's rightful owner. It was a one-sided judgement because no fine was levied on Grankel for beating up Harek of Thjotta's servants. Showing no sign of chagrin, Harek seemed reconciled to the case going against him, declaring that there was nothing shameful in accepting the king's decision.

When Harek was with Olav on the Helge River campaign and in Sweden, King Olav asked him to join his army on the march back to Norway and to leave his ship behind. He responded with determined excuses. 'I am old and heavy, and little accustomed to walking,' he claimed.

'We will carry you when you grow tired of walking,' said Olav.

But Harek still refused, saying, 'I am unwilling to part with my ship; for on that ship and its apparel I have bestowed so much labour that it would go much against my inclinations to put her in the hand of my enemies.'

After waiting for a favourable wind, Harek sailed back to his island home on Thjotta. Disguising his ship as a run-down merchant vessel, covered in a grey tarpaulin beneath which he hid his house-carls, taking down the sail and relying on oars he passed without hindrance through the close blockade mounted by Knut's fleet. When he had done so, in full view he hoisted the sail again, snow white and striped in red and blue, and replaced the gilded vane on top of the mast. Strangely, the Danes made no attempt to pursue and plunder such an opulent looking craft.

Later, it became known that Harek had reached a friendly understanding with Knut. However, few realised this at the time. Fellow travellers like Harek of Thjotta were far more dangerous than the callow Thorir Olvirsson or even that other murderous old Viking, Thorir Hound.

15

Norway Rejects Olav Haraldsson

Skirnir spoke to his horse:
'Dark it is without, and I deem it time
To fare through the wild fells
(To fare through the giants' fastness;)
We shall both come back, or us both together
The terrible giant will take.'

Skirnir's Journey[1]

Early in 1028, King Olav heard that Knut had returned to England from his pilgrimage and was assembling another fleet. Snorri, who in this case exaggerates wildly, says that it numbered over 1,400 vessels. The *Anglo-Saxon Chronicle*'s 'fifty ships' sounds a more likely figure. Probably most were big knarrer commandeered for use as troop transports. Knut had prepared the way for the invasion with his usual cunning, sending large sums of money to the magnates and 'earnestly entreating them to reject and depose Olav and, submitting to him, accept him for their king,' says John of Worcester. 'They greedily accepted his bribes, and caused a message to be returned to Knut that they were prepared to receive him whenever he chose to come.'[2]

Olav sent to Sweden for his own fleet, including the great *Bison*, that he had left at Gotland in King Anund Jacob's care, but it was unable get through the Øresund, still blockaded by Danish warships. Going down to Tønsberg in southern Norway, on the west of the

Oslofjord near the Skagerrak, he ordered a leidang. A mere handful of bonder responded to the levy and their boats were too small for a naval battle. All were men living in the immediate locality, who feared the royal anger if they disobeyed. Scarcely anyone came from far off. 'It was soon found that the people had turned away from the king,' Snorri tells us.

The news of Knut the Mighty's imminent invasion had spread all over the country and, aware of his resources and his army's fearsome reputation, the Norwegian bonder did not intend to risk their lives in a hopeless cause.

> Our men are few, our ships are small
> While England's king is strong in all,
> but yet our king is not afraid –
> Oh, never was such king betrayed . . .
> 'Tis money that betrays our land.[3]

Sigvat Thordarson sang mournfully. No doubt this was an echo of Olav's own feelings.

Olav asked his hird men for advice about what he should do, holding several House Things. 'We must not conceal from ourselves that Knut will come here this summer,' he told them bluntly. 'He has, as you all know, a large force, and we have at present only a few men to oppose him, and as matters stand we cannot depend too much on the fidelity of the country people.' No one had any answers. Stressing that the real enemy was treachery within, Sigvat said that it would be no dishonour to take refuge from such a powerful foe.

Just how far King Olav's authority had collapsed was shown by the behaviour of Harek of Thjotta, who took the law into his own hands. Telling everyone he was bound for Trondheim, he sailed through the night (on a ten-oar cutter instead of his smart longship which was too well known) to surround Grankel's house with eighty housecarls and then set fire to it. Grankel was burned to death, together with most of his servants. Those who escaped from the flames were killed outside. At least thirty men lost their lives. After this, Harek sailed back to Thjotta, resuming his peaceful existence as a farmer, secure in the knowledge that it was no longer in the king's power to punish him.

When Knut was fully satisfied with his invasion force, he assembled it at the Limfjord on the Jutland coast and set sail for Norway. News of his coming accelerated the end of Olav's regime. Landing at Agder in the extreme south, the Dane summoned a Thing where the southern bonder hailed him as king 'and no man opposed him'. Then he sailed north, past Tønsberg and along the west coast, putting in to hold Things where 'people came to him from all the districts, and promised him fealty'. He also visited Egersund where Erling Skjalgsson joined him with many men, promising to give Erling a large swathe of territory to rule over.

At Trondheim the Thing acclaimed Knut the Mighty as undoubted King of Norway. Thorir Hound and Harek of Thjotta were both appointed as sheriffs, taking an oath of fealty to him, while each was given a great fief and allowed to share the exclusive rights to the valuable Lapland trade. As for the lendmenn and the rich bonder, Snorri says that Knut 'enriched all men who were inclined to enter friendly accord with him, both with fiefs and money'. They were also given much wider powers than they had ever possessed under Olav, which to some extent satisfied their wish to recover their old independence.

Knut had taken care to make the Thing as inclusive as possible, ensuring that it was attended by leading men from all over the country. He told it that his kinsman Jarl Hakon was to be his viceroy, while Einar Tambarskjelve, who was Hakon's brother-in-law, would be given back all the fiefs that he had ruled in the days when the Lade jarls governed the country. Einar would also be the first man in the land after Hakon.

Having added the kingdom of Norway to his empire with such astonishing ease, Knut the Mighty departed for Denmark.

* * *

Yet without Knut or even had Knut seemed a little less certain to win, except for a few men such as Einar Tambarskjelve or Thorir Hound, the majority of lendmenn and rich bonder who dictated opinion in Norway would have remained loyal to King Olav, however much they disliked his meddling new monarchy and arrogant ármenn. At bottom, it was a question of backing the winner in order to stay alive and keep one's property. Everybody knew that the terrifying Anglo-Danish king was revengeful and had no time for former enemies, inflicting gruesome punishments. 'Now it was seen those who had been King Olav's true friends, for they followed him, but those who had served him with less fidelity separated from him, and some showed him even indifference, or even open hostility,' says Snorri.[4]

Despite his world disintegrating around him, for some months Olav refused to despair. Believing he was the rightful heir of Harald Fair Hair, he could not believe that the White Christ for whom he had done so much would let his kingdom be taken away from him. If he suspected that his downfall was due to angry demons, as he may well have done, he was certain his new Christian god would have no trouble in defeating them, even though Knut might have been blessed by the pope himself.

Why we know so much about Olav during these months and in such detail is because Snorri was able to consult a now lost chronicle by a well-informed Icelander of the previous century, the priest Are Thorgilsson. Snorri says that Are was 'the first who wrote [about them] and he was both faithful in his story, of so good a memory, and so old a man that he could remember the men, who were so old themselves that because of their age they could recall these events . . . and he named the men from whom he received the information.' This is plausible since we know that Are died in 1148.

Meanwhile, in Sweden, in response to Olav's summons the skippers whom he had left behind to look after his ships, picked out the best ones, burning the others. Then they sailed them through the Øresund which Knut no longer thought worth guarding, and joined the king at Tønsberg. While his enemy was up at Trondheim, the king took his thirteen vessels, all that remained from his fleet of sixty, into the Oslofjord, where they lay hidden in the long Drafn inlet. Here he waited until his enemy, 'having conquered Norway without stroke of sword', should go back to Denmark.

King Olav's seaborne army amounted to 1,000 men at most, probably less. Yet if too small to risk a full-scale confrontation with the new regime's mighty forces, this was still a fighting force to be reckoned with. Besides the 200 superlatively armed veterans of his hird, it included a fair number of chieftains and lendmenn with their own well-equipped following, whose best chance of regaining their lands lay in the king's restoration. Most formidable of all, it had Olav as leader.

When he emerged from the Drafn inlet, he sailed around the coast of the Oslofjord, in the illusory hope of recruiting more men. However, the only ones to join him were a few solitary eccentrics who lived on lonely islands or isolated promontories and had not yet heard of Knut's conquest. Otherwise, Norway had abandoned him.

Sheltering with his ships in the Sel isles northwest of the Naze, he met some merchants who told him that Erling Skjalgsson was collecting a large force of armed bonder at Joederen with a fleet made up of fishing smacks because his three sons were away at Knut's court and the only longship that he possessed was his own. Clearly, Erling's intention was to hunt down and kill his former king, whom he had always disliked. Having heard that Olav was near the Naze, he had stepped up his preparations.

Instead of taking flight, Olav thought he might be able to turn the situation to his advantage. Just before Yule, he left the Sel isles and deliberately sailed through the icy sea past Joederen. According to Snorri's imaginative version of what took place, he meant to explore some out-of-the-way fjords a little further to the north, in the unrealistic hope of finding money and recruits. Snorri even tells us that 'the weather was rainy with dark flying clouds', which made the former king's ships very hard to see.

However, warned of his approach by spies, Erling's lookouts identified them without any difficulty. The jarl commanded the war horns to sound, ordering his followers to go on board his makeshift fleet. They were to make ready for battle.

In fact, it is more likely that King Olav, always a resourceful tactician, was trailing his coat before Erling, challenging him to come out and fight. If he did, then the jarl reacted exactly as Olav had wanted, pursuing the king as fast as he could. Steering towards Bokn, Olav's fleet went through a narrow sound and waited in ambush behind a rocky promontory.

Jarl Erling, whose longship had outsailed the little fishing smacks that formed his own scratch fleet and was far ahead, followed Olav's vessels through the sound, where suddenly he found himself surrounded. Despite being hopelessly outnumbered, he and his men fought heroically when Olav's hird boarded his ship. Eventually, the hird killed, disabled or threw overboard Erling's entire crew, until he was alone. Undaunted, the jarl battled on, neither looking for an escape or asking for quarter. The king's hird had never seen such courage nor anyone fight off so many enemies for so long and with such skill.

Finally, Olav called off his hird. 'You have turned to face me today, Erling,' he told him.

'Eagles stand face to face to claw each other,' replied the jarl.

'Will you enter my service, Erling?' asked the king.

'That I will,' said the jarl, taking off his helmet, putting down his sword and his shield, and then going over to Olav who stood on the forecastle. Elated, the king could not resist scratching Erling's chin with the sharp edge of his battleaxe, saying triumphantly, 'But I shall mark you as a traitor to your ruler.'

Without warning, Aslak Fitjaskalli, an elderly lendmann of high birth who was among Olav's most faithful followers as well as the skipper of one of his few remaining ships, suddenly rushed forward with a hatchet he had hidden under his cloak and struck Erling on the head with it, straight through the brain pan. The jarl fell down dead on the deck. A close cousin who resented the power that he had acquired over western Norway, Aslak had long born him a grudge.

'Damn you for that blow,' said the king to Aslak. 'You have just struck Norway out of my hands.'[5]

'It is bad enough if the stroke displeases you,' answered the wretched Aslak Fitjaskalli. 'For I thought it was striking Norway into your hands. None of your enemies was so powerful as this one. If I have given you offence, sire, by this stroke and have your ill will for it, then it will go badly with me, for I will incur so many men's enmity.'

Through his teeth, King Olav promised Aslak that he would have his protection against revenge. He could not afford to lose a single fighting man, especially the skipper of a longship.

Whether Olav really did say 'struck Norway out of my hands' or whether Snorri put the words into his mouth, there was some truth in them. Erling had been Olav's last chance of finding a powerful ally who would fight with him against Knut. Admittedly, they would have been outnumbered, but Erling was someone who could be relied on to keep his word once he gave it. He and the king would have made a formidable team. 'For better man than he ne'er died,' was Sigvat Thordarson's epitaph on Erling.

When the fishing boats of Erling's scratch fleet arrived on the scene, there was little fight left in their crews after they found they had lost their leader, and that everyone on board his ship had been killed. They were quickly routed or fled out to sea. So ended the battle of Bokn. A handful who had been taken prisoner were allowed to take the jarl's corpse home where there was fierce and widespread anger at the news of so well-loved a chieftain's murder. When they returned Erling's sons, together with their many followers, they had no difficulty in assembling ships and filling them with men who were eager to pursue Olav. However, they never found him.

Anchoring at the islands off Herøy, he not only learned of the preparations made by Erling's sons for his pursuit but that Jarl Hakon had gathered an even bigger fleet at Trondheim for the same purpose, 'a great war force'. Some of his men, notably the two-faced Kalv Arnason, begged him to go up there and challenge the Lade jarl to battle regardless of being so heavily outnumbered. Others disagreed. Hakon soon took the decision out of their hands.

Olav sailed on to anchor in the islands near Ålesund at the mouth of the Geirangerfjord. Next morning, Aslak Fitjaskalli, Erling's murderer, who had gone ashore to spend the night in comfort at a farmhouse, was killed by one of Erling's grandsons as he was returning to his ship. At the same moment that the king received news of Aslak's death, he was told that Jarl Hakon's fleet had been sighted. Olav ordered men to climb a hill and see if it was true. They came rushing back, reporting that a vast armada was approaching from the north.

The king put out to sea as fast as he could while, led by Kalv Arnason, most of the lendmenn who for some time had been waiting for an opportunity to desert, took advantage of the confusion to sail off and make their peace with Hakon. Olav himself did not stop until he reached the mouth of the Norddalsfjorden, where he landed. By then he had only five ships.

Snorri and others say that shortly after Yule the king abandoned his remaining ships but, apart from describing one or two incidents, they do not go into much detail about his unplanned journey across the mountains. This must have taken many days and during a Norwegian winter can only have been nightmarish. We should not underestimate the hardship involved.

Accepting, for the moment at least, that his cause was lost, Olav asked the local bonder if there was a path leading eastward to Lesja – across the highest mountains in northern Europe. He knew there was a pass from Lesja into Gudbrandsdal from where he could reach Sweden, although this would entail a long, gruelling trek through the snow for which his men were not properly equipped. Refusing to believe the bonder's insistence that no such path existed, he ordered them to harness their wagons and haul his baggage over the first mountain. When this proved impossible he decided that the only solution was to build a rough track up and over the mountain. Next morning, fearful that Jarl Hakon's ships would arrive at any moment, his men and the bonder whom they conscripted began clearing away huge rocks, stone slabs and trees. After superhuman efforts they completed the job within two days.

On the evening they finished, Olav sat down and had a last good meal with his hird. He enquired if there was a herdsman's hut on the far side of the first mountain where they might spend the next night. A bonder told him there was certainly a hut on the mountainside, a *saeter* or shelter for shepherds during the summer, but that it had been abandoned by the shepherds as too dangerous to sleep in on account of the trolls 'and other evil beings' who lived there. Unperturbed, the king said that he was going to sleep in it.

On the following day, the fugitives crossed the first mountain, apparently without too much trouble. Before they set out, looking down on the fjord where he had landed Olav was heard muttering to himself, 'You have forced a hard expedition on me, you lendmenn who changed sides, yet only a short time ago you were my friends and loyal to me.' Despite the herdsman's warnings, he slept in the demon-haunted saeter and during the middle of the night a hideous voice was heard outside, howling amid the wind. 'Olav's prayers are burning me,' it shrieked, 'so that I can no longer live in my dwelling – I must flee and never come back.'

Unlike his recent trek back from Sweden, his men did not have any time in which to prepare for this new ice march, lacking equipment and adequate food. Later in winter, it was undertaken in even harsher weather through deep, ever falling snow with its drifts and flurries, always at the mercy of sudden, blinding blizzards that were unpredictable and implacable. In the intermittent howling of the wind even the Christians among them – or perhaps the Christians most of all – no doubt fancied that, like the king in the haunted shieling they could hear the voices of mountain trolls screaming in the wind.

Packing clothes, weapons and what food they had on horses, they went on foot including Queen Astrid and Alvhild with their children, Ulfhild and Magnus, who had rejoined Olav on his return from Sweden. There cannot have been enough skis or snowshoes to go round as the bonder would only have been able to supply a few while the only shelter appears to have been Olav's 'land tent'. At night, when the temperature plummeted, except for rare occasions when they were lucky enough to find farm buildings or herdsmen's huts, everybody (apart from the royal party in their tent) must have crawled into snow holes roofed by brushwood when in forest terrain. In open country they simply burrowed under the snow, using as groundsheet a deerskin coat if they were lucky enough to own one, where they dozed rather than slept for fear of suffocating.

Olav's men were tough Vikings, well accustomed to harsh weather, but they would have suffered miserably. Anyone who lagged behind, whether exhausted or crippled by frostbite, froze to death. So would others during the nights under the snow. The sole trek over similar terrain at this time of year of which we have detailed information is the 'Death March' of the Swedish General Count Carl Gustaf Armfeldt, who on New Year's Eve 1718 set off from Norway to Sweden with 5,000 troops. Hit by a freak blizzard, he lost 3,000 of them in four days.

Doggedly, Olav and his followers plodded on, pushing their way through the drifts, all but overwhelmed by snow whenever a gale blew, going first up into Gudbrandsdal and then down into Hedmark.

When he reached Hedmark, the king was so badly shaken by that terrible journey that he advised those of his followers who had left children or lands in Norway to remain in shelter and then go home as soon as the weather improved, because their families and farms might be in danger from the new regime. It is likely that he asked them to act as sleepers, to prepare for his return and spy for him. Among those who went back was Bjorn the Marshal. To those who stayed, Olav explained that he intended to leave Norway and go to Sweden, where he would decide what to do next. At the same time, he made it clear that he was determined to reconquer his kingdom.

He told them he was convinced that one day the Norwegian people would want him back, adding, 'I think Jarl Hakon will possess Norway for only a short time.' He added that most of his former subjects were bound to agree with his opinion if only because 'Hakon has had but little luck against me.' (Even Olav did not foresee the full extent of the jarl's ill fortune.) He also prophesied that when King Knut died, which he said was certain to happen fairly soon, 'all his kingdoms will vanish and there will be no risings in favour of his family'. Then he admitted frankly to his hearers that nowadays few Norwegians would be inclined to put much trust in anything he foretold. Yet this is precisely what happened.

King Olav and his remaining followers then marched eastward, at as fast a pace as they could manage if only to keep warm. They were not pursued, for the simple reason that nobody else had any idea of where they had gone or where they were going. Among them were a handful of lendmenn and three of the four Arnason brothers (Kalv having joined Hakon). The largest contingent were the 200 hird men, who could be depended upon to stay loyal under any circumstances.

Entering the dense woods of a vast forest, they began the last lap of their journey through the mountains and past the great lake Eidavatnet that is almost an inland fjord. 'Eida's forest ways are rough', Thordarson had grumbled in his song *Austrfaravísur* after crossing the forest in summer on his Swedish mission, 'on each foot sole a bleeding sore', and to him it seemed as if it stretched for 'a hundred miles' – in reality forty.[6] Beneath tall trees whose branches were still heavy laden with snow, led by their defeated king the long, mournful procession continued its icy march into exile.

16

Exile in Viking Russia

Where shall the stranger sit? . . .
Fire he needs who with frozen knees
Has come from the cold without;
Food and clothes must the [way] farer have,
The man from the mountains come.

Hávamál[1]

King Olav crossed into Sweden safely with his remaining followers and went on to Närke in Svealand where they recuperated until the spring, given refuge by a wealthy Swedish magnate named Sigtryg. As soon as weather permitted, they sailed on to the land of 'Rus' – Russia. Olav took with him his son Magnus, but left behind Alvhild and Queen Astrid with her daughter Ulfhild, who stayed in Sweden, in the care of her brother King Anund.

Snorri says that Olav went to Russia in a ship which he found for himself, but an Icelandic chronicle of the Norwegian kings, *Morkinskinna* (or 'rotten parchment') tells a different story. His future host, Grand Prince Yaroslav had insulted his consort, Ingegerd Olofsdotter, once Olav's betrothed. Yaroslav had built a magnificent hall, 'ornamented with gold and precious stones . . . hung with rich fabrics and costly tapestries', of which he was extremely proud. Then, during a banquet, his wife told him that Olav Haraldsson's wooden mead hall was far more impressive.

Enraged, Yaroslav slapped her across the face in front of her retinue, shouting, 'Once again, you have given way to your love for King Olav!' Threatening to leave him and go home, she only forgave her husband on condition that he sent a ship to fetch Olav and his son from Sweden. She also made him promise to become the boy's foster-father.[2]

Whoever provided the ship, it must have been reasonably large, since at least 200 men went on board her with Olav, as they included his hird. Some time during the early summer, after a lengthy voyage across the Baltic they reached the Viking city of Aldeigjuborg (today's Starya Ladoga), where Olav received a hearty welcome from its prince who was none other than his old Swedish ally, Jarl Ragnvald Ulfsson. Then they sailed up the River Volkhov, to arrive at an even greater princely city, Holmgard as Vikings called it – today known as Veliky Novgorod, 'Old Novgorod'.

Famous for skilful carpenters, save for a few Byzantine churches, Old Novgorod's buildings were log huts while the muddy streets were paved with planks. It was also very large, rich from the Vikings' traffic in slaves from the Baltic to Constantinople, as well as from selling the Byzantines exotic furs such as polar bear, sable or seal, and the amber, whale bone, beeswax and whetstones of the North, brought down the River Dnieper with the slaves. Understandably, the streets were lined with tradesmen's shops and booths. The most imposing edifice was its 'kremlin', a mile outside the walls – a fortified palace for the prince and his hird, defended by earthworks and a stockade.

Novgorod was a principality, part of the country known by the Vikings as 'Gardariki' or by the Slavs as 'Rus' from a Finnish word for Swede. Historians argue as to whether Rus was a Viking or a Slavonic land, ignoring the main cultural influence. This was Constantinople, the Byzantine capital, which had a million inhabitants and was ten times bigger than any other city in Europe. The world's commercial centre, its gold solidus had for centuries been the only stable currency – a coin coveted by Vikings. Greedy for

Byzantine luxury, the people of Gardariki were drawn to it as if by a magnet, while they supplied the Varangians, the axemen of the emperors' bodyguard. A case can even be made for seeing 'Old Russia' as a vassal state of Byzantium.

Constantinople was also the heart of Orthodox Christianity so that throughout the land of Rus the recently built churches and monasteries resounded with chanting, not Latin plainsong, but the deep, bell-like notes of Orthodox chant, sung in Church Slavonic. There were Catholic places of worship, too, as this was before the schism between Eastern and Western Christendom. However, it is likely that the Byzantine priests were better educated and more persuasive than those from the West. In consequence the Grand Princes were so strongly inclined to Orthodoxy that Western rite worshippers were a minority.

Furthermore, it is unlikely that Olav failed to visit Kiev, Yaroslav's capital. There he would have experienced another culture shock. Still nominally a tributary of Sweden with whom it kept close commercial ties – Swedes called Rus 'Greater Sweden' – the city was enormously rich because of its role as a key staging post on the River Dnieper between the Baltic and Constantinople. What Olav had seen in London and Rouen paled into insignificance by the wealth he saw at Kiev. It had a population of 50,000 (London's was under 20,000) and behind massive earthen walls and stone gateways stood churches, monasteries and palaces, with new buildings going up all the time. The inhabitants were mainly Slavs, but by now the Viking boyars were intermarrying and speaking Slavonic.

When Yaroslav's father Vladimir had become Grand Prince, the Slavonic thunder god Perun had stood on the Starokyievskaya hill overlooking Kiev, a gigantic wooden idol with a head of silver and a beard of gold. Very popular among the housecarls of the Grand Prince's hird (who identified him with Thor), Vladimir sometimes celebrated a victory with a group sacrifice to him of freemen. He was worshipped no less fervently by the ordinary people of Kiev, who regularly sacrificed children to Perun – including their own sons and daughters.

But after being baptised in 988 Vladimir had Perun pulled down and dragged at a horse's tail through the streets of Kiev, beaten with rods as he passed to insult the demon inside, before being thrown into the Dnieper. Then Vladimir made the people convert to Christianity, importing Orthodox priests from Constantinople who brought ikons and held mass baptisms in the rivers. He also employed Byzantine architects to build churches, not only in and around Kiev but at Novgorod.

Presenting himself at the Novgorod kremlin, Olav was warmly welcomed by its ruler, Yaroslav, Grand Prince of Kiev as well as Prince of Novgorod, who being of Swedish origin spoke fluent Norse, perhaps as his first language, and whose name was unquestionably Norse – 'Jarisleif Waldemarsson'. However, as Grand Prince, he dressed like a Byzantine Caesar in a long, richly jewelled and furred kaftan (or *scaramangion*) which was how, seated on a golden throne, he appeared before his people unless he was going to war.

Like Olav, he had had to fight for his inheritance. As his father Vladimir's appointed heir, he had ruled at Novgorod until his sister at Kiev warned him his father was dead and that his brother Sviatopolk had seized the throne, murdering three other siblings in the process. It took him a three-year war to defeat Sviatopolk the 'Accursed', who in the end fled to the land of the wild Pechenegs where he died.[3] Despite this violent beginning, his benevolent rule had already earned him the name of 'Yaroslav the Wise'. As in his father's later days, due to Byzantine influence there was a surprisingly modern penal code that dispensed with the death penalty, while food was distributed to the poor, the sick and the old on a regular basis.[4]

When Olav saw Yaroslav's consort, the Grand Princess Irene, once Ingegerd Olofsdotter and his former betrothed, he must have thought that he was looking at a creature from another world.

Like her husband she would have worn Byzantine court dress, which for her sex and rank meant a long, heavy silk gown, stiff with gold embroidery, encrusted with pearls and precious stones, in winter trimmed with rare furs. Her face was mask-like, painted white with rouged cheeks and lips, while there was mascara around her eyes whose pupils were dilated by belladonna. The fashion for ladies of the Byzantine court, the use of belladonna as a cosmetic had been introduced to Kiev by her mother-in-law, a sister of the mighty Emperor Basil the Bulgar Slayer.[5]

By now twenty-eight, happily married, Irene had given her husband several children and was eventually to have six sons and four daughters (one of whom would marry an exiled son of King Edmund Ironside). The Grand Princess was famous for her piety, a great builder of churches and monasteries, who was going to end her life as a nun and after her death be canonised as St Anna, the Wonder Worker of Novgorod. She too gave Olav a warm if no doubt formal welcome.

Olav may just possibly have composed verses in her honour, although the attribution is questionable. They praise a woman with beautiful eyes and lovely arms who takes away the author's peace of mind, while the imagery is pagan. They refer to 'Gefn of the path of hawks' and 'Mardöll' – pseudonyms for Freyja. A historian arguing that Olav was not a true Christian, claims that to write like this was scarcely the behaviour of a missionary king, yet it is more probable that if he did write the poem, he was simply thanking her for welcoming him as a homeless exile.[6] *Flateyjarbók* (written nearly four centuries later, but using earlier material) suggests 'he had more kindly feelings towards Ingegerd than towards other women', which merely implies deeper gratitude.

Irene's husband Yaroslav became very fond of Olav's son, Magnus, as he showed after Olav left the child in his care, in an incident described in *Morkinskinna*. During the evening carousals of Yaroslav's hird, the boy liked to walk on his hands up and down the long table in the hall. The housecarls found this amusing except for one old man who grew increasingly irritated. An evening came when he snarled that he had had enough, giving Magnus such a strong shove that he fell off on to the floor.

Later that night, when the Grand Prince had gone to bed but the housecarls were lingering over their drink, the child returned with a hatchet which he embedded in the old man's brain. The dead house-carl's friends wanted to kill him, but a courtier picked up Magnus and ran with him in his arms to Yaroslav's bedroom, where he dropped the boy on his bed, saying, 'There's your little jester – take better care of him.' Hearing what he had done, the Grand Prince roared with laughter, saying 'a right royal deed, foster-son!', and paid the compensation due to the dead man's kindred. *Morkinskinna* adds that Yaroslav brought the boy up 'with great affection'.[7]

Olav had further reason to be grateful to the Grand Prince and his consort, who invited not only him but all his hird to stay for as long as they liked, offering each one a substantial farm so they could support themselves. Later, Yaroslav and Irene suggested that Olav should become king of a country that Snorri calls 'Vulgaria'. East of the Volga in what is now Tatarstan, this was the former territory of the Bulgars, most of whom had emigrated to a new home in the Balkans. (Centuries would pass before it was occupied by Tatars.) Olav seems to have taken the proposal seriously but his hird, who thought there was a good chance of his restoration in Norway, were against it. Bewildered, he could not decide what to do.

Snorri believed that Olav's entire character altered during his stay in Rus. 'When he saw his own power diminished, and his adversaries' augmented, he turned all his mind to God's service.' The implica-tion is that while he had always been a strong believer, his time as an exile was when he felt his way towards a truer understanding of his faith.[8]

An odd incident hints at this. One day, as the king sat at a table carving a piece of fir wood with a knife, a servant said tactfully, 'Tomorrow is Monday, my Lord.' Suddenly Olav realised it was Sunday and that, so he thought, he was profaning it by work. He ordered a lighted candle to be brought and, sweeping the shavings into the palm of his hand, lit them to burn there. It was the reaction of a very simple man who was trying to live according to a creed he still had difficulty in grasping. Even so, away from Norway he was at last able to drive her native gods out of his mind, exorcising the demons.

What a medieval Icelander writing after the schism between East and West did not take into account was the potential influence of Orthodoxy. Its Liturgy had an extraordinary impact on the Vikings of Rus. When still a pagan Vladimir sent ambassadors to investigate the churches at Constantinople they reported, 'We did not know whether we were in heaven or on earth; nowhere else is there such splendour and beauty.' It is not impossible that, deprived of Grimkel, Olav consulted a Byzantine *starets*, a 'spiritual physician', who explained Christianity in a new, gentler way, teaching him to pray to the guardian angel keeping guard over his 'despondent soul and passionate life'.

Snorri says that the people of Kiev noticed a change in their guest's behaviour, especially after he healed a sick boy. He had already cured more than one person in Norway and the Grand Princess told a woman whose young son was dying from a poisoned abscess on his neck to ask Olav for help. After prodding the abscess until the boy howled, he fashioned a small cross from bread that he made him swallow and within a few days the abscess vanished. He also restored the sight of a man named Valdemar. As a Westerner, Snorri thought that all kings possessed healing powers *ex officio*, but the Orthodox Christians of Rus probably saw Olav as a thaumaturge – a saint through whom God works miracles.

For a time Olav thought of going on pilgrimage to Jerusalem and becoming a monk, to disappear into a monastery for the rest of his life, unknown and forgotten. After all, this was what Olav Tryggvason was said to have done.

Yet he found it impossible to abandon hope of returning to Norway, despite his many enemies. For long, he could not make up his mind. Then one night, dozing off after worrying feverishly about what to do, he had another of his dreams. A tall, majestic man was standing by his bed whom Olav instinctively knew must be Olav Tryggvason.

'It is a wonder to me that you let your thoughts become so confused as to think of laying down the kingly dignity God has given to you, and of remaining here and accepting a realm from a foreign king,' said Tryggvason. 'Go back to that kingdom you received as an inheritance, then rule over it with all the strength God gives you and do not let your inferiors take it,' he told him. 'It is the glory of a king to be victorious over his enemies. Return to your country and God will give testimony that the kingdom is yours.'

By now awake, Olav thought he glimpsed the apparition as it left the room. He decided that the command must be Heaven sent and, come what may, he would go home since it was so obviously God's will. His hird were delighted when he informed them while, heartened by their enthusiasm, he began to think it likely that many Norwegians were bound to rally to him.

He was encouraged still more when Bjorn the Marshal arrived at Novgorod. After leaving Olav in Hedmark he had gone home and lived quietly on his farm. Then, eager to secure the loyalty of the former commander of Olav's hird, Jarl Hakon sent a messenger who assured Bjorn of Knut's friendship, presenting him with two gold arm rings and a bag of English silver in token of the king's sincerity. In a weak moment Bjorn took the money, swearing fealty to Hakon.

But not long afterwards, the marshal heard rumours that Hakon was reported lost at sea. Sailing to Norway from England on his way to his marriage, the jarl's ship had last been seen off the Orkney Islands, caught in a bad storm. He had sworn never to fight against Olav again, yet when the king was driven out he accepted Knut's commission to rule Norway as his viceroy. Bjorn saw Hakon's death as divine punishment, proof that God was on Olav's side. Taking only a few men with him, travelling night and day by horse and then by ship, he never halted until he reached Novgorod, where the king and his hird were overjoyed to see the old warrior.

'All is in your power, sire, and in God's,' said Bjorn the Marshal, who as soon as he came into Olav's presence fell on his face before him, clutching the king's foot. 'I have taken money from Knut's people and sworn oaths of fealty to them,' he confessed. 'But now I will follow you, and not part from you so long as we both shall live.'

'Stand up, Bjorn, you shall be reconciled with me, but you must also reconcile your perjury with God,' said King Olav. 'I can see that few men in Norway can have held fast by their fealty when such men as you could be false to me.'

Olav questioned the marshal on the situation at home. Bjorn explained that few of Norway's magnates remained loyal to him, most having gone over to Knut. In his view the king's principal enemies were Einar Tambarskjelve, Kalv Arnason, Thorir Hound, Harek of Thjotta and Erling Skjalgsson's son at Joederen. These five would oppose his return with all their might. There were other, less important enemies, so many that he did not bother to name them.

Even so, it was clear beyond doubt that Bjorn the Marshal was not only ready to risk everything he possessed, including wife, children and home if it would help to bring about King Olav's restoration, but that he was convinced a restoration was feasible. So, too, were the king's housecarls, who had all left lands and family in Norway.

Timothy Bolton argues plausibly that what made up Olav's mind to go back was the news of Hakon's drowning, which wrecked Knut's entire policy in Norway. Confirmation came of the death of the last Lade jarl, who was now known to have drowned in the 'Péttlandsfjord' (Pentland Firth) between the Orkneys and Caithness, a 'bottomless whirlpool or maelstrom' according to a contemporary – probably the tidal race known as the Swelkie.[9] For the moment Norway was without a central government. Understandably, Olav and his followers saw this as a good omen.

Knut had based his policy on insisting that the Lade jarls possessed an older right of tenure than Olav, but Hakon was childless and with him the Lade dynasty died out.[10] What made the situation so worrying from the Dane's point of view was that there were Norwegian magnates who were its heirs through the female line. The most important were Einar Tambarskjelve and Kalv Arnason.

When Olav informed the Grand Prince and his consort of his decision to go back, the couple were horrified and did their best to dissuade him, arguing that with a mere handful of men he was going to certain death by putting himself within reach of enemies who were implacable. Again and again, they offered him the kingdom in Old Bulgaria, promising that he would have full independence, and each time he declined their offer. Then he told them of his dream, insisting it must be God's will that he should return to his homeland.

In the end, accepting that nothing would change Olav's mind, Yaroslav and Irene gave him all the help they could for his journey, equipment and provisions, and no doubt money as well. They also promised to take good care of his small son and heir, Magnus.

17

Olav's Homecoming

Now I am glad of our meeting together,
As Odin's hawks, so eager for prey,
When slaughter and flesh all warm they scent,
Or dew-wet see the red of day . . .

Helgakvitha Hundingsbana II [1]

Immediately after Yule, King Olav and his hird, who still numbered 200 men, prepared to leave Rus. With them, as well a handful of recruits from Novgorod and Kiev went Bjorn the Marshal and the king's 'inseparable companion' Rognvald Brúsason, the son and heir of Jarl Brusi of the Orkneys. Snorri tells us that Grand Prince Yaroslav and Irene said farewell to Olav 'with all honour'.

In March 1030, although it was still winter, the little army set off down the broad Volkhov along the ice, slaves hauling their longships behind them over the frozen river. Then, suddenly, it was April and spring, which is when the ice breaks up in northern Russia, and they were able to rig their vessels and sail on to the coast. As soon as they reached it, finding a fair wind they put out to sea. Reaching Sweden, they sailed into Lake Mälaren and up to Östra Aros (modern Uppsala). Knut had briefly occupied the area around the lake, even striking coins in his name at Sigtuna, but by now Anund had recovered it. The Swedish king gave his old ally a hearty welcome. He had brought with him Queen Astrid and her household, 'and great was the joy when they met', records Snorri.

The rejoicing was marred by discouraging news. 'King Olav was in Sweden that spring and sent spies from thence into Norway,' says Snorri. 'All accounts from that quarter agreed there was no safety for him if he went there.'[2]

Warned by his own spies in Rus or Sweden that Olav was returning, Thorir Hound had collected a large levy of armed bonder, joining forces with Harek of Thjotta who had also gathered a substantial contingent including lendmenn and rich bonder. The pair had made it known that they would fight to the death to prevent the king's restoration. On good terms with the Sami in western Lapland with whom he traded, Thorir had ordered twelve magic reindeer coats to be made by their witches for himself and his housecarls. As everybody knew, coats like this were completely proof against swords, spears or arrows, or indeed any other weapon.

Meanwhile, learning of Jarl Hakon's death, Einar Tambarskjelve had sailed as fast as he could to England where he reminded Knut that he had been appointed the second man in Norway after the jarl and that, as the king had promised, he expected to govern the country in his place. His claim was strengthened by his Lade blood. However, Knut replied that he had decided to make his young son Sveinn the heir to his Norwegian kingdom.

'You shall retain my friendship,' he glibly told Einar Tambarskjelve. 'You shall be the lendmann with the biggest fiefs, and raised above all other lendmenn.' Feigning the deepest gratitude in a suitably submissive tone but always ready to play the long game, Einar's reaction was to delay going home. He could see no point in fighting Olav if he was not to gain from it.

Most Norwegian lendmenn had no such reservations, and when their spies in Sweden reported that Olav had arrived there, they sent round the war arrow. Erling Skjalgsson's sons from Joederen took a force to guard the east of the country while, together with other lendmenn, Aslak of Finnö and Erlend of Garde watched the north. All had sworn an oath to King Knut 'to deprive Olav of life' should they have the opportunity.

Meanwhile, Olav's friends in Norway were preparing to join him. The most interesting of these and, if still only fifteen, potentially the most formidable was his half-brother, the future King Harald Hardrada ('Hard Counsel'), of whom Snorri says that he was already 'manly of growth, as if fully grown'. Snorri tells us, too, that, 'Many other brave men were there.' But a mere 600 set off through the forest to join the king in Sweden.

Despite his supporters in Norway having warned it would be particularly dangerous for him to go into the northern areas, that was where he decided to open his campaign. He asked Anund Jacob for as much aid as he could give, but the Swede did not want to commit himself to full-scale war. 'We know the Norsemen are warlike, and that it is dangerous to carry hostility to their door,' he explained frankly. Even so, he lent Olav 400 picked men from his hird. He also allowed him to march through Sweden when he launched his invasion, and to recruit anyone who cared to join him. Leaving Astrid and Ulfhild in Anund Jacob's care, Olav said farewell.

According to a legend (only recorded in the seventeenth century) when he left Anund, Olav sailed to northern Sweden, landing at the bay of Selånger near Sundsvall. Wherever he came from, *Fagrskinna* says he had a 'very rough journey' after he reached 'Járnberaland' – modern Dalarna – which is on the borders of Hedmark and the Trøndelag. He and his men 'went through forest and lakes, in many places carrying their ships on their shoulders between the lakes', and 600 Norwegians emerged from the woods to join him.[3] Among them was Harald Hardrada who brought a band of kinsmen. Yet Olav's force still amounted to no more than 1,200 men.

Some recruits seemed to be of little value, such as Olav's distant kinsman, Dag Ringsson. His father, the exiled King Ring, had settled in Sweden but Dag hoped to regain their former estates in Norway. Snorri calls him 'a quick speaking, quick resolving man who mixed in everything, eager to speak, but of little understanding'. However, Olav could not afford to be particular and had sent

Dag a message in which he promised that if he came, he would get back all his family's ancestral lands.

The brothers Gauka-Thórir and Afra-Fasti were an even more dubious asset, highwaymen who brought with them thirty other well-armed 'forest robbers', saying they were curious to see a pitched battle. It is more likely that they were attracted by the prospect of unusually rich loot. When asked his religion, Gauka-Thórir replied he was neither Christian nor heathen. In response, Olav told 'these brave slaughtering fellows', as he politely called them, that if they let themselves be baptised and then joined him they would be rewarded with rich lands and high office – otherwise they must be content with remaining highwaymen. The brothers still refused to convert. Even so, they and their band followed at the rear of the king's little army.

As Olav rode on, he fell into a strange mood, dreaming one of his dreams that he later described. Standing in the mountains, looking down on Norway as the country stretched westward, recalling how marvellously happy he had once been there, he suddenly had a vision. He could see the entire Trøndelag, and then all Norway, and for as long as the dream continued he saw further and further, until eventually he could see the whole of the world, both land and sea. He recognised places that he remembered visiting and other places that he had only heard about, together with still others of which he had never even heard the name.[4]

As soon as King Olav crossed the Norwegian border and began marching down Verdal into the north Trøndelag, he received reports of a bonder army advancing in his direction. He would have done better to go to the southeast where he had solid support. Clearly it was an army that intended to find and destroy him, but his spies could not give an accurate count of its numbers.

Inspecting his own army, when he found he had 3,000 men of whom 900 were pagans, he insisted on baptising them. 'We put our confidence in God, not numbers,' he declared. 'I will not mix heathen people with mine.' Finally, 400 agreed to be baptised while the rest went home. His wish cannot have been enforced too strictly, as there must have been pagans among the Swedish housecarls, while he seems to have kept berserkers who were invariably worshippers of Odin.

'I will go into the battle and take part on one side or the other, and I do not care much in what army,' the highwayman Afra-Fasti confided in his brother.

'I shall help the king, for he has most need of help,' replied Gauka-Thórir. 'If I must believe in God, why not in White Christ.' So the two highwaymen had themselves baptised, and then confirmed by a bishop. They were immediately taken into the royal hird by King Olav, who promised they should fight under his personal banner. Sigvat Thordarson may have doubted their sincerity when he wrote not long after, 'Some warriors trusted in God, some not, in Olav's troop.'

Later, Sigvat, who was devoted to the king, bitterly regretted having been absent from his side, but he was away on a pilgrimage. As he later explained,

> Tired of war, I left my home.
> And took the saving road to Rome.
> No more the wild wolf's jaws to fill,
> No more the blood of man to spill.
> The gold-entwined sword I left.
> The blue-steel sword – the king's own gift;
> And with the pilgrim's staff in hand,
> I took my way through many a land.[5]

Aware that the decisive battle could not be far off, Olav addressed his troops. Snorri's words make him sound like a Roman general, but his tactics were sound enough. 'I shall let my banner go forward in the centre and beneath it will be my hird and my henchmen [*gestir*], with the forces who joined us in the Upplands and any who may join us from around Trondheim,' said Olav. 'On the right of my

banner will be Dag Ringsson with the men he has brought. He flies
the second banner. On the left beneath the third banner will be the
men lent to us by the King of Sweden.'

Friends and kindred were to form groups and fight side by side to
recognise each other in the heat of combat, while all should paint a
white cross on their shields and helmets to distinguish them from
the enemy. In action, they were to shout only one war cry, '*Fram!*
Fram! Kristmenn, krossmenn, kongsmenn!' – 'Forward! Forward!
King's men, Christ men, Cross men, King's men, Bonder men!' To
avoid the enemy outflanking them, they must form a very long
front, which would be only two ranks deep, as they had fewer men
than their opponents. Everybody was to stay fully armed night and
day until the battle, to escape being taken by surprise.

Then Olav held a council with his commanders. Men who had
been sent to recruit bonder were reporting a worrying lack of success
– everyone capable of bearing arms had joined the enemy army or
stayed at home. Finn Arnason suggested burning their houses so
that the smoke and flames would make them worry about what was
happening to their wives and children. The meeting welcomed the
proposal, arguing that it would persuade many of the enemy to
desert. A skald stood up, Thormod Kolbrunarskald, a big, gloomy
looking Icelander, who sang pleasantly,

> Fire house and hut throughout the land!
> Burn all around, our mountain band . . .
> The Trondheimers should nothing find
> But ashes whirling in the wind.[6]

Finn's advice made sense yet Olav flatly rejected it. He had used fire
and sword against bonder in the past, he said, but because they had
gone on sacrificing to the old gods. Treason was a lesser crime while
loot, especially cattle, would be an encumbrance. He ordered that
no lives be taken, no damage done to villages and no livestock driven
off. This refusal to cow the bonder may have cost him the battle. His
other orders were less open to question. Advancing down the long

valley of the Verdal, Dag Ringsson's men were to go along the north side to flush out ambushes while the rest of the troops went along the main track. Any spies were to be killed. Both forces would rejoin and pitch camp together every evening.

Next morning, a few bonder came into the king's camp, asking to fight for him. They confirmed reports that the lendmenn had a big army and were preparing for battle. Olav handed one of them a large sum of silver, telling him to give it to the priests with instructions to pray for those who would be killed fighting against him. When the bonde suggested it might be better spent on Masses for his own casualties, the king said there was no need – anyone who fell fighting for him would certainly save his soul.

Still advancing down the Verdal valley, King Olav did not halt until he reached a hilltop in the lower part of the valley, about fifty miles from Trondheim. From here he looked down on Stiklestad, which in those days was not even a hamlet but just a large farm with a few smaller farms nearby. On the plain sixty feet below, he could see the enemy army, spread out over the fields around the big farm. Recruits were still joining it, whole crowds coming from every direction.

Olav's scouts then ran into an enemy reconnaissance party of thirty men returning from spying on them, led by Rut of Vigga whom the king recognised. 'I hear that in Iceland it is the custom for the bonders to give the servants a sheep to slaughter,' he told a group of Icelanders near him, making a pun on Rut's name. 'Now I give you a ram to slaughter.' Taking this for an order, they immediately chased and caught Rut, killing him with all his spies.

Dismounting, Olav told everybody on a horse to follow his example. Then he gave orders for his banner bearer Thord Folason to display the banner and for his army to make ready for battle. Thord, who had held his post for many years, was a man never known to flinch in combat, although to carry the banner was so dangerous that he wore extra armour. Since Dag Ringsson's force had not yet caught up with the royal army, the king ordered the Uppland men to take its place on the right wing until Dag arrived. He tried in vain to stop his brother Harald Hardrada from joining in what lay ahead because he was still a boy. 'If I am supposed to be so weak that I can't handle a sword, I know a good plan, which is tying the hilt to my hand,' said Harald.

Thorgils Halmeson, who owned the big farm at Stiklestad, came into the royal camp and asked if he might fight for the king. 'I had much rather you did not,' said Olav, after thanking him. Instead, he requested Thorgils to take care of the wounded and see that the dead were properly buried. 'Should it happen, bonde, that I fall in this battle, bestow the care on my body that may be necessary, if that is not forbidden.' By this he hoped to ensure that he would receive the last rites of the Church and be given Christian burial. Thorgils promised the king he would do so.

Another recruit who arrived at the last moment was so tall that most other men stood no higher than his shoulder. Handsome-faced, he was well-armed, wearing a costly helmet and an equally expensive chain-mail byrnie, with a fine sword at his belt, while the gold mounted spear he carried was so thick that any ordinary man could only just grasp it. He was Arnljót Gellini from the Jämtland forest who, although a robber, had once rescued a band of royal henchmen from being eaten by a witch. When the king asked if he was a Christian, he answered, 'My faith has been this, to rely upon my power and strength, which has so far satisfied me, but now I will put my faith in you.'

'If you put your faith in me, you must also put faith in what I teach,' Olav told him. 'You must believe that Jesus Christ made heaven and earth, and all mankind, and that to him shall all those who are good and rightly believing go after death.'

In reply, Arnljót said, 'I have heard of the White Christ, but neither know what he proposes, nor what he rules over, but now I will believe all that you say to me, and put my fate in your hands.'

The king then had Arnljót Gellini baptised and in the few moments he could spare tried to teach him the basics of his new faith. Then he placed Arnljót in front of his banner, flanked by Gauka-Thórir and Afra-Fasti with their forest bandits.

Olav sat down and slept, his head on Finn Arnason's knee. After only a short time Finn woke him to say the bonder were advancing, with banners flying.

'Why wake me, Finn, and stop me from finishing my dream?' Olav grumbled. 'They are not so near, and it would be better to have let me sleep.' Finn asked him to describe the dream. Olav answered that he had seen a high ladder which he climbed, so high up into the air that heaven itself seemed open. 'When you woke me, I had reached the last step.'

Finn thought it had been a bad dream. 'I think this means you are fey, unless it be want of sleep.' (Norsemen used the word 'fey' for a man aware that he was about to die.)[7]

Thormod Kolbrunarskald would long be remembered as one of the two heroes in *Fóstbraedra saga* ('Saga of the Sworn Brothers'), the other hero being a psychopathic killer who committed his first murder when only fifteen and after dying in a revenge slaying had been bloodily avenged by Thormod, a formidable fighting man as well as a skald. He preferred to fight with an axe, using both hands and without a shield. A trusted friend of many years standing, he slept near the king.

Olav spent most of the night in prayer and only fell asleep just before dawn. When he opened his eyes, it was on a beautiful, sunny day. He asked Thormod to sing him a song. In a voice so loud that it woke the entire army, Thormod sang the Icelandic version of an ancient berserker song, *The Old Lay of Bjarkamál*:

> I wake you not to wine
> Nor to women's cheer.
> Here awaits you
> Hrolf of the bow!
> Har of the blow!
> Brave men
> Battle ne'er forsaking![8]

It was an odd song to sing at such a moment since it told of a band of doomed housecarls who long ago had fought to the death for their king, scarcely, one would have thought, calculated to raise men's spirits. Yet the army was put into such good heart that they named it 'The Hird's Awakening'.

Olav took an especially valuable gold ring from off his arm and gave it to the skald. 'We have a good king, but it is not easy to say how long the king's life may be,' said Thormod Kolbrunarskald, thanking him.

'It is my prayer that you should never part from me, either in life or death,' replied Olav. 'We shall go on together while I rule and if you will follow me.'[9]

Thormod then sang how everybody was waiting to be joined by the skald who owned the wonderful gold-hilted sword the king had given him. 'When think you he will come, great lord?' he asked, knowing very well that Sigvat Thordarson was away on pilgrimage. In contrast, Thormod the faithful skald can be relied on to never show fear whether 'he feasted the greedy raven' or lay with the dead on the battlefield. Jealous of Sigvat and a secret pagan, he did not see the value of pilgrimages.

Determined that no one should ever forget the battle, another skald, Gizur Gullbrá – 'Golden Eyelash' – chanted:

> From me shall bonder girl ne'er hear
> A thought of sorrow, care or fear.
> I wish my girl knew how gay
> We arm us for our Viking fray.
> Many and brave they are, we know,
> Who come against us there below;
> But, life or death, we, one and all,
> By Norway's king will stand or fall.

The song of a third skald, Thorfin Munr – or 'Mouth' – was:

> Dark is the cloud of men
> Slow moving up through Verdal's fields.

These Verdal folk presume to bring
Their armed forces against their king.
On! Let us feed the carrion crow –
Give her a feast in every blow . . .

Finally, Thormod Kolbrunarskald sang:

The whistling arrows pipe to battle,
Sword and shield their war cry rattle.
Up! Brave men, up! . . .

Snorri says that Olav's army quickly learned the songs by heart. The king was so pleased that he invited the three Icelanders to stand next to him at the shield-wall.

He armed himself, putting on a gold-mounted helmet and a byrnie of steel ring-mail while at his belt hung the gold-hilted sword Hneitr ('Sting'), whose blue blade was even sharper than Baesing's had been. In his right hand he carried a spear and in his left a white shield with the cross inlaid in gold. Obeying his orders, all his men had painted a white cross on their shields.

Then he made a final speech to his army who by now numbered 4,500. 'We have many men, and good men they are too, and while the bonder may have a larger force than we, fate decides the victory,' he told them. 'I promise you solemnly that I shall never run away from this battle, but shall either be victorious over the bonder or fall fighting.' Again, he explained his strategy. Because of their superior numbers the enemy must be cut to pieces as soon as they struggled up to the top of the hill. Otherwise it would be difficult as unlike their opponents no reserves were available. But if the royal army could hit them hard enough immediately after their ascent, their front rank would turn and run, causing those behind to panic and do the same. That was the way to win.

* * *

According to Snorri, the army of the enemy magnates was bigger than any ever seen in Norway. Estimates of its size vary, from 7,000 to 14,000 men, but the most likely figure is just over 8,000, so it outnumbered the king's army by nearly two to one. In view of later claims that Olav had been a martyr, it is clear that, mainly recruited in the Trøndelag or Hålogaland, there can be no doubt that it included a large pagan element whose members undoubtedly came to fight for Odin and Thor. Many others not necessarily committed to either the old or the new faith, such as those from the west coast, resented the ban on fornication and eating horse meat, as well as the fast days, fish days and Lenten penances, and the interfering priests.

However, far from being combat-hardened Vikings, most of what Snorri calls the 'bonder army' consisted of poorly armed labourers who had never fought in a battle before. Whether they were pagans or revengeful kinsmen of those killed in Olav's missionary rampages or loyal to the Lade jarl, their leaders knew very well that if the king's veterans and the Swedish contingent could defeat the comparatively few experienced men in their front line, the rest were going to bolt.

The Danish Bishop Sigurd, Grimkel's replacement as court bishop and not to be confused with Grimkel's English assistant, did his best to whip up the enemy's fighting spirit. The mouthpiece of the magnates who brought down Olav, in a speech delivered shortly before their army reached Stiklestad he denounced Olav 'for bringing strife and war' to Norway, adding that from his earliest youth Olav had been 'accustomed to plunder and kill'. There may have been some truth in this, but it was no less true of men such as Harek or Thorir Hound.

Sigurd then voiced his patrons' grievances. Olav had driven Jarl Sveinn and Jarl Hakon from their heritage, and even his own cousins, the Uppland kings, some of whom he had mutilated besides stealing their kingdoms and 'ruining every man in the country with an honourable name'. He had murdered worthy lendmenn, forced others into exile and roamed far and wide with robber bands, burning and plundering houses, killing people. Now he was in Norway again, with an army 'of forest men, vagabonds and marauders'.

Everybody must defend the liberty that King Knut had brought with him. 'Cast forth these malefactors to become meat for the wolves and the eagles,' ranted the bishop. Their corpses must be left to rot on the ground where they fell – no one should think of dragging their bodies into churches, 'because they are all robbers and evil doers'.

Since Erling Skjalgsson was dead and Einar Tambarskjelve was in England, the enemy's three main leaders had difficulty in choosing who should command their army in combat. When Kalv Arnason said that it ought to be Harek of Thjotta who was not only of Harald Fair Hair's blood but had killed Grankel and had most to lose should Olav win, Harek hastily declined the honour on the grounds that he was old and decayed, and 'lacking in vigour'. He proposed Thorir Hound who had been driven off his lands as an outlaw. Thorir had promised both Knut and his own family to avenge the killing of Asbjorn Slayer of Seal and other relatives, and he would never have a better opportunity.

But Thorir was no keener. While the old pagan agreed that he had a sacred duty to avenge his kindred, he said that the haughty Trøndelager who formed most of their army would never obey a leader from Hålogaland. If he were not in command, he would be better able to fight, having chosen eleven of his toughest housecarls to help him kill Olav. They would all wear the magic coats of reindeer hide he had bought from the Sami and be invincible.

Kalv Arnason then argued that while Olav's force might be smaller than their own, its leader was a veteran warrior who did not know the meaning of fear and whose men would follow him to the death. 'Yet if we three show the slightest hint of lacking confidence, ours will lose their nerve and run.' So he proposed that he, Kalv, with Harek and 'friend Thorir' should lead their army jointly under the same banner. If they did, then the bonder would fight for them well enough. Wisely, the other two accepted Kalv's proposal.

As it was, Kalv emerged as the real leader. Grouped round him were the toughest men in their army. Among them was Thorstein Knaresmed ('Shipbuilder') who had a reputation for being hot tempered and 'a great man slayer'. He bore a special grudge against Olav for seizing a new ship from him as a fine for a murder, telling Thorir that 'if I and King Olav meet, I shall be the first to drive a weapon at him'.

The northerners, Trondheimers and Hålogalanders, were stationed in the centre, the western men from Rogaland, Hordaland, Sogn and the Fjord regions on the left. The rest formed the right wing. Everyone was told to keep his place in the formation, which was a simple line several ranks deep, and to shout as their battle cry '*Fram! Fram! Bonder!*' – 'Forward, Forward, bondermen!'

Kalv addressed them, appealing to everyone who wanted to revenge himself on Olav to join those who were going to attack the king's banner. He warned them to fight with all their strength. They faced 'people who will show no mercy to you if you show any mercy to them'.

Earthquakes have altered the landscape at Stiklestad since Olav's time, but we know that his army was deployed on the brow of a hill standing about sixty feet above the flat plain occupied by the enemy. The two sides were so close that they could see each other's faces, recognising former comrades – or old enemies. 'Why are you here, Kalv Arnason, for we parted good friends in Møre?' Olav shouted down. 'It is surely not right for you to fight against us.'

'Many things have come to pass in a different way from what had been expected,' Kalv replied. 'You left us so we had to come to terms with those who had stayed behind in our country. Now, each of us must remain where he stands, but in my opinion we ought to make peace.' Hearing him, Finn, Kalv's brother, warned Olav, 'When Kalv speaks fair words, it is in his mind to do ill.'

'It may be, Kalv, that you yourself would like a reconciliation,' the king shouted back, 'but it looks to me that the bonder with you do not appear to be quite so peaceful.'

Then another lendmann, Thorgeir of Kvistathir, interrupted them, yelling up at Olav, 'You shall have the sort of peace all too many have received at your hands, and for which you are now going to pay.'

'There is no good reason for you to be so eager to meet us,' the king answered him. 'Fate never decreed that today is the day you will win a victory over me, who raised you up to power and dignity from a very mean station.'

After that, there was no more talking and the battle began. It was 29 July 1030.

18

The Old Gods' Revenge: Stiklestad

I thought a bloody sword was pulled out of your shirt,
it's painful to have to tell such a dream to a man so close to one;
I thought I saw a spear pass right through you,
wolves were howling at both its ends.

The Greenlandic Lay of Atli[1]

Some revisionist historians argue that the battle of Stiklestad is a fantasy dreamed up by clerics who wanted to turn Olav into a martyr. They reject Snorri's account as fiction, citing Adam of Bremen who in 1070 wrote that the king was killed in an ambush. In reality Adam says – wrongly – that Olav was killed by his own men, but adds that he was 'crowned with martyrdom'. They distort the *Anglo-Saxon Chronicle* to support their theory, although its sole entry for 1030 is plain enough – 'King Olav returned to Norway, and the people united to oppose him and fought against him, and he was there slain.'[2]

They also dismiss the testimony of skalds such as Sigvat Thordarson, who shortly after the battle wrote a noble poem in the king's memory, *Erfidrápa Óláfs Helga*. They also ignore the likelihood that Snorri made use of eyewitness accounts by men who fought in it, passed down orally in their families into his own time.

In contrast to the revisionist view, here is a reconstruction.

*   *   *

The battle was fought on 29 July 1030, starting well after noon. Sigvat, who had met survivors, says that there was no sunlight, because the day 'did not achieve full colour.' This has been wrongly interpreted as an eclipse of the sun, which did not happen until a month later. Sigvat meant merely that the sky had been unusually overcast and cloudy.[3]

As one might expect from a commander who had fought eighteen pitched battles, Olav had chosen his hilltop position very well. In front and on the left, it could only be reached after clambering up a steep and muddy slope without any shelter from arrow fire, while a river protected the right. His opponents would in consequence be forced to launch their assault along a narrow frontage, making it hard for them to exploit their advantage in numbers.

The enemy advanced to the foot of the hill, the battle opening with the customary exchange of spears, arrows and 'stones' – lethal slingshot. From above, the royal army shouted down Olav's war cry, '*Fram! Fram! Kristmenn, krossmenn, kongsmenn!*' Unused to battle, some of the bonder on the other side thought that their comrades were shouting it too and must be traitors, so they attacked them, killing many before they recognised each other. At the same time, the wind blew back their *fleindriver* (arrow storm) while boosting the king's.

Looking down on the confusion, some of Olav's troops in the front rank could not restrain themselves and rushed downhill, charging the enemy. Whether they were men without combat experience who lacked discipline or berserkers in a frenzy is not clear. The entire royal army followed, abandoning their shield-wall and an impregnable position, throwing away a carefully planned strategy. No doubt pagans among the enemy thought the old gods were fighting on their side, making Olav's troops go mad – Odin could still be relied on to bring victory.

The king must have realised that his men had almost certainly lost the battle for him before it had properly started, but his only option was to charge with them. There was still a chance he might win, by eliminating the three leaders who stood beneath Kalv Arnason's banner. At first the inexperienced bonder who formed the bulk of their army recoiled before the wild charge, so much that the king's force crashed through their ranks and they were on the point of running for their lives. However, Dag Ringsson's contingent had still not arrived on the battlefield, while some of Olav's 'forest bandits' went off in search of loot. These two factors seriously weakened the royal army, which in any case for a brief but disastrous moment was without any sort of cohesion.

In the meantime, unlike the bonder, the enemy lendmenn's housecarls stood their ground. After the first shock, they managed to rally the bonder fairly quickly. Then, together, they surrounded the best of the royal troops who had grouped themselves around Olav, attacking them from all sides. It was now that his opponents' numbers began to tell. 'Those [of the enemy] at the front hewed with their swords,' Snorri tells us. 'They who stood next thrust with their spears, and they who stood hindmost shot arrows, cast spears, or threw stones [slingshot], hand axes or sharp stakes.'

'There was a great fall of men,' continues Snorri. 'Many went down on both sides.'[4] Soon the casualties in the royal army included such irreplaceable warriors as Arnljót Gellini, Gauka-Thórir and Afra-Fasti with all their forest bandits, although only after each one of them had killed an enemy and often more. The king's ranks began to thin dangerously. Because of their heavy losses, Olav's housecarls, men who knew how to make the most lethal use of their weapons, formed a circular shield-wall around him and his battle banner.

The skald Sigvat says that Olav refused to stay inside it, going out in front to attack the enemy, many of whom shrank back because he looked so terrifying with his serpent-shining eyes – 'the king seemed terrible to them'.[5] He dealt Thorgeir of Kvistathir a lethal blow across the face with all his force, his sword smashing the nosepiece of the lendmann's helmet and splitting his skull almost in half so that his eyes nearly fell out. The king shouted, 'Was it not true, Thorgeir, what I told you, that you would not be the victor when we met?'

By now the enemy were taking an increasing toll of Olav's men. His banner bearer Thord Folason was killed, although the king's banner continued to fly defiantly – just before he died, Thord had stuck its gilded staff firmly in the ground. Two of the Icelandic skalds standing next to the king, Thorfin Munr and Gizur Gullbrá, fell, a couple of the enemy setting upon Gizur who cut one down but only wounded the other before he himself received his own death wound. Afterwards, another skald, Hofgard Refr, praised Gizur for having stood 'firm and stout as a forest tree'.

For some reason – Snorri says it was the darkness – when Dag Ringsson finally arrived, he was confused about whom to attack. The king's men were by now a beleaguered ring growing ever smaller because of casualties, rather than the long line of a shield-wall, and at first Dag could not distinguish between friend and foe. When he did, however, he and his force hurled themselves at the enemy, killing many.

Then Kalv Arnason and Thorir Hound, supported by their house-carls, targeted Olav. Seeing Thorir, the king aimed a cut at the old villain's shoulder, delivered with all his strength, but – as if dulled by Odin – his sword seemed to be deflected by the magic reindeer tunic that Thorir had bought from the Sami, merely raising a puff of dust. Olav only managed to wound him very slightly, in the hand.

'Beat the Hound on whom steel will not bite,' the king shouted to Bjorn the Marshal, who turned his axe round and, with the back of the axehead, gave Thorir such a mighty blow on the shoulder that he reeled. At the same time, the king killed a kinsman of Kalv. However, recovering his balance, Thorir Hound stuck his spear right through Bjorn, shouting, 'This is how we hunt the bear.' (Bjorn means bear.)

Then the shipbuilder Thorstein swung his axe and hit Olav above the left knee, inflicting a severe wound. Finn Arnason killed Thorstein immediately, but too late to save the king. The axe severed leg muscles and tendons, probably smashing his femur as well, while quantities of blood came spouting out. He fell over and, crouching against a rock, threw his sword away, commending his soul to God – Christian, not Viking, behaviour in the face of death. Then, with an axe or a sword Kalv Arnason or one of Kalv's cousins gave him a mortal wound, this time on the left of his neck, gashing his throat. Finally, Thorir Hound delivered an agonising *coup de grâce* with the spear that had killed Asbjorn Slayer of Seal, thrusting it beneath the king's mail tunic and up into his belly.

What many contemporaries would have found so shocking about King Olav's death was the way he faced it, the reverse of 'Laughing shall I die', as his ancestor Ragnar Lodbrok had sung to the adders in the Northumbrian snakepit. Instead of snarling defiance at his killers, Olav had thrown away his sword and prayed to the White Christ. Those on the battlefield who were still pagans, openly or secretly, must have been shocked.

Unaware of the king's death, Dag Ringsson, of whom elsewhere Snorri speaks so disparagingly, went on fighting, and with such ferocity that survivors remembered his onslaught as 'Dag's Storm'. He and his men killed three lendmenn and many bonder, hurling down the banner beneath which they fought. Large numbers of the other bonder fled.

However, Kalv, Harek and Thorir came over from their part of the battlefield and finally, overwhelmed by numbers, Dag retreated with his men into the hills. Here they caused such havoc, burning and looting that, some days after the battle and at the local bonder's frantic request, Thorir Hound pursued them with a force 600 strong. But by then Dag's men had taken refuge high up in the mountains or deep in the forest where Thorir did not care to follow.

Most of the lendmenn's bonder were too tired to do anything other than search the battlefield to see if any of their wounded kindred and friends had survived. Snorri says that dead men from both sides lay in heaps, while many who lived were so exhausted that they were fit for nothing. The victors had lost over 4,000 men, around half of their strength while Olav's army had lost about the same – which means a good two-thirds of their total number.

The seriously wounded were taken into farms or tent for medical attention. There was also a species of field dressing station in a large barn at the main Stiklestad farm.

A large number of fugitives from Olav's army were hunted down and killed, although a fair number survived. Among them were Finn Arnason, the skald Thormod Kolbrunarskald and the dead king's young half-brother Harald Hardrada. After the battle, Finn and Thorberg Arnason collapsed, not from wounds but out of sheer exhaustion. When their brother Kalv found them, Finn threw his dagger at him, yelling that he was a man who broke his word and a traitor. Ignoring the insults, Kalv had his brothers carried to a ship that took them to safety.

The skald Thormod, who after being badly wounded by an arrow in the side of his body had dropped his axe but broken off the shaft and gone on fighting with his sword, staggered towards the barn which was the dressing station. A bonde named Kimbi came out, sneering, 'It is very bad in there with all the howling and screaming, a shame that such brisk young fellows cannot bear their wounds.' He was referring to Olav's supporters.

Then Kimbi looked closely at Thormod. 'You are a king's man,' he said. 'Give me your gold arm ring and I shall hide you – the bonder will kill you if they see you.'

Thormod replied, 'Take the ring if you can, I have lost something more valuable,' by which he meant King Olav, and when Kimbi reached for the ring, suddenly swung his sword, cutting off his hand. Much amused, Snorri comments dryly, 'It is told that Kimbi behaved no better with his wound than did those whom he had been deriding.'

Thormod went into the barn and found a woman who was warming water to clean wounds. She examined his own but at first could not find the arrowhead. However, after boiling leeks, garlic and other herbs that she made him swallow, she knew from the smell that it was in his chest. When she failed to pull it out with a pair of tongs, Thormod took the tongs and pulled it out himself. (They would have been red hot to avoid infection and stop bleeding.) On the arrowhead were pieces of flesh from the heart, some white and some red. 'The king has fed us well, I am fat even at the heart-roots,' he remarked. Then like the pagan he was, he sang a final, defiant song before falling down dead.[6]

The fifteen-year-old Harald Hardrada, who had had his helmet knocked off, had also been badly wounded. Luckily for him, on the night after the battle one of his brother's hird Rognvald Brúsason, the future Jarl of Orkney, found the boy hiding near the battlefield. Later Harald wrote some verses in which he describes how the pair contrived to escape unnoticed into the surrounding forest, while the enemy bonder were busy killing their wounded comrades who lay helpless on the battlefield:

> From copse to copse I crept along
> Unnoticed by the bonder throng.
> 'Who knows, I thought, a day may come,
> My name may yet be great at home.'[7]

Rognvald took the boy to a bonde loyal to King Olav's memory who dressed his wounds and sheltered him until he was well enough to make the long, dangerous journey to safety. Then the bonde's son, unaware of his identity, guided him along secret paths through dense, uninhabited forests and across desolate bogs to a safe refuge in Sweden. There he rejoined Rognvald Brúsason with many others of Olav's men.

Those who kept the old Norse faith, of whom there were plenty, must have been certain that there was no welcome in Valhalla or in Freyja's Folkvang for Olav. They thought that Hel would claim as her own a man who had died praying to the White Christ instead of fighting to the death. They must have fancied, too, that there was joy among the gods at the news of Stiklestad, with Odin chuckling, Thor reaching for his hammer and Freyja no longer shedding her 'tears of gold', but combing her golden tresses as she admired her reflection in a bronze mirror. They had overthrown their most dangerous enemy.

Or had they?

19

Olav's 'Return from the Dead'

One morning early on a hill,
The misty towns asleep and still,
Wandering, I thought upon the fields,
Strewed o'er with broken mail and shields,
Where our king fell – our kind, good king

Sigvat Thordarson[1]

Despite overwhelming defeat at Stiklestad and the slaughter of his supporters, Olav Haraldsson was the ultimate victor. In death, he became invincible, driving Knut and his family out of Norway within a very few years. It was as if he had returned from the dead.

After Stiklestad, in place of the drowned Jarl Hakon, Knut had appointed his fourteen-year-old son Sveinn as Norway's ruler with as regent his English mother Aelgifu of Northampton, whom the Norsemen named 'Álfífa'. Since he would inherit the country when his father died, Sveinn bore the title of king. Álfífa, Knut's former wife whom he had cast off to marry Ethelred II's widow, was the real ruler. Arrogant and inept, she and her son only survived because of Sveinn's Danish hird.

Even when Sveinn came of age, Álfífa kept control. Her son, says *Fagrskinna*, was 'a very young man, fair in appearance, not fierce in temperament or ambitious'.[2] She was bound to fail. Not only did Einar Tambarskjelve and Kalv Arnason both resent Knut's failure to appoint them as Jarl Hakon's successor, but King Olav would soon assert himself.[3]

After the battle, with their belief that there were demons everywhere, heathens among the enemy must have feared that the late king might have turned into a draugr – one of the undead. Nobody knew where he was buried while a month after the battle, on 31 August, there was an eclipse of the sun that seemed to confirm their worst fears.

On the evening of 29 July, Thorgils Halmeson, the Stiklestad bonde who before the battle had been asked by Olav to ensure he was given Christian burial, had hurried to the battlefield to look for his body. Hearing the enemy talk of burning it or throwing it into the sea, he moved fast. When he and his son Grim found the corpse, they removed its clothes, washed off the blood, wrapped it in a linen shroud and hid it under logs in a hut near their farm. In words from the *Songs of the Sun*, 'Longer than all was that one night, when stiff on straw I lay'.[4]

Searching for a place to spend the night, a blind beggar who crept into the hut slipped on some liquid. Picking up his hat which had fallen off, then touching his eyes by mistake, he found his hands wet from some liquid on the floor. Going outside, he saw it was twilight and that the liquid on his hands was blood – and realised he could see. Going to the farm at Stiklestad, he told everybody how his eyes had been healed, describing the hut. Fearful that the man might guide the enemy to where the king lay, Thorgils moved the corpse to another hiding place in a garden.

Thorgils' caution was justified. Five days later, when the dead and badly wounded were still being carried off the battlefield, Thorir Hound came searching for Olav's corpse and asked Thorgils in his capacity as the local landowner if he knew where it was. 'There are many reports abroad, and among others that King Olav was seen in the night up at Staf [farm] and a troop of people with him,' replied the wily bonde. 'But if he fell in the battle, then your men must have hidden him in some hole or under a heap of stones.'

Having personally given the king his *coup de grâce*, Thorir knew perfectly well that he was dead but, as had happened with King Harald Tryggvason after Svoldr, there were many who believed he was still alive. Rumours spread that Olav had escaped and would return with a large army. No doubt others subscribed to the theory that he had become a draugr and was preparing to emerge from some unknown howe to wreak a spectacularly horrible revenge.

When Thorir went home with the rest of the bonder army, Thorgils and his son made two coffins. One they filled with stones and straw, so that it weighed as much as if a man's body was inside, and told their neighbours they were taking it to Nidaros for burial. They did not tell anyone that the other coffin, which contained the real body, was hidden beneath their ship's floorboards.

As soon as he heard of Thorgil's arrival at Nidaros, Bishop Sigurd, informed by spies that a bonde from Stiklestad was on his way with Olav's body, sent housecarls down to the pier to demand that it be handed over to them. Thorgils gave the housecarls the coffin with the stones, and on the bishop's express orders they immediately rowed far out to sea where they dropped it overboard.

That same night, Thorgils and his son took the other coffin to a lonely place that was a little upstream from Nidaros. They buried it there, on the bank of the River Nid, under a sandbank. They hoped a time would come when they would be able to see that it was given a proper burial.

Meanwhile, all over Norway, even in the Trøndelag, opinion changed with extraordinary rapidity. The eclipse on 31 August was interpreted as divine disapproval, whether that of the old gods or the White Christ, and when a spectacularly bad harvest, another certain sign of supernatural distaste, followed it many of Olav's former enemies questioned whether they had done the right thing. More and more people decided that far from being evil, Olav had been a good man and a martyr. They were increasingly unimpressed by Bishop Sigurd's ranting.

Norwegians now began praying to the king to bless a dangerous journey or heal a serious illness, and it seems that some of their prayers were answered so that he came to be seen as a miracle worker. How complete was this change was shown by Einar Tambarskjelve, who had finally returned, publicly declaring that Olav had been a saint. As Norway's most powerful nobleman, Einar's opinion counted for a good deal and everyone knew that he had not been at Stiklestad. Men started to curse those responsible for Olav's downfall. In particular they cursed the loud-mouthed Bishop Sigurd, who grew so alarmed that before the end of 1031 he fled the country.

As soon as Bishop Sigurd ran away, the Trøndelagers, once King Olav's bitterest enemies, sent a message to Bishop Grimkel who was living in the Upplands, having returned from Russia during the late king's exile. They asked him to come to Nidaros and take Sigurd's place. If anyone had known Olav well it was Grimkel who had been at his side for over a decade as his closest confidant and intimate adviser.

When Bishop Grimkel arrived, he and Einar Tambarskjelve 'talked over many things,' Snorri tells us, 'and found themselves in complete agreement'. We know the bishop believed that Olav had been a martyr and a saint while as a subtle politician Einar would have concurred even if he was less certain – his priority was to enlist the dead man's help in driving out the Danes. Grimkel told Einar he was certain that the miracles were divinely inspired and that they must have occurred at his burial place. Informed that Thorgils was widely suspected of knowing where it was, he sent for him. Thorgils and his son came at once and told their story.

Grimkel and Einar then went to King Sveinn and his mother the regent, asking for permission to recover Olav's body. Sveinn said they might do as they pleased. When they reached the sandbank by the river, they found that the coffin had risen to the surface of its own accord and looked as if newly made. Everybody agreed that it should be reinterred in the stave church of St Clement's, which had been Olav's favourite place of worship.

On 3 July 1031, before reburying the coffin, Grimkel had it opened. Not only did the body give out a pleasant odour instead of the stench of putrefaction, but it looked as if the king had only just fallen asleep, with ruddy cheeks, while his hair and nails had grown very long, as though he were still alive. The skald Sigvat wrote later:

> I lie not when I say the king
> Seemed as alive in everything.
> His nails, his yellow hair still grew . . .[5]

Similarly, in *Glaelognskvida* ('The Sea Calm Poem') Thorarinn Loftunga, who attended the exhumation, says:

> . . . nails and hair
> Grow fresh and fair,
> His cheek is red
> His flesh not dead . . .[6]

Álfífa refused to be impressed, commenting ungraciously, 'Those buried in sand rot very slowly.' When the bishop had trimmed the beard and hair, he told King Sveinn and his mother, 'Now the king's hair and beard are as they were when he gave up the ghost.'

Álfífa replied, 'I will believe in the sanctity of his hair if it will not burn in fire, but I have often seen men's hair whole and undamaged after lying much longer in the earth than this man.' At her request, Grimkel burned a few hairs with some incense, but it remained unconsumed.

Álfífa then asked the bishop to burn the hair in 'unconsecrated' fire, by which she meant without incense. Einar told her to keep quiet, rebuking her for her lack of belief. 'Something else more suitable might be put on the fire, such as yourself,' he added.

'You have a broad neck, Einar,' she retorted furiously. 'But I have seen big fish like you caught in a net.'

Uncowed, he answered, 'My neck is not so very broad, while if too many like me are caught in the net, then perhaps the net may break.' This time she made no reply.[7]

Bishop Grimkel then declared that beyond all question, King Olav Haraldsson was a saint, as had been amply proved by the incorruptibility of his body and the increasing number of his miracles of healing. While he did not say so openly, it was also because Olav had finally made Norway a Christian country and died a martyr for doing so. Nor did the bishop say that in his view anyone who disputed the king's martyrdom must admit that he had died a Christian death.

Álfífa was forced to dissemble her scepticism, realising that most of her son's subjects believed in the late king's sanctity. As Bolton points out, she and Sveinn then tried to appropriate the cult for its political benefits.[8] They installed Grimkel as court bishop in place of the fugitive Sigurd, and had Olav's body placed next to the high altar at St Clement's under a golden canopy where it lay in silent reproach to their regime. Its menace was reinforced by the Norwegians' firm conviction that killing a king was the reason for their bad harvests.

Olav's cult grew steadily, with further claims of miracles. A spring of fresh water, that had suddenly gushed up from beneath the sandbank where his body had been buried, and went on flowing, was said to cure the ailments and infirmities of many people, especially those who were cripples or lepers. Soon a stave chapel was built next to it.

Thorarinn Loftunga's poem *Glaelognskvida* is a vivid eyewitness testimony to the dramatic growth of Olav's popularity as a healer:

And crowds do come,
The deaf and dumb,
Cripple and blind,
Sick of all kind,
Cured to be
On bended knee;
And off the ground
Rise whole and sound . . .[9]

Knut's skald Thorarinn, who had accompanied him during his conquest of Norway and been present at Sveinn's acclamation as king, remained at Sveinn's court until 1032. (He describes him as 'our gold-giver'.) That he could write in such glowing praise of Olav's miracles shows how keen the Danish regime was to take over his cult. Otherwise he would never have risked Álfífa's displeasure.

A stave church was built at Stiklestad on the spot where Olav fell, while the rock on which he rested during his last moments was enshrined inside the altar. The rock is still there, under the altar of the stone church that replaced the wooden one in the twelfth century. The king's banner, planted in the ground by Thord Folason just before his own death, remained standing after the battle and was kept flying for hundreds of years by the people of the district. (Since 1954, the *Slaget på Stiklestad* has been re-enacted annually in an open-air theatre nearby, in the *St Olav Drama*.)

Snorri describes King Sveinn as no better than a child in years and understanding, and Álfífa as singularly stupid, telling us that she saw the Norwegian people as 'her great enemies'. *Fagrskinna* is still more disapproving, recording how 'she decided most things for the king and everyone said that she did damage in every situation'. She was even compared with the witch Queen Gunnhild.[10]

Harsh new laws may well have made the Norwegians think that she hated them. No ship might leave Norway without royal permission – if an owner or a skipper did so, his land and goods were forfeit to the king. Forfeiture of goods and lands were also among the penalties for committing a murder, instead of just a fine as formerly. In legal disputes a single Dane's witness counted more than that of ten Norwegians. Danes in Norway, which meant King Sveinn's Danish housecarls, were given precedence over Norwegians and behaved as though they were conquerors.

Further ill feeling was aroused by swingeing new taxes and labour dues. At Yule every farmer in the land had to pay the king fifteen litres of malt, the leg of a three-year-old ox and a bucket of butter, and each housewife a thick skein of wool or flax. All fishermen were bound to give the king's men five good fish out of their catch every time they returned from the sea, while anybody who went to Iceland must pay a tax.

All households had to pay for arming and equipping men for military service. Whenever required, bonder were obliged to build houses for the royal farms. 'It was almost as if there was no peace for any man's property, because of payments and taxes.'[11] Bolton says these exactions should be seen in the context of King Knut's vast tax on England in 1018, as a one-off 'levy taken by a conqueror or an incoming ruler at the beginning of his reign'.[12] But that is not how they were remembered by the Norwegians.

A succession of bad harvests accompanied by what in consequence must have been an exceptionally high death rate in winter made matters worse. Looking back, Sigvat says that a young man would long recall the days of Álfífa when they were forced to eat cattle fodder as goats eat tree bark, but it had been very different in Olav's time, when there were plentiful stocks of grain. Another source writes of the 'oppression of the Danes'.[13] Even so, most observers thought that Knut would ensure Sveinn's survival.

In 1033 Sveinn faced a serious challenge from a pretender named Tryggvi, who declared he was Olav Tryggvason's son and claimed the throne, although some said he was a priest's bastard. Whoever he was, he was a tough, courageous leader, and like his supposed father impressed his men by being able to throw a spear with each hand at the same time. Gaining solid support, he assembled a substantial army and fleet. So did King Sveinn, the two forces meeting in a battle at sea off the island of Bokn – where Olav Haraldsson had ambushed Erling Skjalgsson.

Surprisingly, the young Danish king survived, his men defeating and killing Tryggvi, with many followers. For a short time an uneasy peace prevailed in Norway. But it was significant that Einar Tambarskjelve and Kalv Arnason had failed to come to Sveinn's help against Tryggvi, Kalv declaring ominously, 'I have done enough, if not too much, when I fought against my own countrymen to increase the power of Knut's family.'

The writing was firmly on the wall. Great Norwegian nobles such as Einar and Kalv, with the vast majority of the bonder, were finding the new Danish monarchy intolerable. When they overthrew Olav, they had expected to recover the semi-independence they had enjoyed under the Lade jarls. But now they had less freedom than ever, besides having to pay unheard-of taxes.

Then Sveinn held a Thing at Nidaros to demand yet heavier taxes. In the presence of the king and his mother Einar Tambarskjelve told the assembled bonder, 'I was no friend to King Olav, but the Trønder got a very bad bargain when they gave away their king to receive a mare and a foal in exchange.' He spoke again, telling the bonder that the Thing was a complete waste of time and they had better go home. Before storming out, he added that they were being punished for deposing Olav – 'a most shameful deed'.[14]

The only way for the Norwegians to escape from Danish rule was to place Olav's ten-year-old son Magnus on the throne, even if it meant incurring King Knut's wrath. In the spring of 1034, Kalv Arnason and Einar Tambarskjelve, with a large company of bonder from the Trøndelag, went through the forest to Sweden where they found ships that took them to Lake Ladoga. From there they sent a message to Grand Prince Yaroslav, declaring that they had come because they wanted to make Magnus King of Norway. Yaroslav invited them to Novgorod where every member of the embassy swore an oath of loyalty to Magnus, who in return promised them 'peace and reconciliation', and became Kalv's foster-son.

The Trøndelagers sailed back to Sweden in spring 1035, accompanied by Magnus who was reunited with his mother Alvhild. The young shepherd poet, the Icelander Arnor Jarlaskáld, wrote how the boy

In blood will make his foemen feel
Olav's sword Hneitr's sharp blue steel.

A Thing was held at Hangrar near Sigtuna where Magnus's step-mother Queen Astrid, Olav's widow, offered to pay with her jewels anybody who would help him to recover his father's throne. She made such a rousing speech that, according to Arnor Jarlaskáld, 'many a dark red Swedish shield' was eager to join his army when it came. Astrid told them, 'If you have lost kindred or friends fighting at the side of King Olav, or been wounded doing so, now is the time for you to show a real man's heart and courage, and go to Norway and take vengeance.' Sigvat Thordarson, who may have heard her speak, commented that such good stepmothers are rare.[15]

In the summer, bringing Magnus with them, a large Swedish force crossed the border, entering Norway 'over the keel-ridge of the country', coming down into the Trøndelag, where everybody gave them a delighted welcome. Sveinn's few supporters fled into hiding. At a Thing, Magnus was unanimously acclaimed King of Norway, 'as far as his father Olav had possessed it'. His advisers then appointed new lendmenn as well as new bailiffs for every royal office and estate.

King Sveinn, who was in South Hordaland when the news of Magnus's arrival reached him, sent round the war arrow to raise an army, which had little effect. He then summoned a Hordaland Thing, asking the local bonder to join him with ships and men, to drive out Magnus. His Danish housecarls also made 'long speeches'. In response a handful of Hordaland bonder agreed to follow Sveinn to war with a marked lack of enthusiasm, but most refused while some stayed silent or spoke openly of their intention of joining Magnus.[16] Realising he had almost no support, Sveinn Alfífuson abandoned the struggle and sailed back to Denmark, taking his mother and his hird with him. He bragged of returning with a Danish army, but died in October 1035.

We can take it for granted that Knut had every intention of recon-quering a kingdom he saw as his by right. But on 12 November 1035 at Shaftesbury in Dorset he died a month after his son, suddenly and unexpectedly like his own father, Sveinn Forkbeard, from a massive stroke. His heirs proved incapable of holding together his North Sea empire, which quickly fell apart – as Olav had once prophesied to a disbelieving audience.

Meanwhile, Magnus 'appointed his retinue and established himself in Nidaros with a great multitude of followers and great joy and festiveness', records *Morkinskinna*.[17] By the time he died at only twenty-three, he had made himself one of medieval Norway's hero kings. In an ironic reversal of fortune he also became King of Denmark, invited by the Danish nobility. Some said he should be named 'the Good' because he forgave Olav's enemies, which is questionable.

When Harek of Thjotta came to Nidaros, he was seen landing from his ship by the murdered Grankel's son Asmund, who was standing on a balcony with the king. Asmund told Magnus he wanted to kill Harek and produced a hatchet. Instead of restraining Asmund, the young king lent him an axe as heavy as a club, saying, 'There are hard bones in that old fellow.' Finding Harek in a Nidaros street, Asmund smashed his skull, scattering his brains over the ground. Later, Magnus gave him a valuable fief in Hålogaland.

Thorir Hound had left Norway shortly after Stiklestad. Both the *Legendary Saga* and Snorri tell us he went to Jerusalem, to atone. The *Legendary Saga* adds that God opened Thorir's eyes and he saw angels accompanying Olav's soul 'clad in royal purple' as he ascended to heaven in a blindingly bright light. The same source also says that Thorir claimed his fingers had been almost severed during the battle, until a drop of the king's blood touched them and they healed at once, 'as though a silk thread had been wound around them'.

Snorri merely comments that people said that he never returned. Wherever Thorir went, he disappears from history – he may even have died peacefully at home in his bed. Yet his change of heart may really have happened since his sons were allowed to inherit his estate of Bjarkøy which, as will be seen, would otherwise have been unlikely in the new Norway of King Magnus.

*   *   *

Kalv Arnason saw no reason to fear Magnus, who had agreed to become his foster-son and gave him an important role in governing Norway. Kalv made a bad mistake. When the king was hearing petitions at Nidaros and too busy to listen to one from a bonde from Suul in Verdal, the man shouted, 'Listen, my lord, to my plain speaking. I was there and had to bear a bloody head from Stiklestad for I was then with Olav's men. Listen to me,' he went on. 'Well did I see the men you trust thrusting the dead corpse out of their way as it lay dead and striding o'er your father's gore.'[18] Magnus called him over, granting his petition, and promising 'favour and friendship'.

Shortly after, in the middle of a banquet the king suddenly ordered Kalv to ride with him to Stiklestad and show him over the battlefield. Realising his life was in danger, Kalv whispered instructions to his footboy. These were to go and tell his servants at his great farm of Egge, which was on the bank of the Trondheimsfjord nearby, to make his ship ready 'before sunset' for a long voyage. They were to put on board all his moveable treasure and valuables.

When they reached Stiklestad, Magnus asked, 'Where is the spot where the king fell?'

Kalv pointed with his spear, saying, 'He lay there when he fell.'

'And where were you, Kalv?' enquired Magnus.

'Here, where I am standing,' answered Kalv.

'So your axe could have reached him?' said Magnus, whose face had turned blood red.

'My axe came nowhere near him,' replied Kalv.

Before the housecarls could seize him, he jumped on his horse and galloped to Egge.

Arriving at Egge late that evening, Kalv sailed off down the fjord in the darkness. After taking refuge with his son-in-law in the Orkneys, he spent the next few years as a Viking, raiding in Ireland, Scotland and the Hebrides. Unwisely, he returned to Norway after Magnus's death. In 1051 during a campaign in Denmark, King Harald Hardrada arranged for him to be sent on a hopeless mission during which he was killed in an ambush.[19]

After Kalv Arnason's flight, Magnus appropriated Egge together with any valuables that Kalv had left behind. He also confiscated the lands of the late Rut of Vigga and Thorgeir of Kvistathir, as well as those of several well-to-do bonder who had been killed fighting against his father. Others who had taken part in opposing Olav were given ruinous fines or else chased out of Norway. Finally, after the remainder threatened to rise in rebellion against the king as they had done against his father if he continued to seek revenge, he left them in peace.

Nevertheless, Magnus's victories in the many wars that he fought won the respect of the most truculent bonder, especially in 1043 when he wiped out the Jómsborg Vikings, destroying their stronghold at Wolin, and then on the way home defeated a great army of pagan Wend invaders. In berserker style, throwing off his mail and in a red silk shirt, brandishing his father's axe Hel, he led a charge in which '15,000' Wends died. During the night, he had dreamed that his father told him, 'Attack the Wends when you hear my trumpet' and men from Nidaros among his troops claimed that before the battle they heard the chiming of Olav's bell at St Clement's church – the trumpet.

Three years later, on the brink of an expedition to conquer England, King Magnus died from a mysterious illness.

20

The Triumph of Olav Haraldsson

Then would the lid [of his shrine] fly open and he would arise.
With his axe in hand he would stride down this mighty church;
and up from the paven floor, up from the earth outside, up
from every graveyard in Norway's land would the dead yellow
skeletons arise – they would be clothed in flesh and would
muster themselves round their King.

Sigrid Undset, *Kristin Lavransdatter*[1]

Throughout his reign King Magnus did his utmost to encourage
veneration of his father as a wonder-working saint, ordering the
construction of a shrine for his body that was placed next to the high
altar at St Clement's. In 1066, before sailing from Nidaros on a
doomed attempt to conquer England, King Harald Hardrada visited
the shrine, unlocked it, cut the corpse's hair and clipped the nails
which were still growing, relocked it and then, for some inexplicable
reason, threw the keys into the River Nid. Soon after, Olav told him
in a dream that his death was near and his body would feed the crow
– 'the witch wife's steed'.

Snorri says the shrine resembled a coffin and was made of gold
and silver – in reality, silver gilt – studded with jewels. Eventually,
there were three shrines, the later two enclosing the first. We have
some idea of what it looked like from a small thirteenth-century
box-reliquary (or *châsse*) in the stave church at Hedalen in Valdres
modelled on the Nidaros shrine, that is in the form of a church

rather than a coffin with a dragon-head gargoyle at each end of the roof. In 2021, a shrine designed by the British architect Anthony Delarue was installed in the Catholic cathedral at Oslo, to house the sole surviving relic from the king's body. This is the so-called 'Arm Relic', encased in a massive silver reliquary shaped like a forearm, that ends in a great silver hand. (The relic is in fact a calf bone.)

Everybody was obliged to abstain from work and hear Mass on 29 July, *Olsok* or 'Olav's Wake', the anniversary of Olav's death, which was the most important saint's day in the Norwegian calendar. Increasingly, pilgrims came to Nidaros from all over the country, while later it became the most popular pilgrimage in northern Europe. The majority of pilgrims came in search of a cure for their ailments or infirmities, and large numbers were said to have been healed. By the Reformation, more than fifty churches in Norway had been dedicated to the king.

His canonisation was recognised by Orthodox Christians as it took place before the schism between Eastern and Western Christendom, with a church at Constantinople of Our Lady of the Varangians and St Olav where the Varangian guard prayed before going on campaign. No doubt Grand Princess Irene helped to secure its dedication. The church's most precious relic was Olav's sword Hneitr, presented by Emperor John II Comnenus. Having dropped his own weapon at Stiklestad, one of the Swedish housecarls had picked up the sword and fought his way clear with it. The sword remained in his family's possession for a century until a member became a Varangian and sold it to the emperor for a large sum in gold.

At home, Olav's body was moved from St Clement's to another church at Nidaros, Christ Kirke, built on the sandbank under which he had first been buried and above the holy well. Finally it was placed behind the high altar of a cathedral, Nidarosdom, that began to rise during the mid-twelfth century over and around Christ Kirke on the initiative of Archbishop Eysteinn Erlendsson, but which was not completed until about 1300. English master builders worked here and the nave is in the English High Gothic of the later thirteenth century, with resemblances to the Angels' Choir at Lincoln Cathedral that housed the body of St Hugh of Lincoln. There are also similarities to the transept at Westminster Abbey, rebuilt to house that of King Edward the Confessor.

In about 1150 the future Archbishop Eysteinn commissioned (may even have written) the *Passio et miracula beati Olavi* to celebrate the creation of the archdiocese of Nidaros.[2] An account of Olav Haraldsson's death and miracles, better known as the *Passio Olavi*, begins by evoking a frozen northern landscape in the hands of the devil, and ends with its thawing and redemption by a warm southern wind – Olav. If unmitigated hagiography, the *Passio* shows the extent to which veneration of the king had reached by the mid-twelfth century. At the same time, he became Norway's national hero, an Arthurian figure who was popularly credited with slaying countless trolls and giants in personal combat.

About the year 1153 one of the three kings who then ruled Norway jointly asked the Icelander Einarr Skúlason, a famous skald, to compose a poem in honour of Olav. This was *Geisli* ('Sun Ray'), which Einarr chanted at Christ Kirke in the presence of the three rulers.[3] Reflecting the *Passio*, it has been called the most beautiful poem to emerge from the Scandinavian Middle Ages. *Morkinskinna* claims that the church was filled with a delightful scent and other indications that King Olav himself was well pleased by it.

Archbishop Eysteinn secured Olav's beatification as his country's patron saint and national hero – *Norges evige Konge*, the 'Eternal King of Norway'. When in 1164 he crowned the infant Magnus V Erlingsson at Nidaros in the country's first coronation, the record drawn up by Magnus's council put words into their new ruler's mouth that refer to 'the glorious martyr King Olav who next after the Lord [Jesus Christ] . . . confers the Norwegian kingdom in perpetuity'. Ever since then, and as they still do today, the kings of Norway have held their kingdom as vassals of Olav – *Rex Perpetuus Norvegiae*.[4]

*   *   *

Olav's cult spread all over northern Europe, especially in the British Isles where at least forty churches are known to have been dedicated to him, not only in areas of Scandinavian settlement such as the Danelaw, Yorkshire, East Anglia, the Orkneys or Dublin, but at London, Winchester, Chester and Chichester. A Mass of St Olav was being said at Exeter Cathedral within twenty years of his death.[5] Up to the Reformation he remained popular in these islands. As well as in Britain, medieval manuscript copies of the *Passio* have been found in Finland, Austria and France.

Snorri singles out the story of a cripple in western France only able to walk on his knees and elbows, who dreamed that a magnificent looking person told him he would be healed if he went to St Olav's church in London. Somehow, he begged his way across the Channel and made his way to the City, but when he reached London Bridge, no one could tell him where to find it, leaving him crouching in the street. Then a man came up and said, 'We two shall go together to Olav's church,' and took him over the bridge to it. As soon as they arrived, the cripple rose to his feet sound and strong. His guide had vanished, but he realised that it had been the king himself.

In her novel *Kristin Lavransdatter*, Sigrid Undset imagines the feelings of her fourteenth-century heroine as she kneels as a pilgrim before the choir at Nidaros: 'Behind the golden grated doors St Olav's shrine gleamed in the darkness, towering high behind the altar.' Kristin then has a vision of him, of a face with flaming eyes that see to the very depths of her soul, as he declares 'with my blood did I, Olav Haraldsson, write Thy Evangel in the Norse tongue for these my poor freedmen'.[6]

The pilgrimage to Nidaros came to rank only after Rome, Compostella and Jerusalem, attracting thousands from not just the Scandinavian countries, but from Germany, the British Isles, the Baltic lands and the land of Rus. There were several pilgrims' ways. The two most popular started from Oslo (then known as Anslo). The western went through Gjøvik, the eastern via Hamar, joining each other just north of Lillehammer. Both took twenty-five days to complete on foot, pilgrims setting out early in July to reach Nidaros in time for Olav's feast day on the 29th and the *Olsok* celebrations.

On the way were wells credited with miraculous properties, some of which can still be seen, although the hospices providing food and shelter have long since disappeared. Eventually the pilgrims came to Feginsbrekken, the 'Hill of Joy', from where they caught a first glimpse of Nidaros. As at other shrines, leaden badges were given to them when they arrived, showing the king holding the axe that struck him down. They also took home stone jars of healing water, drawn from the holy well in the cathedral fed by the stream flowing from beneath his grave.

Nobody had been more of a Viking than Olav Haraldsson, yet he destroyed the Viking way of life in Norway by exorcising its gods and forbidding his subjects to rob other Christians. To die as he did, begging God for mercy instead of snarling defiance at his killers, denied its whole ethos while the code of law he approved at Moster, telling slave owners to free a slave each year and tacitly rejecting slavery, meant an end to people trafficking. His swaggering half-brother Harald Hardrada, who had become an anachronism by the time the English killed him at Stamford Bridge in 1066, is sometimes called the last Viking, but the title really belongs to Olav, who refashioned pagan Norse predators into the forebears of the eminently sane and kindly folk we know today.

Olav Haraldsson was a martyr and he made Norway a Christian country, but was he really 'a glorious saint' as Thorarinn Luftunga calls him in *Glaelognskvida*? Clearly Bishop Grimkel, who knew him as well as anybody, thought so. Yet no one can deny that the king 'fed the raven' during his battles, that on missionary forays he killed, mutilated and blinded, that his attitude towards attractive women was far from saintly. Even Snorri rejected any tales of miracles before his overthrow. However, Snorri also believed that misfortune changed Olav, a transformation that, as I suggest, may have been due to some unknown Byzantine priest.

We should also remember that while to us King Olav's methods of conversion seem the reverse of saintly, for medieval men a saint was someone who was generally believed to have been accepted into heaven, regardless of past sins, the supreme example being the good thief crucified with Christ. They would have thought entirely plausible the story of the last-moment repentance of a man killed by falling from his horse and his forgiveness:

Betwixt the saddle and the ground
Mercy I ask'd: mercy I found.

Olav's contemporaries did not think his shortcomings in any way an obstacle. To their minds the proofs of his saintliness were his incorrupt body and his healing miracles. We may question the miracles, attributing them to mass hysteria or to sympathetic magic, but medieval men were fully convinced that they took place. Even today many people still believe in such cures. 'To one who has faith, no explanation is necessary,' wrote Thomas Aquinas. 'To one without faith, no explanation is possible.'

Epilogue

The Eternal King of Norway

In 1536 the last Archbishop of Nidaros, Olav Engelbrektsson, opened the king's coffin, to find that instead of crumbling into dust his body had stayed largely intact. Skin and flesh remained on the face, and although the eyes were a little sunken the eyebrows were still there. The tip of his nose was missing and his lips were twisted, yet his teeth remained white, while if he lacked a beard his jaw was in place. When his thighs were prodded through the shroud you could feel flesh. Only his toes were withered. Instead of a lingering stench of ancient putrefaction, there was 'a goodly scent'.

However, in 1537 Christian III, King of Denmark and Norway, introduced Lutheranism, outlawing 'Popery', and Archbishop Engelbrektsson fled into exile. The shrine was broken up, its precious metals sold as bullion. In 1564 Swedish soldiers stabled their horses in the cathedral, already badly damaged by fire, stealing 'King Olav's helmet and spurs', which they presented to the Storkyrkan church at Stockholm. These remain in Sweden today at the Swedish History Museum, analysis having shown that they date only from the fifteenth century.

Regardless of despoliation, in 1567 a Norwegian writer could still call Nidarosdom the 'crown, flower and ornament of the realm'. The king's body had been reburied but went on attracting pilgrims until the following year, when it was hidden to stop them from coming. There is a strong tradition that it lies in a secret grave beneath the cathedral and only a few years ago a priest historian claimed that one or two families in Trondheim still know its location.[1]

For nearly three centuries, Nidarosdom was no more than Trondheim's parish church, increasingly neglected in a decaying city. A storm blew down the spire in 1708, the damage compounded by another fire. Even so, the lion in Norway's coat of arms went on grasping the golden axe – Olav's emblem. Following the uneasy union with Sweden after the Napoleonic Wars, Charles XIV John of Sweden was crowned there as King Charles III of Norway in 1818, in response to a plea by the Norwegian Storting, the first coronation that the semi-ruinous cathedral had seen since Christian II of Denmark's crowning here in 1514.

In the nineteenth century Olav became more than ever the symbol of Norway and a full-scale restoration of the cathedral began in 1869 (only completed in 1969). When Norway regained its independence in 1905 King Hakon VII was crowned at Nidaros, while in 1930 *Olsok*, Olav's Day, was declared a national holiday. During the Second World War, Norway's Nazi party, the anti-Christian Nasjonal Samling, tried to take over Olav's cult, issuing a stream of pamphlets portraying him as a pagan chieftain while the monument erected at Stiklestad in 1807 was replaced in 1944 by another topped with a swastika that Vidkun Quisling personally unveiled. This was demolished and the old memorial re-erected as soon as the war was over.

Since 1958 the service of blessing the new sovereign that replaces a coronation has taken place in Nidarosdom, which houses the Norwegian crown jewels. Impressively restored, the magnificent cathedral is Norway's national shrine, in much the same way that Westminster Abbey is for the people of Britain.

In 1994 two of the medieval pilgrims' main routes from Oslo to Nidaros were reopened and signposted on the initiative of the Lutheran Church, and since then Nidarosdom has attracted a growing number of pilgrims, including Catholics and agnostics as well as Lutherans. Walking the pilgrims' way is occasionally recommended by Lutheran pastors as therapy for violent criminals in the hope that Olav will understand their problems and ask God to cure them. Whether he does so or not, at the right time of year the *Olavsleden* is a beautiful and not too arduous journey of slightly over 600 kilometres through a glorious landscape.

Acknowledgements

I am especially grateful to Frederick and Kristin Lesser for their memorable hospitality at Oslo during many visits to Norway over the last few years, in particular for first introducing me to the Vikingskipshuset with its three wonderful longships, to the medieval gallery at the Universitetets Kulturhistorisk Muséer, and to the Norsk Folkemuseum with its stave church and timber houses, and for accompanying me to Nidarosdom. I am also grateful to Stella Lesser for unfailing encouragement.

In addition, I should like to thank Andrew Simmons, Birlinn's editor-in-chief, for some extremely helpful comments while I was writing the book.

Another debt is to the staff of the London Library, who so often went out of their way to help me locate obscure sources.

Note on Translations and Spelling

I try to strike a balance between the literal if rather ugly translations now in favour and the old-fashioned, less precise versions by Samuel Laing, Benjamin Thorpe, Olive Bray or Henry Adams Bellows that sometimes I even prefer to such beautiful modern renderings as those by W. H. Auden, Ursula Dronke or Carolyne Larrington. References to *Heimskringla* are to the latest, most faithful version by Alison Finlay and Anthony Faulkes which is from the original Icelandic, but I also quote Laing's version from a Norwegian translation when reasonably accurate, slightly modernising it for the sake of clarity, as he is so much more atmospheric. (I give references to both sources in the notes.) Where dialogue or verse is unattributed, it is nearly always from Snorri, using Laing.

I have omitted the letters 'eth' and 'thorn' since they are unfamiliar to those who do not read Old West Norse, Icelandic or Anglo-Saxon. I also use simplified, modern versions of personal and place names.

Notes

PROLOGUE

1. '*Thetta svaerd haetir Baesengr*', from *Olafs saga hins Helga, en Kort saga om Kong Olaf den Hellige* (eds Keyser and Unger), p. 5
2. Some historians believe his birth may have been a few years earlier, *Store Norske Leksikon*
3. Not Greenland but a coastal area around Norsø in Lower Telemark
4. *Grettis saga Ásmundarsonar* (trans. Morris and Magnússon as *The Saga of Grettir the Strong*), ch. xvii
5. The light is obviously a later, Christian interpolation

INTRODUCTION

1. Sigvat Thordarson, *Erfidrápa Óláfs Helga – Memorial Poem to St Olav* (trans. Lindow), from 'St Olaf and the Skalds' in *Sanctity in the North* (ed. DuBois), p. 125
2. For an analysis of Snorri's methods, see Sverre Bagge, *Society and Politics in Snorri Sturluson's Heimskringla*; and, more concisely, in Bagge, *Cross and Scepter*, pp. 209–14

1 THE WORLD OF A YOUNG NORSE CHIEFTAIN

1. *Harbard's Song*, from *The Poetic Edda* (trans. Larrington), stanza 24
2. *Helgakvitha Hjorvarthssonar*, from *The Poetic Edda* (trans. Bellows), stanza 9

3. *The Lay of Sigrdrifa*, from *The Poetic Edda* (trans. Larrington), stanza 6

4. There are good examples in the medieval gallery of the Historical Museum at Oslo and in the Scientific Museum at Trondheim, but so rusted after centuries in the earth that they give little idea of what they must have been like at their prime

5. *Ágrip af Nóregskonungasogum*, p. 6

6. Hjardar and Vike, *Vikings at War*, pp. 163–5

7. Snorri Sturluson, *Heimskringla*, Finlay and Faulkes, vol. 2, ch. 33, p. 25; Laing, ch. 138

8. Foote and Wilson, *The Viking Achievement*, p. 145

9. *Hávamál*, from *The Poetic Edda* (trans. Olive Bray), stanza 141

10. Price, *The Children of Ash and Elm*, p. 143

11. Price, *The Viking Way*, p. 19

12. Jesch, *Women in the Viking Age*, p. 180

13. Price, *The Children of Ash and Elm*, p. 330

14. *Helgakvida Hundingsbana II* (44–55), from *The Poetic Edda*, vol. i, *Heroic Poems* (trans. and ed. Dronke), p. 153

15. For an impressive translation see *The List of Rig*, from *The Poetic Edda* (trans. Larrington), pp. 238–44

16. *Heimskringla*, Finlay and Faulkes, vol. 2, chs 23–4, p. 18; Laing, ch. 22

17. Bagge, *Society and Politics*, p. 119

18. *Ágrip af Nóregskonungasogum*, p. 21

19. Thordarson, *Erfidrápa Óláfs Helga* (trans. Lindow), in *Sanctity in the North* (ed. DuBois), p. 125

20. Shippey, *Laughing Shall I Die*, p. 262

2 HARALD FAIR HAIR AND HIS SUCCESSORS

1. C. Krag, 'The Creation of Norway', in Brink and Price, *The Viking World*, p. 647

2. *Old Norse Poems* (ed. L. M. Hollander)

3. *Hákonarmál*, in Orchard, *Cassell Dictionary of Norse Myth and Legend*

4. *Historia Norwegie* (trans. Fisher), ch. xvi

5. *Ágrip af Nóregskonungasogum*, p. 21

6. Theodoricus Monachus, *Historia de Antiquitate Regum Norwagensium*, p. 9

7. *The Saga of the Jómsvíkings* (trans. Blake), pp. 36–7

8. Bagge, *From Viking Stronghold to Christian Kingdom*, p. 27

9. Shippey, p. 245
10. Oddr Snorrason Munkr, *The Saga of Olav Tryggvason* (trans. Andersson), p. 81
11. *Fagrskinna*, p. 121
12. Adam of Bremen, *Gesta Hammaburgensis ecclesiae pontificum* (trans. Tschan)
13. Oddr Snorrason Munkr, *Saga of Olav Tryggvason*, pp. 92–4

3 THE VIKING OLAV HARALDSSON

1. William of Jumièges, *Gesta Normannorum Ducum* (trans. Van Houts), p. 19
2. Bagge, *From Viking Stronghold to Christian Kingdom*, p. 34
3. Shippey, p. 14
4. J. Bill, 'Viking Ships and the Sea', in Brink and Price, pp. 176–7
5. For longships see Ibid., pp. 172–6; and Hjardar and Vike, *Vikings at War*, pp. 136–52
6. Sigvat Thordarson, *Austrafaravísur*, in *Heimskringla*, Finlay and Faulkes, vol. 2, ch. 71, p. 59; Laing, ch. 70
7. *All-wise's Sayings*, from *The Poetic Edda* (trans. Larrington), stanza 24
8. *Hávamál*, from *The Poetic Edda* (trans. Bellows), stanza 157
9. *Historia Norwegie* (trans. Fisher), ch. xviii
10. *The Saga of the Jómsvíkings* (trans. N. F. Blake)
11. *Historia Norwegie* (trans. Fisher), ch. xviii
12. *The Saga of Gunnlaug Serpent-tongue*, in *Sagas of Warrior-Poets* (ed. Whaley), p. 124
13. *Heimskringla*, Finlay and Faulkes, vol. 2, ch. 15, p. 13; Laing, ch. 14
14. *The Chronicle of John of Worcester* (trans. McGurk); and *Anglo-Saxon Chronicle* (trans. Garmonsway), pp. 142–3
15. *Anglo-Saxon Chronicle*, p. 142
16. *Heimskringla*, Finlay and Faulkes, vol 2, ch.15, p.13; Laing, ch. 14

4 OLAV ABANDONS THE GODS

1. *Songs of the Sun*, stanza 32, in *Edda Saemundar Hinns Froda* (trans. Thorpe)
2. *Heimskringla*, Finlay and Faulkes, vol. 2, ch. 20, p. 16; Laing, ch. 19
3. J. Renaud, 'The Duchy of Normandy', in Brink and Price, p. 455

4. Winroth, *The Conversion of Scandinavia*, pp. 140, 142
5. *The Poetic Edda*, vol. ii, *The Mythological Poems* (trans. and ed. Dronke)
6. *Heimskringla*, Finlay and Faulkes, vol. 2, ch. 17, p. 14; Laing, ch. 16
7. Christys, *Vikings in the South*, pp. 96–7
8. *Anglo-Saxon Chronicle*, p. 144
9. *The Saga of Gunnlaug Serpent-tongue*, in *Sagas of Warrior-Poets* (ed. Whaley), pp. 124–6
10. *Anglo-Saxon Chronicle*, p. 152

5 THE BATTLE OF NESJAR, 1016

1. *Reginsmol*, from *The Poetic Edda* (trans. Bellows), stanza 24
2. *Fagrskinna*, p. 137
3. Ibid., p. 132
4. Ibid., pp. 137–8, and *Heimskringla*, Finlay and Faulkes, vol. 2, ch. 30, pp. 22–3; Laing, ch. 27, give identical accounts of this conversation
5. *Fagrskinna*, p. 138
6. Sigvat had fought in the battle, so this is eyewitness testimony

6 BUILDING A KINGDOM

1. *Heimskringla*, Finlay and Faulkes, vol. 2, ch. 57, p. 45; Laing, ch. 45
2. Bagge, *From Viking Stronghold to Christian Kingdom*, p. 30
3. Hjardar and Vike, *Vikings at War*, pp. 97–9
4. Bagge, *Society and Politics*, pp. 38–9
5. Bagge, *Cross and Scepter*, pp. 68–9

7 THE TERRIBLE ONE AND OTHER GODS

1. *Grimnir's Sayings*, from *The Poetic Edda* (trans. Larrington), stanza 54
2. *Hávamál* (trans. Olive Bray), stanzas 137, 138
3. *Loki's Quarrel*, from *The Poetic Edda* (trans. Larrington), stanza 24
4. *Grimnismol*, from *The Poetic Edda* (trans. Bellows), stanza 19
5. Price, *The Children of Ash and Elm*, p. 43
6. *Second Lay of Hunding*, from *The Poetic Edda* (trans. Bellows), stanza 33

7. *Thrymskvitha*, from *The Poetic Edda* (trans. Bellows), stanza 25
8. *Loki's Quarrel* (trans. Larrington), stanza 32
9. Most of the comparatively little we know of Norse paganism comes from Snorri, who was biased by Christian distaste as well as by theories of his own
10. *Hávamál* (trans. Olive Bray), stanza 136
11. Price, *The Children of Ash and Elm*, p. 174
12. N. Price, 'Sorcery and Circumpolar Traditions in Old Norse Belief', in Brink and Price, p. 245
13. Shippey, p. 82
14. *Hávamál* (trans. Bellows), stanza 156

8 THE NEW RELIGION

1. Hallfrod Ottarsson, *Óláfsdrapa*, in *Poetry from the Kings' Sagas*, vol. i, *From Mythical Times to c.1035* (ed. Whaley), p. 392
2. F.-R. de Chateaubriand, *La Génie du Christianisme*
3. 1 Corinthians, x. 20, 28
4. C. Raudvere, 'Popular Religion in the Viking Age', in Brink and Price, *The Viking World*, p. 235
5. Foote, 'A Note on Thrandur's kredda', in *Aurvandilstá: Norse Studies*
6. Price, *The Children of Ash and Elm*, pp. 448–9
7. *Heimskringla*, Finlay and Faulkes, vol. 2, ch. 73, p. 64; Laing, ch. 72
8. Ottar the Black, *Höfudlausn*, in *Heimskringla*, Finlay and Faulkes, vol. 2, ch. 75, pp. 68–9; Laing, ch. 74
9. *Heimskringla*, Finlay and Faulkes, vol. 2, ch. 85, p. 83; Laing, ch. 86

9 OLAV'S EMPIRE

1. 'early greens the wood'
2. 'where the hart goes yearly'
3. *Orkneyinga saga* (trans. Pálsson and Edwards), ch. 4
4. Ibid., ch. 12
5. Ibid., ch. 19
6. Wylie, *The Faroe Islands*, p. 26
7. *Historia Norwegie* (trans. Fisher), p. 69
8. Foote, *Aurvandilstá: Norse Studies*, pp. 209–21

9. *Faereyinga saga*, ch. 23
10. Ibid., ch. 3
11. Ibid., ch. 48
12. J. V. Sigurdsson, 'Iceland', in Brink and Price, p. 572
13. *The Saga of Bjorn, Champion of the Hitardal People*, in *Sagas of Warrior-Poets* (ed. Whaley), p. 153
14. For Stein Skoptason's story see *Heimskringla*, Finlay and Faulkes, vol. 2, ch. 138, pp. 162–6; Laing, ch. 148
15. Hollander, 'Sigvat Thordarson' in *The Skalds*

10 OLAV AND THE SWEDISH PRINCESSES

1. *Skirnir's Journey*, from *The Poetic Edda* (trans. Bellows), stanzas 11–12
2. *Heimskringla*, Finlay and Faulkes, vol. 2, ch. 91, p. 89; Laing, ch. 92
3. Ibid., vol. 2, ch. 88, p. 84; Laing, ch. 89
4. Ibid., vol. 2, ch. 122, pp. 139–40; Laing, ch. 131. Norwegian historians claim that she came from Bergen, but William of Malmsbury says she was English

11 A WAR ON DEMONS

1. This chapter is largely based on Snorri Sturluson's account which although a reconstruction of what actually took place gives the best description we have of Olav's missionary methods. *Heimskringla*, Finlay and Faulkes, vol. 2, chs 107–13, pp. 116–24; Laing, chs 113–19
2. Theodoricus Monachus, p. 15
3. In 1966 archaeologists found evidence under the twelfth-century stone church at Maere showing that its timber predecessor had been a *hof* taken over by Christians – a rare example of a Norse temple adapted for use as a church
4. *Heimskringla*, Finlay and Faulkes, vol. 2, ch. 111, p. 119; Laing, ch. 117
5. Quoted in Valebrokk and Thiis-Evensen, *Levende Fortid de utrolige Stavenkirkene*
6. *Heimskringla*, Finlay and Faulkes, vol. 2, ch. 113, p. 124; Laing, ch. 119
7. *Saga of Hallfred Troublesome Poet*, in *Sagas of Warrior-Poets* (ed. Whaley), pp. 84–5

8. '*adversarius vester diabolus tamquam leo rugens circuit quaerens quem devoret*', from the First Letter of St Peter, 5–8, in the Vulgate Bible
9. Page, *Chronicles of the Vikings*, p. 223

12 THE KILLING OF ASBJORN SLAYER OF SEAL

1. *Fagrskinna*, p. 146
2. Bagge, *Society and Politics*, p. 68
3. *Heimskringla*, Finlay and Faulkes, vol. 2, ch. 181, p. 221; Laing, ch. 192
4. Bagge, *Cross and Scepter*, p. 19
5. Bagge, *Society and Politics*, p. 203

13 THE SHADOW OF KNUT THE GREAT

1. *Heimskringla*, Finlay and Faulkes, vol. 2, ch. 131, pp. 148–50; Laing, ch. 140
2. Bolton, *Cnut the Great*, p. 209
3. W. Hunt, 'Canute', in *Dictionary of National Biography*, 1887
4. Theodoricus Monachus, p. 22
5. *Heimskringla*, Finlay and Faulkes, vol. 2, ch. 131, pp. 148–50; Laing, ch. 140
6. Foote and Wilson, *The Viking Achievement*, pp. 280–2
7. *Heimskringla*, Finlay and Faulkes, vol. 2, ch. 219, p. 249; Laing, ch. 281
8. Ibid., vol. 2, ch. 133, p. 156; Laing, ch. 143
9. Ibid., vol. 2, ch. 139, p.169; Laing, ch. 149
10. Bagge, *Society and Politics*, p. 67

14 WAR WITH KNUT

1. *Heimskringla*, Finlay and Faulkes, vol. 2, ch. 150, p. 189; Laing, ch. 160
2. *Historia Norwegie* (trans. Fisher), p. 87
3. *Anglo-Saxon Chronicle*, p. 157
4. *Fagrskinna*, p. 152
5. *Songs of the Sun*, stanza 13, in *Edda Saemundar Hinns Froda* (trans. Thorpe)

6. Bolton, p. 91

7. Sigvat Thordarson, *Vestrfaravísur*, in *Heimskringla*, Finlay and Faulkes, vol. 2, ch. 161, p. 198; Laing, ch. 171

8. *Fagrskinna*, p. 164

9. Sigvat Thordarson, *Vestrfaravísur*, in *Heimskringla*, Finlay and Faulkes, vol. 2, ch. 162, p. 199; Laing, ch. 172

10. *Hávamál* (trans. Bellows), stanza 1. Bellows' translation differs considerably from others

15 NORWAY REJECTS OLAV HARALDSSON

1. *Skirnir's Journey* (trans. Bellows), stanza 10

2. *The Chronicle of John of Worcester*

3. *Heimskringla*, Finlay and Faulkes, vol. 2, ch. 168, p. 204; Laing, ch. 178

4. Ibid., vol. 2, ch. 180, p. 219; Laing, ch. 190

5. *Fagrskinna*, p. 156

6. *Heimskringla*, Finlay and Faulkes, vol. 2, ch. 91, p. 88; Laing, ch. 92

16 EXILE IN VIKING RUSSIA

1. *Hávamál* (trans. Bellows), stanzas 3–4

2. *Morkinskinna*, pp. 89–90

3. *The Chronicle of Novgorod 1016–1471*

4. *The Russian Primary Chronicle*, (trans. Cross and Sherbowitz-Wetzor)

5. J. Shepard, 'The Viking Rus and Byzantium', in Brink and Price, p. 508

6. Lindow, 'St Olaf and the Skalds', in *Sanctity in the North* (ed. DuBois), pp. 109–10

7. *Morkinskinna*, p. 90

8. 'delivering the hagiography in concentrated form, towards the end of Olav's life … enables him [Snorri] to give a vivid account of Olav's conflicts, and one that does justice to the point of view of his adversaries as well as to that of his devotees'. Bagge, *Cross and Scepter*, pp. 210–11

9. Theodoricus Monachus, p. 23

10. Bolton, p. 185

17 Olav's Homecoming

1. *Helgakvitha Hundingsbana II*, from *The Poetic Edda* (trans. Bellows), stanza 42
2. *Heimskringla*, Finlay and Faulkes, vol. 2, ch. 197, p. 232; Laing, ch. 208
3. *Fagrskinna*, p. 159
4. *Heimskringla*, Finlay and Faulkes, vol. 2, ch. 202, p. 235; Laing, ch. 213
5. Sigvat Thordarson, *Lausavísur* (trans. Laing), in *Heimskringla: The Norse King Sagas*
6. *Heimskringla*, Finlay and Faulkes, vol. 2, ch. 205, p. 238; Laing, ch. 217
7. Ibid., vol. 2, ch. 214, p. 246; Laing, ch. 226
8. Ibid., vol. 2, ch. 208, p. 242; Laing, ch. 220
9. For an imaginative analysis of Thormod's motives and Olav's reaction, see Shippey, pp. 258–9

18 The Old Gods' Revenge: Stiklestad

1. *The Greenlandic Lay of Atli*, from *The Poetic Edda* (trans. Larrington), stanza 24
2. *Anglo-Saxon Chronicle*, p.157
3. Thordarson, *Erfidrápa Óláfs Helga* (trans. Lindow), stanza 15, in *Sanctity in the North* (ed. DuBois)
4. *Heimskringla*, Finlay and Faulkes, vol. 2, ch. 226, p. 254; Laing, ch. 238
5. Thordarson, *Erfidrápa Óláfs Helga* (trans. Lindow), stanza 13, in *Sanctity in the North* (ed. DuBois)
6. *Heimskringla*, Finlay and Faulkes, vol. 2, chs 233–4, pp. 259–63; Laing, chs 246–7. Another source says that Thormod was killed by a mysterious arrow, shot by the dead king so that he could join him in the next world
7. Ibid., vol. 2, ch. 231, p. 295

19 Olav's 'Return from the Dead'

1. *Heimskringla*, Finlay and Faulkes, vol. 2, ch. 254, p. 300
2. *Fagrskinna*, p. 161
3. For Aelgifu, see Bolton, pp. 186–7
4. *Songs of the Sun*, stanza 47, in *Edda Saemundar Hinns Froda* (trans. Thorpe)

5. Thordarson, *Erfidrápa Óláfs Helga* (trans. Lindow), stanza 23, in *Sanctity in the North* (ed. DuBois)

6. Thorarinn Loftunga, *Glaelognskvida*, stanza 5, in *Heimskringla*, Finlay and Faulkes, vol. 2, ch. 245, pp. 271–3; Laing, ch. 258

7. *Heimskringla*, Finlay and Faulkes, vol. 2, ch. 244, pp. 269–71; Laing, ch. 258

8. Bolton, p. 187

9. Thorarinn Loftunga, *Glaelognskvida*, stanza 8, in *Heimskringla*, Finlay and Faulkes, vol. 2, ch. 245, pp. 271–3; Laing, ch. 258

10. *Fagrskinna*, p. 161

11. Ibid., p. 162

12. Bolton, p. 188

13. *Fagrskinna*, p. 169

14. Ibid., p. 166

15. Sigvat Thordarson, *Kvaedi um Ástrid dróttning*, in *Sagas of the Norse Kings* (trans. Laing), part ix, ch. 1

16. *Morkinskinna*, p. 100

17. Ibid.

18. *Heimskringla*, Finlay and Faulkes, vol. 3, ch. 13, pp. 14–15. Snorri quotes the bonde's speech as verse but it reads better as prose

19. *Norsk biografisk leksikon*

20 THE TRIUMPH OF OLAV HARALDSSON

1. Undset, *Kristin Lavransdatter* (trans. Archer and Scott), p. 374

2. *A History of Norway and The Passion and Miracles of the Blessed Óláfr* (trans. Kunin)

3. *Morkinskinna*, p. 393

4. Tollefsen, *Norwegian Kingship Transformed*, p. 54

5. Lindow, 'St Olav and the Skalds', in *Sanctity in the North* (ed. DuBois), p. 107

6. Undset, *Kristin Lavransdatter*, p. 374

EPILOGUE

1. Ekroll, *St Olavs skrin I Nidaros*

Bibliography

TEXTS AND TRANSLATIONS

Adam of Bremen, *Gesta Hammaburgensis ecclesiae pontificum*, trans. F. J. Tschan (New York: Columbia University Press, 1959)

Ágrip af Nóregskonungasogum: A Twelfth-Century Synoptic History of the Kings of Norway, trans. M. J. Driscoll (London: Viking Society for Northern Research, 2008)

The Anglo-Saxon Chronicle, trans. G. N. Garmonsway (London: J. M. Dent and Sons, 1962)

The Chronicle of John of Worcester: The Annals from 450 to 1066, trans. P. McGurk, vol. 2 (Oxford: Clarendon Press, 1991)

The Chronicle of Novgorod, 1016–1471, trans. R. Mitchell and N. Forbes, Camden Third Series, vol. xxv (London, 1914)

The Complete Sagas of Icelanders, ed. V. Hreinsson, 5 vols (Reyjkjavik: Leifur Eiríksson, 1997)

Dudo of St Quentin, *Historia Normannorum: The History of the Normans*, trans. E. Christiansen (Woodbridge: Boydell Press, 1998)

The Edda or Poetic Edda, Commonly known as Saemund's Edda, trans. Olive Bray, Part I, *The Mythological Poems* (London: Viking Club, 1908)

Edda Saemundar Hinns Froda: The Edda of Saemund the Learned (trans. B. Thorpe), 2 vols (London, 1866)

The Elder Edda: A Book of Viking Lore, trans. A. Orchard (London: Penguin, 2011)

Faereyinga saga, trans. E. York Powell as *The Saga of Thrond of Gate* (London, 1896)

Fagrskinna: A Catalogue of the Kings of Norway, trans. A. Finlay (Leiden and Boston: Brill, 2004)

Fóstrebraedra saga, trans. M. S. Regal as *The Saga of the Sworn Brothers* in *The Complete Sagas of Icelanders*, ed. V. Hreinsson, 5 vols (Reyjkjavik: Leifur Eiríksson, 1997)

Historia Norwegie, trans. P. Fisher (Copenhagen: Museum Tusculanum Press, 2003)

A History of Norway and The Passion and Miracles of the Blessed Óláfr, trans. D. Kunin (London: Viking Society for Northern Research, 2001)

Ibn Fadlan and the Land of Darkness: Arab Travellers in the Far North, trans. and ed. P. Lunde and C. Stone (London: Penguin, 2012)

Landnámabók, trans. T. Ellwood as *The Book of the Settlement of Iceland* (Kendal: T. Wilson, 1898)

Morkinskinna: The Earliest Icelandic Chronicle of the Norwegian Kings (1030–1157), trans. T. M. Andersson and K. E. Gade (Ithaca: Cornell University Press, 2000)

The Nine Books of the Danish History of Saxo Grammaticus, trans. O. Elton (New York: Norroena Society, 1905)

Norse Poems, trans. W. H. Auden and P. B. Taylor (London: Faber, 1981)

Oddr Snorrason Munkr, *The Saga of Olav Tryggvason*, trans. T. M. Andersson (Ithaca, NY: Cornell University Press, 2003)

Ólafs saga hins Helga, en Kort saga om Kong Olaf den Hellige, eds R. C. Keyser and C. R. Unger (Christiania: Feilberg & Landmark, 1849)

Old Norse Poems: the most important non-skaldic verse not included in the Poetic Edda, ed. L. M. Hollander (New York: Columbia University Press, 1936)

Orkneyinga Saga: The Saga of the Earls of Orkney, trans. H. Pálsson and P. Edwards (London: Penguin Books, 1981)

The Poetic Edda, trans. H. A. Bellows (Oxford, 1923)

The Poetic Edda, trans. & ed. Ursula Dronke, vol. i, *Heroic Poems* (Oxford: Clarendon Press, 1969); vol. ii, *Mythological Poems 1* (1997); vol. iii, *Mythological Poems 2* (2011)

The Poetic Edda, trans. Carolyne Larrington (Oxford: Oxford University Press, 2014)

Poetry from the King's Sagas, D. Whaley (ed.), vol. 1, *From Mythical Times to c.1035* (Turnhout: Brepols, 2012)

The Russian Primary Chronicle, trans. S. H. Cross and O. P. Sherbowitz-Wetzor (Cambridge, MA: Medieval Academy of America, 1953)

The Saga of Grettir the Strong, trans. William Morris and Eiríkr Magnússon (London, 1869)

The Saga of the Jómsvíkings, trans. N. F. Blake (Edinburgh: Thomas Nelson, 1962)

The Saga of King Olav Tryggwason: who reigned over Norway A.D.995 to A.D.1000, trans. J. Sephton (London, 1895)

Sagas of Warrior-Poets, ed. Diana Whaley (London: Penguin Books, 2002)

Skúlason, E., *Einarr Skúlason's Geisli: A Critical Edition*, ed. M. Chase (Toronto: University of Toronto Press, 2005)

Sturluson, Snorri, *Heimskringla: The Norse King Sagas*, trans. Samuel Laing (London: J. M. Dent & Sons, 1951)

Sturluson, Snorri, *Heimskringla: The Olav Sagas*, trans. Samuel Laing, revised J. Simpson, 2 vols (London: J. M. Dent & Sons, 1964)

Sturluson, Snorri, *Heimskringla: History of the Kings of Norway*, trans. A. Finlay & A. Faulkes, 3 vols (London: Viking Society for Northern Research, 2011–16)

Theodoricus Monachus, *Historia de Antiquitate Regum Norwagensium: An Account of the Ancient History of the Norwegian Kings*, trans. D. and I. McDougall (London: Viking Society for Northern Research, 1998)

William of Jumièges, et al., *Gesta Normannorum ducum: The Deeds of the Norman Dukes*, trans. E. M. C. Van Houts, 2 vols (Oxford: Oxford University Press, 1992)

SECONDARY SOURCES

Bagge, Sverre, *Society and Politics in Snorri Sturluson's Heimskringla* (Berkeley: University of California Press, 1991)

——, *From Viking Stronghold to Christian Kingdom: State Formation in Norway, c.900–1350* (Copenhagen: Museum Tusculanum Press, University of Copenhagen, 2010)

——, *Warrior, King and Saint: The Medieval Histories of St. Óláfr Haraldsson*, in *Journal of English and Germanic Philology*, vol. 109, no.3 (July 2010), pp. 281–321

——, *Cross and Scepter: The Rise of the Scandinavian Kingdoms from the Vikings to the Reformation* (Princeton: Princeton University Press, 2014)

Bengtsson, F. G., *Röde Orm*, trans. M. Meyer as *The Long Ships* (London: Collins, 1954)

Bidwell, S. P., *Across the North Sea and Back Again: A Comparative Study between the Cults of St Olav and St Edmund* (Oslo: University of Oslo, 2017)

Bø, Olav, *Heilag-Olav I norsk folketradisjon* (Oslo: Det Norske Samlaget, 1955)

Bolton, Timothy, *Cnut the Great* (New Haven & London: Yale University Press, 2019)

Børtnes, Jostein, *Visions of Glory: Studies in Early Russian Hagiography* (Oslo and New Jersey: Humanities Press International, 1988)

Brink, S. and Price, N. (eds), *The Viking World* (London: Routledge, 2008)

Christys, A., *Vikings in the South* (London: Bloomsbury, 2015)

Davidson, H. R. E., *The Viking Road to Byzantium* (London: Allen & Unwin, 1976)

Davis, R. H. C., *The Normans and their Myth* (London: Thames and Hudson, 1976)

——, *Normandy before 1066* (London: Longmans, 1982)

Dickins, B., *The Cult of St. Olave in the British Isles* (London: Viking Society for Northern Research, 1939)

DuBois, T. A. (ed.), *Sanctity in the North* (Toronto: University of Toronto Press, 2008)

Dumézil, Georges, *Les Dieux des Indo-Européennes* (Paris: Presses universitaires de France, 1952)

Ekroll, Øystein, *St Olavs skrin I Nidaros*, in SPOR no. 2 (2000)

——, *Nidaros Domkirkes* (Trondheim, 2009)

——, Morten Stige and Jiri Havran, *Kirker i Norge*, Bind 1, *Middelalder i stein* (Oslo, 2000)

Foote, P., *Aurvandilstá: Norse Studies* (Viborg: Odense University Press, 1984)

—— and Wilson, D. M., *The Viking Achievement* (London: Sidgwick and Jackson, 1970)

Henriksen, Vera, *Helgenkongen* (Oslo: Aschehoug, 1963); English edition *St. Olav of Norway: King, Saint and Enigma* (Oslo: Tano, 1985)

——, *Hellig Olav* (Oslo: Aschehoug, 1985)

Hjardar, K. and Vike, V., *Vikings at War* (Oxford: Casemate, 2016)

Hollander, L. M., *The Skalds: A Selection of Their Poems* (Princeton: Princeton University Press 1947)

Jesch, J., *Women in the Viking Age* (Woodbridge: The Boydell Press, 1991)

Jones, Gwyn, *A History of the Vikings* (Oxford: Oxford University Press, 1968)

Jónsson, Finnur, *Den norsk-islandske skjalde-digtning* (Copenhagen, 1908)

Kollandrud, M., *Pilegrimsleden til Nidaros: en guide til Vandringen* (Oslo: Gyldendal, 1997)

Langslet, L. R. and Ødegård, K., *Olav den hellige: spor etter helgen-kongen* (Oslo: Gyldendal Norske Forlag, 2011)

Marsden, J., *Harald Hardrada* (Stroud: Sutton, 2007)

Müller, O., *Olav den hellige* (Oslo: UNKF, 1993)

Musset, L., *Nordica et la Normandie. Recueil d'études sur la Scandinavie ancienne et médiévale, les expéditions des Vikings et la fondation de la Normandie* (Paris: Société des Études nordiques, 1997)

Orchard, A., *Cassell Dictionary of Norse Myth and Legend* (London: Cassell, 1998)

Page, R. I., *Norse Myths* (London: The British Museum Press, 1990)

——, *Chronicles of the Vikings* (London: The British Museum, 2014)

Price, N., *The Viking Way: Magic and Mind in Late Iron Age Scandinavia* (Oxford: Oxbow, 2019)

——, *The Children of Ash and Elm: A History of the Vikings* (London: Allen Lane, 2020)

Renaud, J., *Les Vikings et la Normandie* (Rennes: Ouest-France, 1989)

——, *Vikings et noms de lieux de Normandie* (Cully: OREP, 2009)

Simek, Rudolf, *A Dictionary of Northern Mythology*, trans. Angela Hall (Woodbridge: Boydell and Brewer, 1995)

Shippey, T., *Laughing Shall I Die: Lives and Deaths of the Great Vikings* (London: Reaktion Books, 2018)

Store Norske Leksikon, 1998–2005

Sundqvist, O., *The Role of Rulers in the Winding Up of the Old Norse Religion* (University of Sweden, online 14 March 2021)

Tollefsen, T. M., *Norwegian Kingship Transformed: the Succession and Coronation of Magnus Erlingsson* (Oslo: University of Oslo, 2015)

Turville-Petre, E. O. G., *Myth and Religion of the North: The Religion of Ancient Scandinavia* (London: Weidenfeld and Nicolson, 1964)

Undset, S., *Hellig Olav, Norges konge* (Oslo: Some, 1930)

——, *Saga of Saints* (London: Sheed & Ward, 1934)

——, *Norske helgener* (Oslo: Aschehoug, 1937)

——, *Kristin Lavransdatter*, trans. C. Archer and J. S. Scott (London: Abacus, 1995)

Valebrokk, E. & Thiis-Evensen, T., *Levende Fortid de utrolige Stavenkirkene* (Oslo: Boksenteret, 1993)

Winroth, A., *The Age of the Vikings* (Princeton: Princeton University Press, 2014)

——, *The Conversion of Scandinavia: Vikings, Merchants, and Missionaries in the Remaking of Northern Europe* (New Haven: Yale University Press, 2014)

Wylie, J., *The Faroe Islands: Interpretations of History* (Lexington: University of Kentucky, 1987)

Young, G. V. C., *Færøerne: Fra vikingetiden til reformationen* (Copenhagen: Rosenkilde og Bagger, 1982)

Index